FOLLOW, FOLLOW

FOLLOW, FOLLOW

CLASSIC RANGERS OLD FIRM CLASHES

IAIN DUFF

MAINSTREAM
PUBLISHING

EDINBURGH AND LONDON

First published in Great Britain in 2010 by
MAINSTREAM PUBLISHING COMPANY
(EDINBURGH) LTD
7 Albany Street
Edinburgh EH1 3UG

ISBN 9781845966348

A catalogue record for this book is available
from the British Library

Typeset in Big Noodle and Bembo

Printed in Great Britain by
CPI Mackays, Chatham ME5 8TD

1 3 5 7 9 10 8 6 4 2

To Callum and Thomas, and especially to my wife, Georgia,
for all her patience and understanding

CONTENTS

FOREWORD

There is no football match in the world that can compare with the Old Firm derby. As someone who was brought up as a Rangers supporter, to get the chance to play in just one of these games was simply a dream come true.

During my career, I have been lucky enough to have played in lots of big matches in the Premiership (arguably the biggest league in the world), in Europe and at international level for Scotland. But there is absolutely nothing that matches the Old Firm derby.

And to score a vital goal for my boyhood heroes in front of the Rangers fans at Parkhead – well, I have to say, that was the best moment of my career.

My header in the 1–1 draw in 2010 meant so much to me and the team. It helped us in a big way towards the league title. Celtic had scored a couple of minutes earlier and the place was jumping, with the home fans all singing and dancing. It was late in the game and I'm sure they all thought they'd won it. The noise was unbelievable. But we went up the pitch and won a corner, and when the cross came in I met it flush with my head and sent it flying into the goal.

I don't think I've scored a better header and to see the ball hit the net right in front of the Rangers end was so special for me. After I scored, I ran over to the supporters. I knew my brother was in the crowd, so I started to look for him, but before I got a chance to pick him out all the boys jumped on top of me.

FOLLOW, FOLLOW

For a boy who grew up as a bluenose in Lanarkshire, it was a fantastic moment. My whole family were Rangers supporters and my dad would take me to Ibrox every second Saturday on the supporters bus from Motherwell.

The era I grew up in was the late 1980s, and although I was too young to be allowed to go to the Old Firm games, my dad would tape them all for me. Even watching them on TV, you could tell just how special they were. The one that sticks out most is Rangers' 5–1 win in 1988, when Ray Wilkins scored his amazing volleyed goal.

That was the game that made me realise what the Old Firm derby was all about. You could see how the players and supporters celebrated and what it meant to them. The atmosphere was incredible and it summed up everything that young boys like me dreamed about doing when they were older.

The funny thing is that my dad actually knows all the TV commentary from that game off by heart! He can talk it all through and tell you exactly what the commentator's about to say. Of course, he now knows about five minutes of the commentary leading up to the first goal I scored against Celtic as well. It's funny to hear, but it just shows you how much it means to everybody in the family. The passion he's got for Rangers is unbelievable and that was passed on to me and my brothers.

I loved going to Ibrox to see Rangers, but as I got older I missed a lot of the bigger games because I tended to be playing myself. I was turning out for all sorts of different teams – I even played in the Primary 7 school team when I was only in Primary 4. Football has been my life for as long as I can remember.

It was my ambition right from the start to play for Rangers and to play for Scotland. In fact, my mum's still got something I wrote at primary school saying I was going to play midfield for Rangers and midfield for Scotland and buy my parents a limousine! My mum still reminds me about that quite a lot – but it just shows it's all I wanted to do.

I started my career as an apprentice at Motherwell. I always seemed to do quite well when we played at Ibrox and even nicked a couple of goals. It was brilliant to play there. I had grown up with Barry Ferguson and by then he was starting to play regularly for Rangers, so I would come up against him. It was all quite surreal because I'd be in the tunnel in a Motherwell strip but I'd be looking in at the Rangers players and wishing it was me – wishing I could play in that fantastic stadium and win trophies and make some contribution to the history of the club.

I moved down to Wigan but when Rangers eventually came in for me it was a dream come true. They put in a couple of bids that were knocked back and I was almost in tears because I didn't think I was going to get the move. But I dug my heels in, put in a transfer request and eventually it all happened.

The day I signed was one of the proudest football moments in my life. I'll never forget I got a speeding ticket and three points on my licence driving up from England on the motorway to sign. But it was well worth it; it was a brilliant feeling to be joining Rangers. That night, I went back to see my mum and dad and my two brothers, and they were all so happy. It's a time I'll never forget.

My first Old Firm game came a few weeks into my first season at Ibrox and it was a slightly bittersweet experience. In the run-up to the game, the nerves were kicking in and I started worrying about what it would be like to play in a derby and get beat. Thankfully, we won 3–0, which was fantastic, although on a personal level there was some disappointment.

I actually scored at the Copland Road end with a goal that would have made it 4–0, but the linesman gave it offside. I got about 15 text messages after the game telling me the goal should have stood. It took a good few weeks to get over it because I'd missed out on the chance to put my name in the history books as an Old Firm scorer.

For the players, there is a huge difference between the build-up to an Old Firm game and that to any other match. As soon as the final whistle goes in the game before, the boys start looking forward to it. Even in the showers after the game, we'll be saying, 'Right, lads, we're not going out tonight, we've got an important game next week.' It's the same at training all week leading up to the game; the atmosphere is just so focused. If it's an away game, when you arrive at Parkhead on the team bus you are getting things thrown at you, you're getting abuse as you walk in the door, but it all helps you get ready for battle, as they say.

In my first season, there were a few foreign lads who were new signings too, like Jean-Claude Darcheville and Daniel Cousin, and when we were in the dressing-room before the first Old Firm game a few of us Scottish lads were drilling it into them how important it was to win the match. They might not have known much about it beforehand, but they soon did.

It affects everyone. Our masseur gets up at half past five on the morning of every Old Firm game because he can't sleep. Before one game, Barry Ferguson decided he was going to get everything waxed! I don't know if it worked, but players often do things that they think might help them psychologically.

It's hard to describe, but you never feel more aware or up for a game than you do when you're walking out the tunnel at either Ibrox or Parkhead before an Old Firm game. Being Scottish, being a fan and knowing what the club's all about makes it easier to handle. When he became gaffer, Walter Smith brought in a lot of Scottish lads who understand the significance of the Old Firm derby and know what the expectations of playing at this club are. It's worked well for him so far and I hope we'll be able to keep that going.

Depending on their age, everyone has their own favourite Old Firm match and hopefully – like mine – yours is included in this book. The games featured stretch back almost 120 years, and in that time there have been many great moments for Rangers fans to savour. Let's hope there will be plenty more memorable wins in the future for my dad to learn the commentary to!

Lee McCulloch
July 2010

INTRODUCTION

A SPECIAL DERBY

The Old Firm rivalry is one of the oldest and fiercest anywhere in world football.

For more than one hundred and twenty years, Glasgow's two football giants, Rangers and Celtic, have vied for supremacy in a city that lives and breathes the game. Controversy is rarely far away when the two meet but amid the fallout that invariably follows their contests, the actual football is often forgotten – even though it is what happens on the pitch that ultimately matters most to the majority of fans.

The story of the Old Firm begins in 1888, the year of the clubs' first meeting. Celtic Football Club was founded by Marist monk Brother Walfrid in the East End of Glasgow in November 1887, with the stated aim of alleviating poverty in the area, specifically among Irish Catholic immigrants. The club had the backing of businessmen from the city's Irish community who set about offering large financial inducements to some of the best players in the country to persuade them to join the new club.

Rangers had been in existence since 1872, when a group of young students from Argyll got together on Glasgow Green to participate in the fledgling sport of football. Within a few years, they had become one of the best-supported clubs in the country and had achieved a level of success on the field that far outstripped their humble origins. By 1888, Rangers had set up home at the first Ibrox Park in the South Side of the city; they remain in the area to this day.

FOLLOW, FOLLOW

The two clubs first met at Celtic Park in May of that year, in what was also Celtic's first-ever match. The home team won 5–2 against a Rangers 2nd XI in front of a crowd of 2,000. Despite having been founded 16 years earlier, Rangers struggled in their early encounters against the better-funded team from the East End of the city. In fact, it took five years for the Light Blues to record their first competitive victory over Celtic, a 3–1 win in the Glasgow Cup final of 1893.

The victory was a watershed for Rangers, who went on to win the Scottish Cup for the first time against the same opponents the following season. Rangers and Celtic soon began to dominate Scottish football and were attracting huge crowds, which in turn helped boost their finances, making them even more powerful. In the early years of the twentieth century, they even gained the nickname 'the Old Firm' from the widely held perception that they were working together to maximise their income.

It was this belief that sparked off one of the worst examples of crowd disorder ever seen at a Scottish football ground, when Rangers and Celtic followers rioted after the 1909 Scottish Cup final replay at Hampden. Fans reacted angrily when it became clear that the teams, having drawn the match 1–1, would be playing a money-spinning second replay instead of extra time.

Between 1904 and 1931, the clubs enjoyed their longest period of unbroken dominance to date, winning 27 league titles between them, although it's a record that looks almost certain to be surpassed in the coming years. When Rangers secured the 2009–10 SPL title, it was the 25th in a row to have been won by one or other of the Old Firm, and there is little evidence that any of Scotland's other clubs will be seriously challenging for the league any time soon.

Of course, the unique feature of the Old Firm rivalry, and the one that in many people's opinion defines the two clubs, is the religious divide. Rangers' support traditionally comes from the Protestant community in the west of Scotland, while Celtic's fan base is, for the most part, made up of Catholics.

Although Celtic were formed as a Roman Catholic club and had always played on their Irish roots, Rangers were not initially defined by religion. But in the early part of the twentieth century that changed, possibly because a good proportion of the Rangers support came from the Clydeside shipyards and many workers were Protestants who had come over from Northern Ireland when the Belfast shipbuilder Harland and Wolff opened its Govan yard in 1912.

At the same time, Celtic's supporters flaunted their support for Irish nationalism, drawing a backlash from the wider Scottish population. Whether it was down to the background of the club's support or simply the fact that they were already Celtic's biggest football rivals, Rangers became the focus for those who disliked the Parkhead club's mix of religion and politics and became Scotland's 'Protestant club'.

The sectarian tensions undoubtedly added spice to the football rivalry that already existed between the two clubs, but they also contributed to the violence that continues to blight the Old Firm to this day. For decades, the authorities have looked at ways of addressing the problem, and while crowd trouble at games is now a rare occurrence, there is plenty of evidence in A&E departments throughout the west of Scotland that they are a long way from finding a solution.

Critics have accused both Rangers and Celtic of exploiting sectarianism for financial gain. Certainly, both clubs saw crowds increase in the first half of the century, culminating in the New Year derby of 1939, for which 118,730 fans crammed into Ibrox, a world-record attendance for a league game.

The Old Firm has long fascinated observers from south of the border and further afield. Foreign journalists regularly appear in the Ibrox and Celtic Park press-boxes, desperate to see what all the fuss is about, and this is nothing new. In 1969, the chief reporter of *Charles Buchan's Football Monthly* magazine was dispatched north to Glasgow to report on the New Year derby. Peter Morris confessed to having been 'traumatised' by the experience but described the clash – which ended in a 1–0 victory for Rangers – as 'a passionate, exciting struggle for prestige'.

Morris wrote:

> Everywhere the half-bottles of whiskey [*sic*] were out, the
> beer cans, the pint glasses, smuggled in under coats, ready to
> be used as weapons if lunacy prevailed. 'Glas-gow Rangers!
> Glas-gow Rangers! We'll support you ever more!' At my end
> the Rangers following was massed – a vast sea of red, white
> and blue humanity, roaring out the old battle songs – some
> going back half a century – confident that THEIR TEAM,
> the beloved Gers, would triumph. Across the park behind the
> far goal, the Celtic hordes were banked in one vast defiant
> phalanx. Solid they were and by contrast, much quieter.

The reporter was disappointed at the attitude of the home support
towards the away players, hearing 'only vitriolic abuse delivered in
thick Glaswegian accents, coarsened by alcohol and the continual
roaring out of those awe-inspiring anthems. It must have been the
same at the Celtic end.'

Given their rivalry, it's no surprise that the Old Firm have had
numerous memorable encounters over the years and many of the
greatest moments in Rangers' history have come against their biggest
rivals. Notable cup finals, league deciders and treble clinchers have
all been won by the Ibrox club at Celtic's expense. (This book looks
at the greatest Old Firm matches from a Rangers point of view, but
neutrals should be aware that Mainstream, the publishers of this book,
are bringing out a companion volume, *Hail! Hail!*, written by Martin
Hannan, which will tackle the subject from a Parkhead perspective.
Buying both would be doubly instructive, and, for the record, neither
Martin nor I has a clue at the time of writing as to which games the
other is choosing.)

Old Firm derbies have provided a stage for some of the greats
of Scottish football. Ibrox legends like David Meiklejohn, Bob
McPhail, Willie Waddell, Jim Baxter, Derek Johnstone, Davie
Cooper and Brian Laudrup have all made memorable match-
winning contributions over the decades. Rangers' record scorer in
Old Firm matches was R.C. Hamilton, who scored 35 times against
Celtic at the turn of the twentieth century. In modern times, arch-

predator Ally McCoist inflicted more pain on the Parkhead club than anyone else, scoring 27 times in Old Firm derbies. Given the regular movement of players in the modern era, it seems unlikely that his tally will ever be bettered.

The great Rangers teams of the 1940s and early 1960s achieved many triumphs over Celtic, including the Scottish Cup final replay of 1963, featuring a virtuoso performance from Jim Baxter.

Celtic enjoyed a period of dominance in the second half of the 1960s and early 1970s that was difficult for Rangers supporters to bear. Having to watch their biggest rivals win nine successive league championships made the Scottish Cup wins of 1966 and 1973 and the League Cup triumph of 1970 all the sweeter.

The tables were turned in the late '80s when Graeme Souness became manager and set in motion Rangers' own nine in a row. His first trophy as manager came in the League Cup final against Celtic in 1986. When he arrived in Glasgow, Souness infamously dismissed the Old Firm derby as just another game, little more than another two points to be won. But it didn't take him long to realise just how important the Glasgow rivalry is to supporters and players alike.

As a Rangers fan, his assistant Walter Smith understood the significance of the derby from the outset and after moving into the manager's seat on Souness's departure he enjoyed a string of important victories over Celtic. With Rangers moving ever closer to matching their rivals' nine in a row, the tensions between the two clubs reached unprecedented levels, at times boiling over on the pitch and off.

The big spending of the 1990s under Souness, Smith and Dick Advocaat gave way to a new age of austerity in the first decade of the twenty-first century, but still Rangers enjoyed important and memorable wins over Celtic, including the dramatic Scottish Cup final of 2002 when Peter Løvenkrands scored a last-minute winner.

Despite their early struggles against Celtic, Rangers have enjoyed the upper hand over their great rivals over the decades. In the 296 league games up until the end of the 2009–10 season, the Ibrox men have won 116 times, compared to Celtic's 96 victories. Including

FOLLOW, FOLLOW

Scottish Cup and League Cup ties, Rangers' record is played 388, won 155, lost 139 and drawn 94.

Of course, there are many who see the Old Firm's ongoing battle for supremacy as little more than a local skirmish in a footballing backwater. There are many supporters on both sides who would rather see their clubs compete on a bigger stage, where they could break free of the shackles of a rivalry they consider prevents them from reaching their true potential.

Both Rangers and Celtic have explored the possibility of competing in the English Premier League but have been thwarted at every turn. The chances of such a move happening now look remote in the extreme, and the management of both clubs have resigned themselves to a future based in Scotland. Despite all the hand-wringing that surrounds the Old Firm, their meetings will continue to be the most important on the Scottish football calendar.

For all its faults, the Old Firm derby remains one of the most watchable matches in the world, up there alongside Real v. Barça, Boca Juniors v. River Plate, Milan v. Inter and Liverpool v. Manchester United. The football on offer would rarely satisfy the purist, and the madness that often surrounds it is not to everyone's taste. But for passion, excitement, tension, drama and controversy, it's hard to beat.

1

FIRST BLOOD

RANGERS 3 CELTIC 1
GLASGOW CUP FINAL
PLAYED AT CATHKIN PARK, GLASGOW
18 FEBRUARY 1893

Rangers team: Haddow, Hay, Drummond, Marshall, A. McCreadie,
Mitchell, H. McCreadie, Davie, Kerr, Barker, J. McPherson

Rangers scorers: Barker, Kerr, McPherson

The rivalry between Rangers and Celtic today is so strong and so deep-rooted that it's difficult to imagine that the clubs have ever been anything other than the bitterest of enemies. It goes without saying that there is a deep enmity between the two sets of supporters and there have been enough flashpoints on the pitch to suggest that from time to time the players don't get along either. Even in the rarefied atmosphere of the boardrooms, there often appears to be an underlying sense of mistrust between the two clubs, which occasionally erupts into open hostility.

So it may come as something of a shock to many of the modern-day followers of the Old Firm to learn that in the early years of their existence they were actually best of friends. When Rangers beat Celtic in the final of the Glasgow Cup in 1893, the losers were full of praise for their conquerors. During the post-match banquet at a Glasgow hotel, the two clubs swore loyalty to each other, while Celtic president

FOLLOW, FOLLOW

John Glass stated that there was no team Celtic would rather have seen win the competition than Rangers.

Newspaper reports at the time recorded the 'fine spirit of kinship' that prevailed between the two clubs. The *Scottish Referee* sports paper highlighted 'interchanges of mutual good behaviour' and praised the teams for not resorting to 'rough play'. The paper declared, 'Not a regrettable incident occurred on the field to mar the reputation of any player or spoil the harmony which characterised the play.'

Such reports of mutual respect and appreciation are a far cry from the headlines we see after most Glasgow derby matches these days. However, cynics might be inclined to suggest that Celtic could afford to be magnanimous in defeat on this occasion. Although they had been in existence for 16 years longer than Celtic, Rangers were in many ways the plucky underdogs of the Glasgow football scene. After a successful first decade, the 1880s had been a difficult time for the club. The Glasgow Cup victory in 1893 was the first time they had ever won the prestigious trophy and it was their first cup win of any kind since they had lifted the Glasgow Charity Cup 14 years earlier. Even more significantly, the 3–1 victory marked Rangers' first-ever win over Celtic in a competitive match, almost five years after they had first played each other.

Celtic, on the other hand, had hit the ground running after their formation in 1888. The club was set up by the Marist priest Brother Walfrid with the laudable aim of providing assistance to poor Roman Catholics in Glasgow's East End, most of whom were immigrants from Ireland. With the backing of wealthy businessmen, Celtic were quickly able to gather players from other Scottish teams, most notably Edinburgh-based Hibernian, which until Celtic's formation was the pre-eminent Catholic club in Scotland. In an era when professionalism was banned in Scottish football, the financial inducements that lured the Hibs players to Glasgow were met with widespread disapproval and sat uncomfortably with the club's charitable ethos.

The tactic may have been morally questionable, but it had the desired effect, allowing Celtic to quickly establish themselves as a major force in the game. Their first match was a 5–2 win over Rangers' 2nd XI in May 1888, and silverware wasn't long in arriving. A Scottish Cup victory in 1892 was followed the next season by the league title, the first of four championship wins that decade.

In contrast to Celtic's instant affluence, Rangers had been formed in 1872 by a handful of young football enthusiasts, all under the age of 18, with little more than a leather ball to their name. Given their poverty of resources, their early success was remarkable. Within five years, the fledgling club had seen several of its players represent the national team, moved into its first ground, at Kinning Park on Glasgow's South Side, and reached the final of the Scottish Cup.

But after winning their first major trophy, the Charity Cup, in 1879, the Light Blues struggled in the following decade. The 1888–89 season was undoubtedly the worst in the club's history to that point, with 19 defeats and 7 draws from their 39 matches. A 6–1 home defeat to Celtic in the Glasgow Cup was a particular low point.

Despite the relative lack of on-field success, Rangers had grown to be one of the most popular clubs in the country and in 1887 moved to a new, bigger ground at Ibrox, close to the site of the current stadium. The inaugural Scottish League championship was jointly won with Dumbarton in 1891, and although it would be another seven years before Rangers would be champions again, there were signs that good times were on the horizon.

Gradually, Rangers were assembling a line-up that would be capable of competing for the major silverware every season. Kilmarnock-born John McPherson was undoubtedly the star of the team, an inside-forward who would serve the club as a player for 12 years before becoming a director. He has been described as the greatest player of the club's first fifty years, one early history of the club saying of him, 'He delighted in dribbling up to a defender, feinting and swerving round him, before delivering his shot.'

McPherson had scored four goals as Rangers defeated Northern, Linthouse, Queen's Park and Glasgow Thistle on their way to the 1893 Glasgow Cup final. Although both teams were fighting it out for the league title, Celtic went into the final as strong favourites, with some pundits confidently predicting a walkover. They had some justification; Celtic had won seven of the ten previous encounters between the teams, with the other three being drawn. *Scottish Referee* analysed the strengths and weaknesses of the teams and concluded that, despite having a stronger half-back line (Bob Marshall, Hugh McCreadie and David Mitchell), Rangers were generally weaker and would have to rely on the condition of the pitch to restrict Celtic's 'parlour passing'.

The predictions of a one-sided final appear to have had an impact on the attendance. With inclement weather forecast and controversy raging in the press over the cost of admission to football games, it seemed that the anticipated lack of competition persuaded many fans to stay away. It was a lower than expected crowd of 10,000 that gathered for the match at Third Lanark's ground, Cathkin Park, on what turned out to be a mild February afternoon. But what the spectators lacked in numbers they made up for in passion. As *Scottish Referee* recorded, 'Enthusiasm prevailed, especially among the Ibrox contingent, who seemed imbued with exhilarating feelings of confidence in the ability of the Light Blues to win.' And if newspaper reports are to believed, those who stayed at home missed a 'hard and at times brilliant' game.

With the clock approaching 3.30 p.m., Celtic, in their green and white vertically striped shirts (it was to be a few more years before they adopted the horizontally striped jerseys), appeared first from the pavilion, headed by their captain, James Kelly. A minute later, the Light Blues' skipper, Mitchell, led his team onto the field. Both sets of players were given a hearty welcome, according to the *Glasgow Herald*, although *Scottish Referee* indicated that the reception for Rangers was rather more vociferous. It had been so long since Rangers had last won a cup competition that it was no surprise that their followers were excited at the prospect of picking up some silverware.

Since the anticipated bad weather hadn't materialised, it was Celtic who had reason to be happier with the conditions as Neilly Kerr kicked off the match for Rangers exactly on the half-hour. Although the pitch was a little softer than the East End team would have liked, the *Herald* opined that the playing surface was probably the best of any ground in the city. In theory, the conditions should have been ideal for Celtic's passing game, but Rangers' half-backs refused to allow the opposition forwards any time or space to indulge themselves, paralysing the Celtic attack with their dogged defence. Marshall in particular was singled out by *Scottish Referee* for his 'strong, legitimate blocking and tackling'.

In attack, Rangers were 'cool, clever and confident' and once they won the ball ensured that they wasted no time in getting it into the danger areas. The contrast in styles was stark. While Celtic apparently wanted to paint pretty pictures, Rangers adopted a far more pragmatic approach: get the ball, move it forward quickly and test the goalkeeper. That's not to say that they resorted to some sort of prototype Route One approach; the *Herald* reported how fans cheered their 'capital passing' and were treated to the best play Rangers had produced all season.

The supposed difference in playing styles of the two clubs is one of the enduring clichés of the Old Firm legend. The received wisdom, perpetuated through the years by lazy pundits, is that Celtic are the cavalier footballing side, while Rangers rely on brute strength to crush their opponents. Of course, there have been plenty of occasions over the decades when the teams have lived up to their stereotypical reputations, but equally the opposite is true. No Rangers team featuring the likes of Alan Morton, Jim Baxter, Brian Laudrup or Ronald de Boer, to name but four, could ever be accused of not playing football. Dick Advocaat's Rangers of the late 1990s produced some of the most dazzling attacking football ever seen in Scotland, while the Celtic teams of Martin O'Neill relied heavily on pace, strength and aerial power to bludgeon their way to victory.

It was a combination of powerful tackling and speedy passing that saw the Light Blues gradually impose their will on the final and after a string of near misses, it was no surprise when they took the lead after half an hour through a long-range shot from John Barker. Two more goals were added in the second half by Kerr and McPherson as Rangers continued to dominate the game. It was only in the very final moments that Celtic were finally able to breach the resolute Rangers defence, but Sandy McMahon's strike was no more than a consolation, and the final whistle brought scenes of celebration for those in blue.

Fans piled onto the Cathkin pitch to hail their heroes, carrying the players shoulder high in triumph. The celebrations didn't stop there, as *Scottish Referee* reported: 'On the road back to the city, car, brake, cab and other vehicles were eagerly seized upon by enthusiastic Ibroxonians, hundreds of them sported the colours and frantically waved the favourite "blue" to and fro in the evening breeze.'

While the supporters enjoyed their evening, the trophy was presented to Rangers officials at a post-match dinner attended by both clubs at the Alexandra Hotel in Glasgow. Before the banjo band of the Minerva Club began their after-dinner entertainment, Bailie John Ure Primrose, a Glasgow councillor and future chairman of Rangers, urged city fathers to encourage the development of the game of football. His comments were warmly welcomed by *Scottish Referee*, which described them as 'a splendid tonic to the prattling paroquets who are never ceasing in their attempts to belittle and bespatter our pastime'.

Although football crowds were increasing all the time and publications like *Scottish Referee* devoted huge amounts of space to the game, the mainstream media – especially the 'serious' newspapers like *The Scotsman* and the *Glasgow Herald* – remained generally unconvinced of its merits. Match reports were usually short, factual and difficult to find, with more coverage granted to sports like cricket, rugby and horse racing.

Where today the press build-up to big matches begins days in advance, the 1893 Glasgow Cup final received no coverage at all in the newspapers on the morning of the game. The day's headlines were dominated by the ongoing debate in the House of Commons over the Irish Home Rule Bill.

The bill was the second attempt by William Gladstone as prime minister to grant home rule to Ireland, his first try in 1886 having led to him losing power. This time, Gladstone, who drew up the bill in secret, managed to steer it through the Commons but it was eventually rejected by the Conservative-dominated House of

FIRST BLOOD

Lords. *The Scotsman* was strongly against the proposals, deriding their 'feebleness and fatuity', and questioned whether Britain could rely on the 'loyal support and co-operation' of a future Irish government should the country find itself at war with France or America. 'Nobody can honestly or prudently say that we could,' the paper concluded. 'It is necessary to take to the Gladstonian refuge of fatuity, and say that such a war can never arise.'

Although the politics of Ireland were not yet an intrinsic part of the Rangers–Celtic rivalry, officials of both clubs would have taken more than a passing interest in the coverage of the issue over their breakfast that morning. Given their roots, the Celtic camp would clearly want to be up to date with any developments in plans for the future governance of Ireland, while the political views of senior Rangers figures like Primrose were firmly on the Unionist side of the debate.

Scottish Referee was fulsome in its praise of Rangers' victory, enthusing over their 'daring, dashing, play'. An editorial stated:

> Perseverance has had its reward and no one will grudge the Rangers nor will a solitary voice seek to diminish or detract from the play by which this signal triumph was achieved. Pluckily the club has fought against and borne with the knocks of misfortune these 14 years and now that those who defend its honour on the field and those who loyally follow its fortunes round the ropes both rejoice in all the glory that a cup brings in its train, none will deny them enjoying to the fullest measure the fruits of victory. The fact that it was thoroughly deserved adds an additional spice of interest and pleasure to the win.

Rangers were growing in stature as a club, thanks in no small part to the efforts of one of their greatest servants. In May 1889, William Wilton had become match secretary, at the age of 23, a role that effectively saw him become the club's first-ever team manager. For 30 years, until his untimely death in a boating accident on the Clyde in

1920, he was the dominant figure at the club, and without his guiding influence it is unlikely that Rangers would have gone on to become the force in Scottish football that they did. The remit of his job seems to have touched on every aspect of the running of Rangers, not least the development of Ibrox.

The Glasgow Cup victory was something of a coming of age for Rangers on the field. The club's players and supporters had in the past been characterised as having a supreme confidence in their own team's abilities that sometimes appeared misplaced. Now, with this triumph, they had something tangible to back up their self-belief. At last, they had bettered Celtic and, in lifting the Glasgow Cup, were now officially the best team in the city.

2

CUP OF CHEER

Rangers 3 Celtic 1
Scottish Cup Final
Played at Hampden Park, Glasgow
17 February 1894

Rangers team: Haddow, Smith, Drummond, Marshall, A. McCreadie,
Mitchell, Steel, H. McCreadie, Gray, McPherson, Barker

Rangers scorers: H. McCreadie, Barker, McPherson

It may have taken Rangers five years to finally record a win over
Celtic, but that first victory in 1893 proved to be something of a
turning point. The following season saw the Ibrox men play their
rivals from the East End six times, losing only once and scoring fifteen
goals to Celtic's seven. Among the four wins was a 5–0 thrashing at
Ibrox, which saw Hugh McCreadie score a hat-trick.

But by far the most significant Rangers victory over Celtic in 1894
came at Hampden in the Scottish Cup final. In their 21-year history,
the Light Blues had never won the national cup competition and had
only twice reached the final.

Both their previous final appearances had been against Vale of
Leven, one of the early giants of the Scottish game. The final of
1877 went to a second replay, with Rangers eventually defeated
3–2 in a match considered by many at the time to be the greatest
ever seen in Scotland.

FOLLOW, FOLLOW

Two years later, the clubs met again at the first Hampden and drew 1–1 in controversial circumstances. Rangers had a goal disallowed for offside that would have put them 2–0 ahead and were convinced it should have stood. To make matters worse, Vale equalised with three minutes to go. So angry were Rangers that they refused to turn up for the replay, and their opponents won the cup by default. The club officials who took the stance on a point of principle couldn't possibly have imagined that it would be 15 years before Rangers would reach a final again.

By the time the Light Blues made it to their third final, in 1894, Scottish football had already undergone important changes, two in particular which would have a major impact on the future direction of the game. First came the introduction of the league championship in 1890. Although the Scottish Cup remained the most important tournament, the league was rapidly gaining in prestige and before long it would eclipse the cup in significance.

The second change came in the summer of 1893 and was even more significant in the development of the sport. After years of stubborn resistance, the Scottish Football Association (SFA) finally bowed to the inevitable and legalised professionalism. The move brought Scotland into line with the game south of the border and ended the practice of clubs making underhand payments to players. In the first season of the professional era, Rangers paid their first-team players £2 a week, by no means a fortune but still more than the typical worker would have been paid at the time. And it was enough to stop the steady stream of players heading south of the border.

Rangers started their Scottish Cup campaign in this brave new era with a convincing 8–0 win over Glasgow club Cowlairs, one of the league's founding members. Victories in the subsequent rounds over Leith Athletic, Clyde and Queen's Park saw Rangers win through to the final at Hampden, where Celtic lay in wait.

Rangers had been underdogs when they faced Celtic in the Glasgow Cup final the previous season, but this time it was different. The wins over the Parkhead club earlier in the season had given their ever-optimistic fans a real reason to believe they would win the trophy. However, one of the many derby clichés that have grown up over the years is that the form book goes out the window when the Old Firm meet. And with five full Scottish internationals in the Celtic team, Rangers would have been foolish to be complacent.

As an attacking force, Rangers had already proved that they had the firepower to wound Celtic; they had scored nine goals in the three matches between the teams that took place before the cup final. But with only two conceded, the goals-against column showed the Ibrox men were just as strong at the other end of the pitch – thanks in no small part to Jock Drummond and Nicol Smith.

The full-backs played together throughout the 1890s and their partnership was a vital part of Rangers' success at that time. They amassed a huge number of honours playing for the Light Blues and represented Scotland 26 times between them.

Drummond was signed in 1892 from Falkirk, while Smith arrived from junior football in Ayrshire the following year. Both players were tough competitors, not afraid to go in where it hurt. An official Rangers history book, William Allison's *Rangers: The New Era*, published in 1966, said that Smith was 'robust and speedy' and that 'he tackled with explosive power'. The author went on: 'He revelled in a vigorous shoulder charge and seldom failed to win it. He was brave too.'

Tragically, Smith, known as 'Nick', was struck down by illness in December 1905 and died from a gastric infection the following month at the age of just 32. His final game for Rangers had been against Third Lanark in November.

The clash between Rangers and Celtic had captured the public's imagination, especially in the west of Scotland. A week of heavy rain had left the Hampden pitch heavy and there were further downpours on the day of the game, casting some doubt on whether it would be able to go ahead. Queen's Park officials did their best to make sure the pitch was playable, including scattering hayseed on the turf, and the pitch passed a late inspection by the referee. There was a feeling that the soft conditions would suit Rangers. The general belief ahead of the game was that it would certainly be the team with the greatest stamina that would win out.

The miserable weather also had an impact on the attendance, but despite the rain more than 17,000 braved the elements to back their team. As had been the case at the previous season's Glasgow Cup final, Rangers enjoyed the majority of the support and their fans made themselves heard. *The Scotsman* reported, 'As the teams took the field punctual to time, there was no mistaking the fact that the Rangers were favourites with the crowd, their reception being much more hearty than that accorded to the Irishmen.'

As expected, Rangers adapted more quickly to the underfoot conditions, and they started the game well, immediately putting the Celtic defence under pressure. Doyle had to scramble the ball away on several occasions in the early part of the match, and a shot by Hugh McCreadie was fisted away by goalkeeper Joe Cullen. Celtic soon got themselves into the match and before long play was raging from end to end, both sides passing up good chances to break the deadlock.

Celtic made a bright start to the second half, but as the match wore on Rangers' superior fitness told and they gradually assumed the upper hand. After a couple of near misses, they finally took the lead ten minutes into the second half through a low shot by Hugh McCreadie that Cullen failed to stop. McCreadie had reacted quickly after receiving a pass from John Barker. Driven on by their delirious fans, Rangers added a second a few minutes later through Barker, and when John McPherson added a third the Ibrox supporters were convinced that their long wait for cup glory was over.

Celtic refused to give up, though, and managed to pull a goal back in controversial circumstances with 15 minutes to go. A corner to the Parkhead men resulted in a goalmouth scramble, and Willie Maley stuck out a foot and sent the ball goal bound. Celtic insisted the ball crossed the line, and despite protests from the Light Blues the referee, Mr Marshall, allowed the goal to stand. The goal ensured a frantic finish to the game, with Celtic piling on pressure in the closing minutes, but the Rangers defence performed admirably, with Drummond and Smith in particular gaining plaudits.

CUP OF CHEER

When the final whistle blew, Celtic were out on their feet and Rangers had held on to record a famous victory, one which the *Glasgow Herald* said was met with 'unbounded enthusiasm'. It was undoubtedly a popular victory, and not only among the Rangers support. *The Scotsman* said the win was 'as deserved as it was popular' and in the hours after the match, telegrams of congratulation arrived from all over Britain and Ireland.

The victorious players – now, of course, fully fledged professionals – were handsomely rewarded for their cup win with a bonus of three guineas to each of the eleven. The club could well afford the payments. Accounts presented at the 1894 AGM showed that income for the year was £5,227, a fivefold increase since 1889.

Although the players were now relatively well off, they weren't quite in the super-rich bracket yet, so probably wouldn't have found themselves in the sights of the anarchist groups that were springing up across Europe at this time, intent on destroying the bourgeoisie. Newspapers on the day of the cup final were full of the story of Martial Bourdin, a Frenchman who died when the explosives he was carrying detonated prematurely outside the Royal Observatory in London. It was just one of several attempted anarchist attacks to take place across the Continent in 1894, with reports of incidents in France, Spain and Germany, and there were links between the bomb used in London and the one used in a similar, fatal attack in Paris earlier in the year.

Bourdin, a tailor by trade, had travelled by tram to Greenwich Park, apparently with the intention of blowing up the Observatory. As he approached the building, the bomb exploded in his hand, blowing it off and causing serious injuries to his torso. The *Daily Telegraph* said the scene of the explosion was marked by 'great stains of blood' and reported police speculation that he had gone to Greenwich with a 'criminal intention'. The following day, police raided the Autonomie Club – a haunt of foreign anarchists, including Bourdin – in the Tottenham Court Road area. They seized documents and detained around 80 foreigners, according to *The Scotsman*.

FOLLOW, FOLLOW

On a lighter note, the year also saw major developments that would have far-reaching consequences for entertainment. William Kennedy Dickson, a French-born inventor of Scottish descent, received a patent in 1894 for motion-picture film, while in April the same year his boss, Thomas Edison, publicly demonstrated his peep-show device, the Kinetoscope, a precursor to movies.

Dickson later invented the Mutoscope, which created the illusion of moving images – often of demure Victorian women undressing – through a revolving drum. They became known as 'What the Butler Saw machines' after one of the most popular of the reels and could be found mainly in seaside resorts like Blackpool. The year also saw the opening of Blackpool Tower, a tourist attraction that would be visited by millions of Glaswegians over the decades and remains a popular destination for Scots.

Having broken their Scottish Cup duck, lifting the trophy suddenly became second nature for Rangers. In the season 1896–97, they won their second Scottish Cup as well as the Glasgow Cup and the Glasgow Charity Cup. The following season, the Scottish and Glasgow cups were retained and only a 1–0 defeat to Third Lanark in the final of the Charity Cup prevented a repeat of the 'Three Cups' achievement.

But it was the 1898–99 season that saw Rangers achieve a unique record that remains to this day. Captained by the legendary R.C. Hamilton, the team won all 18 of its league matches, a perfect record. Along the way, they beat Celtic 4–1 at Ibrox and 4–0 at Parkhead, as well as inflicting a 7–0 win on Dundee and thrashing one-time title contenders Hibs 10–0.

The achievement bettered that of the Preston North End 'Invincibles' team of 1888–89, which went undefeated in the English league, but at the time arguments raged as to whether this was the greatest Rangers team. The Three Cups feat was seen by some as even more impressive. With only 18 games played, it is difficult to compare the performance with the achievements of the modern era. But no matter how it is judged today, the season remains the high point of Rangers' first three decades.

The last years of the nineteenth century would see big changes off the pitch at the club. Since its formation in 1872, Rangers had been a private club run by members, along similar lines to a bowling or golf club. In May 1899, the decision was taken that the club should become a limited liability company and the Rangers Football Club Ltd was formed. The old committees were replaced with a board of directors, and the president, James Henderson, became chairman.

As had been predicted when the idea of moving out to Ibrox was first mooted, Glasgow's population was growing at a rapid rate and the area was becoming increasingly popular. By the end of the 1890s, Ibrox's capacity had grown and the team was attracting crowds of up to 30,000 for big games.

Rangers decided that they had outgrown their old ground and began drawing up plans for a new home, on adjoining land. On 30 December 1899, the new Ibrox was opened for business, with Heart of Midlothian the first visitors. The new century was bringing with it exciting developments for Rangers, but there would also be many challenges ahead, not least the one presented by their rivals across the city.

3

THE BIRTH OF THE OLD FIRM

RANGERS 1 CELTIC 1
SCOTTISH CUP FINAL REPLAY
PLAYED AT HAMPDEN PARK, GLASGOW
17 APRIL 1909

Rangers team: Rennie, Law, Craig, Gordon, Stark, Galt, Bennett, McDonald, Reid, McPherson, A. Smith

Rangers scorer: Gordon

By the start of the twentieth century, Rangers and Celtic had established themselves as Scotland's two biggest clubs. As the pair grew more successful, competition developed between them on the pitch, and this translated into a strong rivalry between the two sets of opposing supporters. But, despite growing tensions off the field, the two clubs remained firm friends at the administrative level, even gaining the infamous nickname 'the Old Firm' from the widely held perception that they had developed a commercial relationship that benefited both financially.

Rangers started the new century on a high, winning four consecutive league titles between 1899 and 1902. However, their fortunes took a dramatic downturn after the Ibrox disaster of April 1902, when 25 fans were killed and more than 500 injured as part of Ibrox's new wooden terrace collapsed during a Scotland v. England international.

FOLLOW, FOLLOW

The disaster had a devastating effect on the club, both off the field and on. The club's reputation had taken a public battering, while the cost of rebuilding Ibrox was enormous. As a result, the club was forced to put twenty-two players on the transfer market, bringing to an end a glorious era that had seen the capture of four league titles in a row. The sudden decline of the Ibrox club allowed a revitalised Celtic to take advantage, winning six successive titles at the beginning of the new century.

Despite their troubles, Rangers had never been more popular among the paying public. They were now the country's best-supported team. Average league crowds in the first decade of the 1900s ranged from 10,500 to 16,750, and for big games attendances would regularly reach 30,000. Matches against Celtic were now attracting attendances of up to 60,000. A Scottish Cup replay in February 1908 saw 54,000 inside Ibrox, and the same season's Ne'erday derby at Ibrox attracted 60,000.

The huge crowds brought in much-needed money to both clubs, and this led to a growing feeling in the football world that they were working together to maximise their income. The Old Firm nickname is believed to have come from a cartoon published by *Scottish Referee* in April 1904. It depicted a man with a sandwich board bearing the slogan, 'Patronise the Old Firm – Rangers, Celtic Ltd'.

Supporters of both clubs were suspicious of the number of draws that resulted when the teams met in cup ties. Draws meant replays – lucrative for the clubs but costly for fans. This conspiracy theory may have been no more than an early manifestation of Old Firm fan paranoia, but five years later those same suspicions were the catalyst for possibly the worst disorder ever seen at a Scottish football match.

In a place described by Victorian journalist Sir John Hammerton as 'probably the most drink-sodden city in Great Britain', crowd trouble was nothing new. The opening of the first Ibrox was marred by a pitch invasion, while there was trouble at the 1892 Scottish Cup final between Queen's Park and Celtic.

The traditional New Year derby match was often the catalyst for crowd trouble in the early days, with the 1902 clash at Ibrox having to be abandoned because of off-field disturbances. An hour before the scheduled kick-off time, the ground was already full, with thousands more waiting outside. With 30 minutes to go to the start, police decided to allow thousands of boys to move onto the cinder track around the pitch, as both stands and the east terracing were packed to bursting. Supporters soon spilled onto the turf behind the goals to escape the crush. The match finally got under way without any serious injuries, but according to the *Evening Times* 'mob law prevailed' and the referee was forced to bring the match to an early conclusion. Rangers were blamed for not having enough police on duty to control the crowd and for allowing too many fans in.

In January 1909, *The Scotsman* reported 'an unfortunate incident' at the New Year's Day derby. A collection was being made during the game for the East Park Home for Infirm Children when a man took umbrage at being presented with the box, seized it and threw it away. It fell into the stand and struck a spectator's hat, smashing it completely. The box then hit former Glasgow Lord Provost Sir John Ure Primrose behind the ear, inflicting a nasty cut.

But these incidents were nothing compared to the events of April 1909. *The Scotsman* described the Hampden riot as 'one of the most disgraceful blots disfiguring the annals of the game'. More than a century later, it is difficult to argue with that assessment. Marauding fans from both sides invaded the pitch, torched the stadium and attacked police officers and firefighters, leaving more than 100 people injured and doing thousands of pounds' worth of damage to the ground.

Rangers and Celtic had drawn 2–2 in the first final at Hampden. An exciting match ended in controversial circumstances when Celtic scored a late equaliser. The referee ruled that Rangers keeper Harry Rennie had carried the ball over the goal line as he dodged out of the way of the onrushing Celtic forward Jimmy Quinn. Rennie insisted that he had not stepped over the line and wept after the match at the thought that what he saw as a grave injustice had robbed his team of the cup.

FOLLOW, FOLLOW

When they met again for the replay a week later in front of a crowd of 70,000 at the same venue, the teams tied again, this time 1–1. When the final whistle blew at the end of the 90 minutes, there was an assumption among the supporters that extra time would be played. It appears they had been influenced by a newspaper article published earlier in the week in which the Celtic secretary, Willie Maley, had said his club would be in favour of playing extra time after the first replay. This turned out to be impossible; competition rules stated that extra time could be played only after a third match. Unfortunately, this fact was not reported.

The confusion was exacerbated at the end of the game. The official police report stated that while most of the Rangers players immediately returned to the pavilion, the Celtic team lingered on the pitch, giving the fans the impression that there would be more football. A witness later told *The Scotsman*:

> Hay, the captain of the Celtic, stood almost in the centre of the field with the ball in his arm and deepened the general impression that there would be further play. Most of the Rangers players followed the referee to the pavilion but almost the whole of the Celtic team remained on the field.

When the official announcement was made that the game was over and there would be a second replay, all hell broke loose. It started with a few howls of discontent from the terraces ('Play on', 'Continue the game', 'Play the extra half-hour') but very quickly escalated into all-out disorder. Young fans – described later by Sir John Ure Primrose as 'the hooligan element' – tore down barricades and streamed onto the field. Worryingly, it quickly became clear that they were heading for the pavilion, where, by now, both teams were ensconced. Despite being hopelessly outnumbered, the police managed to keep them out, but this only had the effect of the angry mob instead turning their ire on the constabulary. Bricks, stones and bottles were hurled towards the officers, who retaliated by drawing their batons. Hand-to-hand combat ensued, but the sheer weight of numbers ensured that the police were overwhelmed.

The Scotsman reported, 'Stricken men fell with blood streaming from their wounds, and the rage and tumult became more intense. Many of the police were beaten and injured in the most brutal and callous fashion, and the force as a whole were the chief sufferers of the day.' Reserves were called in from other parts of the city in an attempt to quell the riot, and for a while they had some success, especially the mounted police. But soon even they became a target, with rioters surrounding them and forcing one of the officers to dismount. Supporters 'beat man and horse most unmercifully', according to reports.

At one point, a group of fans tore up and down the pitch with a road roller, leaving the turf badly damaged. The goalposts were ripped from the ground and the nets cut up. One crossbar was dragged into the street outside the ground, where a gang of men and boys hacked shards off it for a memento of the day. Police helmets that had been lost in the battle were also cut up into strips and taken home as souvenirs.

Meanwhile, back inside, broken barricades were piled up in a heap and set alight, with whisky being used as ignition fuel. As the huge bonfire raged, the Hampden pay-boxes were set alight. Firefighters called to tackle the blazes were set upon, with one suffering a number of broken ribs. The rioters also grabbed the firemen's hoses and cut them into pieces in an attempt to prevent them dousing the flames.

A Glasgow detective who had been on pickpocket-monitoring duties at the game later described the scenes he encountered when he arrived back at Hampden to help his colleagues. He told *The Scotsman*:

> When I arrived there was a terrible row proceeding. The police and the firemen inside the grounds were being pelted with stones, and similar treatment was being meted out to the police who were on duty outside the barricade. The firemen were struggling with the crowd, who were busy cutting their hosepipes and doing everything they could

> to prevent the work of the extinction of the fire being
> proceeded with. Two of our men arrested an individual for
> stone throwing but they were set upon by the mob and had
> to let their man go.

He added, 'Dreadful excitement prevailed everywhere.'

It took the authorities more than two hours to finally restore order. Police numbers had been swollen to around 200, and gradually they were able to clear the pitch and the surroundings. Outside the ground, the mob continued on its wrecking spree, hurling missiles at the police and smashing every window within reach with stones. Thankfully the rioters were unaware that just yards away officials from the SFA were ensconced in a flat in Somerville Place, directly opposite the main entrance of the ground. In their possession were the £1,400 takings from the match as well as the Scottish Cup itself. One can only imagine the outcome had the crowds discovered their presence.

In the end, around 120 people were injured, mostly police officers. Incredibly, despite the mayhem, just one man was arrested during the battles. He spent a couple of nights in the cells at Queen's Park police station before appearing in court charged with assaulting a plain-clothes policeman and a soldier.

News of the riot made the final editions of Glasgow's evening newspapers, and the next day crowds descended on Hampden again, this time to see the scene at first hand. It was not a pretty sight. The woodwork at the Somerville Place pay-boxes was completely burned away, leaving a mass of exposed, twisted metal. Stones and broken bottles littered the enclosure, and every few yards there were dark patches where fire had scarred the ground.

Condemnation of the fans' actions was immediate and universal, but in the aftermath of the disturbances thoughts quickly turned back to the football and, specifically, what should be done about the Scottish Cup. Needless to say there were those who felt that mob rule should not be allowed to prevail and that the second replay should go ahead, with Sir John Ure Primrose among them. He was critical of the level of policing at Hampden and also questioned why a public announcement hadn't been made ahead of the game on what would happen should the replay end tied.

Despite this view, officials of both clubs agreed that the final should be abandoned. A joint statement issued the following day stated:

> Although it was mooted during the week that extra time might be played in the event of a draw, it was found that the cup competition rules prevented this. On account of the regrettable occurrences of Saturday, both clubs agree to petition the Association that the final tie be abandoned.

The SFA convened a special meeting on the Monday evening after the match to discuss what would happen next. The Old Firm clubs rejected a proposal that the game be played outside Glasgow, and, after a 15–11 vote, it was decided that it should not take place at all. So, for the first and only time in the competition's history, the cup and the medals were withheld.

There will be many looking back at this disturbing episode who will see it as nothing more than an early example of the sectarian baggage that goes with Scotland's two biggest clubs. In truth, there is no evidence to support that assertion. In fact, in many ways this was a rare case where the supporters of both teams were united against a common enemy: the powers that be. Police and firemen were the target of the mob, not rival supporters. And it was a joint sense of injustice that sparked off the trouble in the first place, rather than the bitter enmity that would fuel later violence involving followers of both clubs.

Nevertheless, whatever attempted justification or explanation there may have been, it remains the case that the behaviour of a minority of fans that afternoon was totally unacceptable. Rangers and Celtic were the new powerhouses of Scottish football, but their success meant they were both attracting an unwelcome hooligan element to their support. A century on, it is a problem that both clubs continue to grapple with.

4

···

HOODOO BUSTERS

RANGERS 4 CELTIC 0
SCOTTISH CUP FINAL
PLAYED AT HAMPDEN PARK, GLASGOW
14 APRIL 1928

Rangers team: T. Hamilton, Gray, R. Hamilton, Buchanan, Meiklejohn,
Craig, Archibald, Cunningham, Fleming, McPhail, Morton

Rangers scorers: Meiklejohn, Archibald (2), McPhail

At precisely one minute past four on a windy April afternoon in 1928, Rangers' legendary captain David Meiklejohn stepped up to take possibly the most important penalty kick in the club's history. The vast Hampden crowd of more than 118,000 fell eerily silent as he began his run-up. Moments later, the man known as Meek to his teammates blasted the ball into the net past the Celtic goalkeeper, John Thomson.

There was an explosion of noise from the terraces. The Light Blues were a goal ahead in the cup final and well on their way to ending an astonishing 25-year hoodoo.

When Rangers beat Hearts to win the Scottish Cup in 1903, no one could have predicted that a quarter of a century would pass before they would lift the famous old trophy again. The Ibrox club had reached five finals since the last triumph but lost every one of them.

FOLLOW, FOLLOW

Stalwarts of what had otherwise been a glorious era for the club –
legendary players like Meiklejohn, Alan Morton, Sandy Archibald and
Andy Cunningham – had begun to think they might never collect a
winner's medal in the country's most prestigious cup competition. The
club's cup record had become a music-hall joke. Comedian George
West's show *King o' Clubs* had been running at the Princess Theatre
in Glasgow for several weeks, culminating every night with a gag that
brought the house down. West would produce a replica of the Scottish
Cup and, after puzzling over it for a few moments, declare, 'This is a
real antique. The last name on it is Rangers . . .'

Even some of the Rangers team couldn't resist joining in on the
jokes. Bob McPhail, formerly of Airdrie, and ex-Morton player Jock
Buchanan were the only players at Ibrox with Scottish Cup medals
and would perform a comedy routine to wind up their dressing-
room pals. Many years later, in his autobiography *Legend: Sixty Years
at Ibrox*, McPhail revealed how the jokes met with a frosty reception.
He recalled:

> Our medals were worn, with the pride of youth, on our
> watch chain, which was of course appropriately dangling
> from the slit pockets of our waistcoats. When we went into
> the Rangers dressing-room I'd say to Jock, 'What's that
> on your chain there?' He'd reply, 'This is my Scottish Cup
> medal, Bob. What's that on your chain?' I'd make a pretence
> of examining my medal and say, 'Why, this is my Scottish
> Cup medal, Jock.' The Rangers players were not amused by
> this childish comedy routine.

Rangers and Celtic were by now well established as the giants of the
Scottish game, and their rivalry had developed along the religious
lines that are so familiar today.

In the early years of the twentieth century, William Wilton had
been the dominant force in turning Rangers into the country's
leading football club, but it was his successor as manager who took
the club to the next level. When Wilton tragically died in a boating

accident in 1920, the Rangers board turned to trainer Bill Struth.

Struth grew up in Edinburgh. His sporting interests were varied, but it was as a runner that he excelled. He became a professional athlete in his teens, picking up medals and cash prizes in races all over Scotland and the rest of the UK. Despite having no background in football, at the age of 32 he successfully applied for a job as full-time trainer at Clyde. Rangers tried to bring him to Ibrox as trainer in 1910. He declined the offer, but when veteran trainer James Wilson died four years later, Struth was the obvious choice to take over. Struth's arrival at Ibrox ensured that in the post-war years Rangers would go from strength to strength and dominate the Scottish game for decades.

As they went into the 1928 cup final, Struth's team had won six of the nine league titles available since hostilities had ended in 1918, but, despite their dominance, the Scottish Cup inexplicably eluded them. There was a feeling, though, that this would be the year to lay the hoodoo to rest.

Interest in the cup final was enormous, not least because it was the first time the Old Firm had met in the final since the riot of 1909. In addition, Celtic were the cup holders and Rangers were the reigning Scottish League champions, while both teams were vying to win the league. Stand tickets for Hampden sold out within a couple of hours of going on sale, and a record crowd was expected on the day. For the first time in Scottish football history, police, mindful of what had happened at the last Old Firm final, were drafted in to steward the crowds on the terracing.

Fans began arriving at Hampden at 10.30 a.m., with the *Evening Times* reporting that the first arrivals were a group of Celtic supporters from Ireland, wearing green and white scarves and hats. Another group came straight from work, still covered in soot and dirt. They enjoyed an al fresco lunch of beer and pies on a grassy patch outside the ground before taking their place on the terraces when the gates opened at 1 p.m.

An extra two hundred and thirty tramcars were laid on to transport fans to Mount Florida – four cars a minute, transporting fourteen thousand passengers per hour. There was enormous traffic congestion all around the area – cars, buses and motorbikes queued along Battlefield Road, past Queen's Park and down Victoria Road. Special trains were provided to transport fans direct to Mount Florida station from as far north as Inverness and as far south as Dumfries. Although the vast majority of fans made it to Hampden on foot or by public transport, nearly 900 cars filled the official car park in addition to many parked in the surrounding side streets.

The Celtic team bus was cheered as it made its way through the crowds to Hampden, but Rangers players and officials chose to make a less high-profile entrance, arriving at the ground in a fleet of taxis.

Rangers fans were in a confident mood as they arrived, according to newspaper reports, many belting out their version of the old American Civil War song 'Marching Through Georgia' – better known today as 'The Billy Boys'.

As kick-off time approached, huge queues had formed outside the ground, and it soon became clear that many fans would not get in. Finally, the decision was taken to close the gates, leaving thousands of late arrivals disappointed. Crowds instead gathered on vantage points around Hampden, hoping for a glimpse of the action or at least to be able to hear what was going on.

The attendance was officially given as 118,115, producing receipts totalling £4,792, and was said to be a Scottish, and perhaps British, record for a club match at the time. Despite the crushing on the terraces, remarkably few people needed treatment by St Andrew's Ambulance Association, and thankfully there was no repeat of the violence seen two decades earlier.

A strong wind was gusting round the vast arena, but the rain stayed away, leaving the pitch hard, dry and bare. But fears that this might make for tricky conditions that could handicap the players proved groundless. Both teams mastered the conditions in their own way and managed to serve up what was widely considered to be one of the best Scottish Cup finals ever seen.

Celtic appeared first, followed soon after by Rangers, at which point some over-exuberant young supporters invaded the pitch and had to be chased back to the sidelines before the real action could commence. To the delight of their own fans, Celtic won the toss and, with the wind behind them, were able to exert early pressure. Later, Meiklejohn said, 'Our supporters were glum, but I was pleased about losing the toss. We liked to begin a match against the wind. We were strong and fit and liked to end with massive attacks.'

Rangers' defence suffered several anxious moments in the early part of the game as Celtic's wingers tried to exploit the wind by firing high crosses into the penalty area. Tommy McInally then tried a spectacular long-range shot that was carried on the wind towards the Rangers goal, only to be deflected by a defender's boot for a corner. McInally then had another shot from a free kick, which went narrowly wide.

The Rangers forwards had to work hard to help relieve the pressure on their defenders, with Jimmy Fleming, Archibald and, especially, Morton using their dribbling skills to take the ball out of the danger areas. Morton was beginning to cause the Celtic defence problems and won a free kick after being fouled following a particularly clever run. From the resulting kick, he forced a good save out of Thomson.

The match was now swinging from end to end, and Rangers keeper Tom Hamilton had to produce a terrific save following a swift counter-attack. As half-time approached, Hamilton was called into action again when he pounced on a shot by Adam McLean. As he lay on the ball, a crowd of Celtic and Rangers players piled on top of him, his ordeal ending only when the referee eventually blew for a foul.

The half-time whistle brought temporary relief for the players. It had been a relatively even first half, according to reports, although Celtic would have felt disappointed at not having taken advantage of the wind at their backs.

Rangers came out for the second half in a determined mood and were soon getting the better of exchanges, pushing the Celtic defence onto the back foot. After ten minutes of almost incessant pressure, it looked as if Celtic keeper Thomson had finally been beaten by a shot from Fleming, but with the ball heading towards goal, defender Willie McStay rushed across and cleared it away with his hand. It was a clear handball, and the only decision for the

Motherwell referee Willie Bell to make was to determine whether or not the ball had already crossed the line for a goal. Despite the Rangers protests, after consulting with his linesman he decided it hadn't and pointed at the spot.

With all that had gone before in the cup, Rangers now needed someone with nerves of steel to come to the fore. Meiklejohn was that man. He was standing in as skipper for the injured Tommy Muirhead and, by taking responsibility for the penalty, played a true captain's role.

Meiklejohn's teammates were of the opinion that had he missed, their rivals would have gone on to win the final. The weight of responsibility was enormous, but whatever nerves he was feeling inside, he was calmness personified as he stepped up to the spot with 118,000 pairs of eyes trained on him.

In his autobiography, Bob McPhail recalled:

> There was a strange silence when Meek put the ball on the spot. Seconds later, he had driven it powerfully past Thomson's right side and into the back of the net. A well-taken kick. Later I was told the goal had been scored at exactly 4.01 p.m. It must still rank as the most important penalty kick ever taken by a Rangers player. If our skipper had missed then Celtic would have won that final. Not one Rangers player on the field believed otherwise.

If his teammates had feared what would happen if he missed, when the ball hit the back of the net they knew instinctively that the jinx was about to be lifted. Suddenly the cup was within their reach, and they started to play with even more confidence. The fears of another final failure were swept away.

Rangers piled on the pressure, with Archibald in particular causing the Celtic defence problems. Thomson had to pull off a series of saves to keep his team in the game, but eventually McPhail made the breakthrough, scrambling home a corner from Archibald in the 68th minute. Archibald then added two more spectacular goals to seal the victory – both unstoppable long-range shots that left Thomson with no chance.

Rangers had outclassed their opponents all over the pitch and were deserving winners. Wingers Morton and Archibald had caused all sorts of problems for the Celtic defenders, and they were ably assisted by the inside-forwards McPhail and Cunningham. Penalty hero Meiklejohn was singled out for particular praise by *The Scotsman*, which said he had 'completely subjugated' Celtic's star forward, Jimmy McGrory.

The Rangers fans celebrated the end of the hoodoo. 'The Ibrox choir struck up their favourite anthem,' reported the *Evening Times*, 'and the "Wells o' Wearie" was taken up by the whole west terracing, the old song going with a joyous swing that indicated the seventh-heaven feeling of the champions' following.'

After they posed for pictures on the Hampden pitch with the trophy, the Rangers players battled through boisterous crowds to reach their waiting taxis. They were repeatedly held up as they made their way to the city centre, especially on Cathcart Road. Crowds gathered outside Ferguson and Foster's restaurant, which was booked for the celebratory dinner, and each player was cheered as he arrived.

As for George West, he was forced to come up with a new joke. After their meal, some of the team went to the Princess Theatre with the trophy for the last night of *King o' Clubs* – and the audience was stunned when West produced the real thing on stage instead of the replica. He told the crowd, 'Man, they've shown me up as badly as they did Celtic at Hampden. But even though they've done me out of a gag, I'm not offended. I congratulate them on their great victory – and on the end of the Rangers hoodoo.'

Away from football, newspapers on the day of the cup final had excitedly reported how a skeleton thought to be 4,000 years old had been discovered by well-known archaeologist Ludovic Mann at a sandpit in Mount Vernon, just to the east of Glasgow. Earlier in the week, he had found several handmade clay pots thought to date back to the Bronze Age. Further investigations uncovered an untouched tomb containing the human remains. The bones, which had 40 water-rolled stones placed on top of them, were found only a few feet below ground level.

Former prime minister David Lloyd George was also in Glasgow, to address a Liberal meeting on Saturday afternoon. *The Scotsman* reported that the evening before he had been reunited at Central Station with ex-Royal Engineer P.J. McLoughlin, who had escorted him through the Somme trenches in 1916.

The year also saw one of the most momentous scientific breakthroughs of all time when Ayrshire-born pharmacologist Alexander Fleming discovered penicillin by chance. He had been working on the influenza virus when he noticed that mould had formed accidentally on a culture plate and that it had created a bacteria-free area around itself.

In the US, legendary crimefighter Eliot Ness began his Prohibition crackdown against organised-crime gangs in Chicago, which would many years later become the subject of the film *The Untouchables*. It was also the year that Mickey Mouse made his first screen appearance, in Walt Disney's animated short *Plane Crazy*. Mickey's voice was first heard in his third film, *Steamboat Willie*, released later in the year.

Meanwhile, in Schenectady, New York, General Electric's television station W2XB launched the first regular schedule of TV programming, on 10 May 1928. It would be many years before TV would become part of everyday life for ordinary Scots, but radio was already well established. As well as live commentary of the cup final, Scottish listeners to the BBC on 14 April could have enjoyed such delights as *Something About Canada: Canadians and Canadian Poultry*, *Rifle Shooting in Scotland* and Una O'Connor in *Irish and Cockney Character Studies*.

For most working-class Glaswegians, an annual summer holiday was still out of reach, but for the wealthy there were opportunities for exotic trips overseas. *The Scotsman* of 14 April carried an advert for a travel company offering all-inclusive holidays to Switzerland, Germany, Holland or France ranging from £9 to more than £17. Or for the really well-to-do there was the chance to take a six-week 'grand tour' of Europe for £70.

The Rangers players, who were on a basic salary of £8 a week, each received £20 for winning the cup – enough to pay for a nine-day motor tour of Germany's Rhineland, should they wish. In *Legend*, McPhail recalled a conversation about the final he had with Celtic's inside-left Tommy McInally. McPhail said, 'When I told him what our bonus had been he said, "You didnae win the cup, Bob, you bought it!"' But it was the glory of victory and the honour of finally laying to rest a 25-year hoodoo that was the real reward for the Rangers players.

Seven days later, Rangers clinched the league title by beating Kilmarnock 5–1 and, in doing so, won their first-ever double, but it was the cup win that would mean most to the supporters and players. 'It seemed to me that some malevolent shadow had been removed from the club,' said McPhail.

5

THE BIGGEST-EVER CROWD

RANGERS 2 CELTIC 1
SCOTTISH LEAGUE
PLAYED AT IBROX PARK, GLASGOW
2 JANUARY 1939

Rangers team: Dawson, Gray, Shaw, McKillop, Simpson, Symon,
Waddell, Harrison, Thornton, Venters, Kinnear

Rangers scorers: Kinnear, Venters

Football had never been more popular than it was in the late 1930s, and, despite war looming ever closer, enthusiasm for the game showed no signs of abating. A world-record crowd of 149,547 turned out at Hampden to see Scotland beat England 3–1 in April 1937. The same season, almost 95,000 turned out at Ibrox for the Ne'erday derby. Two years later, that figure was dwarfed when the stadium next hosted the traditional festive-season clash.

The First Division matches on the afternoon of Monday, 2 January 1939 were watched by a total of 268,000 people, including 45,061 for the Edinburgh derby at Tynecastle. But it was the turnout for the Old Firm match at Ibrox that grabbed most of the attention. There were 118,730 paying customers inside the stadium, the biggest crowd the world had ever seen for a league match. Another 30,000 were turned away when the gates were locked.

FOLLOW, FOLLOW

The true number inside the ground was probably even higher than the official figure. The fans who managed to sneak in without paying, combined with the youngsters who got a free lift over the turnstiles, would have increased the crowd by several thousand.

With New Year's Day falling on a Sunday, the public holiday was moved to the Monday, and it seems this, combined with the cold but dry weather, may have encouraged more fans than usual to make their way to the big game. In the hours approaching kick-off time, the scenes in Glasgow made it clear that pre-match predictions of a 60,000 crowd were somewhat wide of the mark.

In addition to the football crowd, thousands of visitors had been encouraged by the bright weather in the early part of the public holiday to descend on Glasgow from the country and outlying towns and villages. The closure of shops and businesses gave the city a Sabbath-like feel, and restaurants and pubs remained shut throughout the day, much to the disappointment of the thousands of out-of-town visitors.

Glasgow Corporation had laid on an extra 120 trams and 45 buses to cope with the demand, but passengers were still left kicking their heels at the side of the road as buses and trams filled with supporters swept past stops. The city-centre underground stations were packed as thousands of supporters tried to squeeze into trains heading towards the South Side. Trains departed for Ibrox every two minutes, but still this wasn't enough. Others decided walking was the best option. It seemed that everyone wanted to be at Ibrox that day.

Long before kick-off, the gates at the traditional 'Rangers end' were closed and mounted police shepherded supporters to the other end of the stadium. The mood was good-humoured as the fans shuffled along to the opposite gates, but it wasn't long before these, too, were closed.

Inside the ground, the fans were in a good mood, lustily belting out 'A Guid New Year' as they waited for the game to get under way. But there were fears that the alarming swaying of the spectators could result in serious injuries. One report described the crowd as 'a seething, swaying mass of humanity, squeezing and manoeuvring for places from which they could glimpse the match spectacle which had set the throng roaring'. *The Scotsman* described how ambulance- and policemen had to help many fans out of the enclosures onto the track to escape the crush.

Thousands who paid their shillings to pass through the turnstiles didn't even manage to reach the rim of the huge Ibrox bowl. They didn't get a glimpse of the game and had to rely on running commentaries of the action being passed down from fans who managed to get a view.

The more adventurous scaled anything they could find. The half-time scoreboard was utilised as a makeshift grandstand by one group of youths, before the police intervened, while other fans climbed drainpipes. Thousands more simply walked around for the duration of the game, unable to see anything other than the backs of those in the top row of the terracing. In spite of warnings broadcast over loudspeakers, passageways were completely blocked, leaving little room for the supporters to move and adding to the crushing problems.

Despite everything, the crowd was remarkably well behaved and there were relatively few serious injuries. Medics treated 80 supporters, mainly for the effects of crushing. Four needed treatment at the Victoria Infirmary, with one sixty-one-year-old man detained for rib injuries. A girl collecting money at half-time for a local charity was also treated by ambulancemen. She was left with a bloodied nose after being hit by a stray penny that was thrown in her direction.

The match itself was well worthy of the massive crowd, with *The Scotsman* describing it as a 'memorable game' and the *Daily Record* praising the players for a 'contest that thrilled and delighted from first kick to last'. Having been heavily criticised for losing the first derby of the season 6–2, Rangers were determined to avenge that defeat. Just as importantly, two points would go a long way to recapturing the league title they had lost to Celtic the previous season.

As is so often the case in Old Firm games, it was played at a frenetic pace, with football sometimes a secondary consideration. The home team had the better of the first half and, after a few minutes, looked certain to record a comfortable victory. Alex Venters, so often a thorn in Celtic's side, and Willie Thornton were the biggest threats to the Celtic defence, with their crisp passing leaving their opponents chasing shadows.

Venters in particular drew praise for his performance, the *Daily Record* saying, 'He gave the impression of having a double on the field, so much ground did he cover, so much was he in the thick of it.' He was signed from Cowdenbeath in 1933 and enjoyed an illustrious thirteen-year career at Ibrox, winning three league titles and two Scottish Cups and scoring one hundred and fifty-five league goals. His total goal tally included an impressive 18 strikes in Old Firm games.

On this occasion, Venters' goal came in the 39th minute, a clinical finish following a clever pass from Willie Thornton. By then, Rangers were already in the lead, Davie Kinnear having fired home the opening goal after racing away from the Celtic defender Bobby Hogg.

The first half may have belonged to the home team, but Celtic fought back after the interval and with 15 minutes to go pulled back a goal through Joe Carruth. Rangers' forwards were struggling to repeat the dominance they had enjoyed before the break and were only occasionally able to relieve the pressure on their defence. When they did break free, however, they showed more threat than their opponents, both Robert Harrison and Kinnear coming close to increasing their lead. Despite the frantic action at both ends, there were no more goals, and when the final whistle blew Rangers had moved eight points clear of their Glasgow rivals.

The win ensured Rangers fans started the New Year in a good mood, and, despite the very real prospect of war, the general public mood going into 1939 was remarkably upbeat. After years of high unemployment, job prospects were picking up and Glasgow had just hosted the hugely successful Empire Exhibition, which had attracted twelve million visitors despite taking place during one of the wettest summers on record. Rangers had hosted the opening ceremony at Ibrox, with most of the events taking place at nearby Bellahouston Park.

The passing of the old year was celebrated vigorously in Glasgow, with city fathers breaking with tradition and hosting a civic

THE BIGGEST-EVER CROWD

Hogmanay celebration to mark the occasion. A crowd of 50,000 revellers gathered in a brightly lit George Square to see in the New Year with the Lord Provost, Patrick Dollan. The chimes of Big Ben were broadcast across the square before he and his wife led the crowds in renditions of 'A Guid New Year', 'Auld Lang Syne' and the national anthem.

Plans for an aeroplane fly-past had to be abandoned because of a heavy overhead fog, but it was otherwise a glittering occasion, the square's trees festooned with coloured lights and the municipal buildings illuminated by floodlights. Four ten-foot-high gas braziers shooting flames into the night sky completed the scene.

In his New Year message, Mr Dollan said 1938 had been a year of 'continuous effort and struggle' to improve conditions for Glasgow's citizens and warned that the New Year would throw up even greater challenges. 'Democracy is on trial at home and abroad,' he said.

As if any reminder was needed of the threat posed by the Nazi regime, Mr Dollan was first-footed in his private room at the City Chambers by 14-year-old Jewish refugee David Gold, who had been given a home in Glasgow after fleeing persecution in Austria.

Events throughout 1939 made war look more and more likely, and in September the inevitable happened. Germany's invasion of Poland was swiftly followed by a declaration of war by Britain and France.

Although football was reorganised into regional leagues during the conflict, it acted as a useful distraction for the public, as did the cinema. Two of the most popular Hollywood films of all time were released in 1939. The classic musical *The Wizard of Oz*, starring Judy Garland as Dorothy, premiered in August, while *Gone with the Wind*, starring Vivien Leigh and Clark Gable, received its first showing in December.

As well as making the record books for the size of the crowd, the Old Firm match on 2 January was significant for another, less well-known reason. For the first time, Celtic officials took part in a ceremony within the famous Blue Room at Ibrox that has become part of the club's folklore.

FOLLOW, FOLLOW

To mark the coronation of King George VI in 1937, industrialist and Stoke City president Sir Francis Joseph had 30 pottery cups cast from an original mould, which was later destroyed. He presented one to each of the English First Division clubs and to the two teams promoted from Division Two. The others he gave to the King himself, the Football League, the FA and the British Museum. The last one he kept for himself until Rangers played Stoke in a benefit match to raise money for relatives of the victims of the Holditch Colliery Disaster.

As a thank you for taking part in the fund-raiser, the cup was presented to Rangers on the condition that, at the first home game of every year, the directors should fill the cup with champagne and toast the health of the monarch. The tradition continues at Ibrox to this day, with the chairman of Rangers' first visitors of the New Year invited to take part in the ceremony. Traditionally, the Old Firm teams have played each other on New Year's Day, so on many occasions the Rangers chairman of the day was joined in the Blue Room by his Parkhead counterpart.

After the 1939 Old Firm game, Rangers chairman Jimmy Bowie was joined in toasting the health of the King by various dignitaries, including Celtic's Tom White, Glasgow's Lord Provost and Scottish League secretary William MacAndrew. After passing the champagne-filled Loving Cup around the assembled guests, Bowie confidently predicted that the day's crowd record would soon be broken and that Rangers would need to increase the capacity of Ibrox. Neither forecast came true. Although huge crowds would still be seen right up until the early 1970s, the general trend was downward.

The vast attendance did, however, prompt inevitable calls for the annual New Year meeting between Rangers and Celtic to be all-ticket. In a *Scotsman* interview the day after the match, Bill Struth said such a move might be advisable if huge crowds were to become a regular occurrence. He was sure, though, that Ibrox would easily be able to accommodate such vast crowds in the future. 'So far as Ibrox Stadium is concerned, by the time the match comes around again, we will be able to take everybody who comes to it,' he told the paper.

'We have alterations going on in the grounds just now that will give accommodation for 20,000 more.'

As it turned out, the outbreak of war later in the year meant that crowds were limited and the days of crowds of more than 100,000 for league games were over. Football continued throughout the war years, and Rangers carried on their domination of the Scottish game.

6

A FORGOTTEN RECORD

RANGERS 8 CELTIC 1
SOUTHERN LEAGUE
PLAYED AT IBROX PARK, GLASGOW
1 JANUARY 1943

*Rangers team: Dawson, Gray, Shaw, Little, Young, Symon, Waddell,
Duncanson, Gillick, Venters, Johnston*

Rangers scorers: Gillick (3), Waddell (2), Young (2), Duncanson

In the world of the Old Firm fan, one-upmanship is everything. So Celtic supporters would have been feeling pretty pleased with themselves when they unfurled a banner during a 2007 derby at Ibrox celebrating the 50th anniversary of their record 7–1 victory over Rangers. But, moments later, the home fans, who were clearly anticipating this taunt, trumped their rivals by producing their own banner. It read 'Rangers 8–1 Celtic. 1st January 1943. If You Knew Our History' and was a reference to a wartime league thrashing dished out by the Light Blues at Ibrox.

The irony is that the banner would not only have taken the visiting supporters by surprise but would also have left many of the home fans scratching their heads. Because the victory took place during the war years, it is considered by most scholars of the game to be 'unofficial' and therefore is rarely included in history books. As a result, the match has been allowed to drift out of the public consciousness, to the extent that the majority of modern-day Rangers fans will never have heard of the achievement.

So, while Celtic followers of all ages continue to bask in the memory of their much-lauded win five decades ago, most of the blue half of Glasgow has no idea that Rangers have actually gone one better.

Despite the outbreak of war in September 1939, football continued and the Old Firm rivals remained the bitterest of enemies. The Scottish Cup was suspended, and leagues were regionalised. Many Rangers players were sent off to fight in Europe, while others found themselves helping the war effort by working in 'reserved' occupations at home. Those working at home were able to play football regularly in the revamped league and cup competitions.

Rangers were hugely successful during the war years under Bill Struth, with legendary players like Jerry Dawson, Jock 'Tiger' Shaw, George Young, Scot Symon and Willie Waddell all coming to the fore. They would go on to be stalwarts of the post-war Rangers team.

In January 1940, Ibrox hosted its first derby since the fighting had begun. Following the record crowd of 1939, the decision was taken to make the match all-ticket, but in the end it was a crowd of only around 40,000 that turned out to see the rivals draw 1–1. Tickets were even being sold outside the ground by supporters who found themselves with too many.

In September 1941, the Glasgow rivals met at Ibrox before a crowd of 60,000 in the Southern League. With half-time approaching, Rangers were leading 2–0 when Celtic were awarded a penalty. Goalkeeper Jerry Dawson, who had conceded the foul in the first place, pulled off a great save but in the process sparked a riot among the Celtic fans massed behind his goal. Hundreds of bottles were hurled towards the pitch and fighting broke out.

A squad of police officers was dispatched into the heart of the crowd, truncheons drawn, and eventually managed to restore order. Rangers finally ran out 3–0 winners, but the scenes on the terracing caused outrage, particularly as they took place during a time of national emergency. Lord Provost Patrick Dollan even threatened to ban Old Firm games for the duration of the conflict in an attempt to prevent further violence. In the end, the matches survived, but the SFA decided to shut down Parkhead for a month and banned Celtic from playing anywhere in Glasgow during that period.

Nowadays, it is not uncommon for football to make the front pages of the newspapers as well as the back pages, and, while we might think of that as a modern phenomenon, it has actually always been the case. Even when the nation was at war, the national game rubbed shoulders on page one with dispatches from the front line.

On 1 January 1943, Glasgow's *Evening Times* reported that the Red Army had celebrated the New Year by making major advances against the Germans on the Russian Front. The paper also told how British submarines in the Mediterranean had sunk two enemy supply vessels and torpedoed a destroyer, and reported on RAF bombing raids in Germany.

The war threw up some peculiar court cases. *The Scotsman* reported on 1 January that an Edinburgh tailor had been fined £15 at the city's Sheriff Court for making suits with too many pockets. The Savile Row Tailoring Co. had breached restrictions introduced after the outbreak of the war aimed at preserving valuable resources. The offending suit jackets had three outside pockets and two inside, instead of the three allowed in total. The waistcoat had four pockets, instead of two, and the trousers, which should have been flat round the ankle, had turn-ups sewn in as well as extra pockets.

In Glasgow, a warehouseman was jailed for 15 months for stealing 14 cases of whisky, which were part of a consignment he was instructed to load at the Clydeside docks. When the load was checked and it was discovered that 168 bottles were missing, police visited Hugh Scott's home and discovered a quantity of the stolen spirits. Having been caught red-handed, he admitted the theft.

Sitting somewhat incongruously on the *Evening Times's* front page alongside all this was a story headlined 'Celtic Players Ordered Off'. It told how that day's Old Firm derby at Ibrox had been afflicted by the 'customary sensations' associated with the fixture. Two of the visiting team had been sent off for arguing with the referee, although, for a change, the scenes on the pitch had not translated to trouble on the terraces.

The placing of the story on the front page demonstrated just how important football remained during wartime, especially matches between the Old Firm teams. So it is slightly surprising that the game in question has been largely forgotten about by historians, particularly as it was the day the biggest ever Old Firm victory was recorded.

The 30,000 fans who defied the New Year's Day travel difficulties could hardly have predicted what was to unfold at Ibrox. By Old Firm standards even during wartime, it was a fairly muted gathering, the *Evening Times* describing the crowd as 'quiet and orderly'.

Rangers were at full strength, with goalkeeper Jerry Dawson making the team despite having been knocked unconscious just six days earlier when he was hit by a bottle thrown by a Hibs fan during a match at Easter Road. Celtic were also able to field a strong team, with Hogg the only notable absentee.

The home team had a whirlwind start, taking the lead in just 30 seconds. Venters swung the ball out towards Willie Waddell on the wing. He took it past the Celtic full-back Henry Dornan before firing it in towards Jimmy Duncanson, who blasted it past the goalkeeper from ten yards. Celtic had barely had a touch of the ball and Rangers were a goal up.

It was a stunning start, and soon Rangers had doubled their lead. Once again, it was Waddell who tormented the visiting defence, leaving Dornan for dead as he raced towards the edge of the penalty area before driving an unstoppable shot into the net.

With less than five minutes on the clock, Rangers already looked to be in full control. However, Celtic didn't buckle and five minutes later were back in the game when Davie Duncan put the ball past Dawson. As one report at the time noted, 'This was indeed an unusual opening for an Old Firm game.'

What had threatened to be a one-sided match had now turned into a real battle, with all the usual derby skirmishes. Celtic defender Malcolm MacDonald was booked for backchatting the referee, Mr Davidson, but his teammates were slowly gaining in confidence in both attack and defence, keeping in check the Rangers forwards who had threatened to run riot early in the game.

However, Rangers did have a chance to increase their lead in the first half, Torry Gillick sending in from the edge of the 18-yard box a powerful header that forced the Celtic goalkeeper, Willie Miller, to scramble across his line as the ball narrowly went wide. Despite plenty of endeavour from both sides, there was no further scoring before half-time, although another Celtic player was booked for dissent. Mr Davidson clearly did not appreciate players questioning his authority, as he was to make crystal clear after the interval.

Rangers had enjoyed a sensational start to the first half, and they were able to replicate this at the beginning of the second period. Once again, Waddell played a vitally important role. His cross was headed home by Gillick after a mix-up between the Celtic centre-back Willie Corbett and his goalkeeper. Both the keeper and the Rangers forward were injured in the melee but after a few minutes recovered and were able to continue.

Although the Light Blues had extended their lead, Celtic were holding their own and forcing the home team to fight for every ball. Then things started to heat up. Rangers won a free kick just across the halfway line, which George Young stepped up to take. The giant defender, nicknamed Corky, may not have been the most obvious dead-ball expert in the Rangers team, but his right foot was a fearsome weapon, capable of propelling the heavy leather ball 50 or 60 yards with the minimum of effort.

With Celtic anticipating a high ball aimed at the head of one of Rangers' forwards, Young instead went for goal, from a full 50 yards. The ball sailed over everyone and didn't stop until it nestled in the back of the Celtic net, behind a bemused Miller. The defenders immediately launched a protest against the goal, apparently on the grounds that one of the Rangers players had strayed offside as the ball floated through the air.

MacDonald, who had been booked in the first half, took his protests too far and found his name being taken again, meaning he had to be sent off. Five minutes later, Matt Lynch joined him in the dressing-room, having also spoken out of turn over another perceived injustice. Celtic's players had found themselves the victims of an SFA crackdown on dissent and protests from players.

The following day's newspapers had little sympathy for Celtic's plight, particularly given the powder-keg nature of the Glasgow derby. Alan Breck in the *Evening Times* wrote:

> I know it is difficult, when you feel your case is right, not to talk, but there must be discipline. Players must learn to take the referee's decision. Especially in a Rangers–Celtic match, the results on the field can be disastrous on the terraces.

With thirty minutes to go, Rangers were 4–1 up and facing just nine men. It would have been easy for them to simply sit back and play out the rest of the game, but, with their opponents on their knees, Rangers went for the kill.

Man of the match Waddell quickly added a fifth goal with a left-foot shot, and, as Celtic imploded, Young scored again, this time from the penalty spot. The award was given after Dornan punched away a net-bound Gillick header. The Rangers forward was not to be denied though, and he completed his hat-trick with two goals in the closing minutes of the match.

The 8–1 scoreline was an abject humiliation for Celtic. They had lost the plot, and their indiscipline was mercilessly exploited by a ruthless Rangers team that swept aside allcomers during the wartime period. The result helped Rangers win the Southern League again, as they did every season during the war. It also demonstrated the huge gulf that existed between the Glasgow giants, one that would continue well into the 1960s.

7

• •

PLUS ÇA CHANGE...

RANGERS 4 CELTIC 0
SCOTTISH LEAGUE
PLAYED AT IBROX PARK, GLASGOW
24 SEPTEMBER 1949

*Rangers team: Brown, Young, Shaw, McColl, Woodburn, Rae, Waddell,
Findlay, Williamson, Cox, Rutherford*

Rangers scorers: Rutherford, Findlay, Waddell, Williamson

Where the Old Firm is concerned, the more things change the
more they stay the same. The post-war years saw Rangers enjoy
a prolonged period of superiority over Celtic that would not be
repeated until the 1990s, but in both decades encounters between
the two clubs were fraught affairs, marred by trouble on and off
the field, rampant paranoia and accusations that the standard of
football was at an all-time low.

Newspaper match reports in the 1940s focused as much on
sectarian singing, missile throwing, complaints about biased
refereeing and the misbehaviour of players as they did on the
actual football. In fact, reading accounts of Old Firm clashes from
that time, it's remarkably easy to imagine the words being applied
to matches of the modern era. This damning paragraph from a
Glasgow Herald article in 1947, highlighting a supposed drop in
standards, could have been written at any time in the subsequent

60 years: 'Rarely has a greater travesty of a sporting function been perpetrated on a football public that is by no means unused to Rangers and Celtic in opposition destroying the good name of the game.'

Despite the press's concerns about the game's reputation, Scottish football was in fact enjoying a post-war boom. Rangers' opening league match of the 1946–47 season at Motherwell saw a crowd of 30,000, and the following week 50,000 turned out at Ibrox for the visit of Hibernian.

The biggest threat to Rangers' stranglehold on Scottish football came not from the East End of Glasgow but from the east of Scotland, where Hibs had assembled an excellent team. That's not to say that the Old Firm derbies had lost their edge – in fact, the opposite was true.

In the years after the war, the ill feeling generated at Old Firm matches seemed to increase with each passing game. Much of the tension centred on refereeing decisions, and as the decade progressed there was clearly growing frustration among Celtic players and supporters that they were somehow being unfairly treated. Of course, this all coincided with an era in which the Parkhead club was in the doldrums, and it would be safe to assume that the feeling of injustice was linked to the general dissatisfaction at the way the team was performing. As many observers have pointed out, Celtic's apparent persecution at the hands of the authorities seems to manifest itself only at times when they have a poor team. Strangely, during successful periods, the conspiracies appear to die off.

The first sign of trouble came in the semi-final replay of the Victory Cup, in June 1946. When Rangers were awarded a penalty with 20 minutes to go, the entire Celtic team protested to the referee, with the inside-left George Paterson eventually going too far and getting himself sent off for dissent.

The protests continued nonetheless, and when the ball was eventually placed on the penalty spot it was promptly booted away by Celtic's left-back, Jimmy Mallan, who was also ordered off. This was all too much for one member of the Celtic support, who invaded the pitch and had to be apprehended by the police after George Young finally converted the spot kick. Several more attempted pitch invasions had to be thwarted before the game could continue, with Rangers eventually winning 2–0.

In September the same year, Rangers fans organised a boycott of the league match at Parkhead in protest at the prices being charged by Celtic's directors. The resulting attendance of 28,000 was less than half of what would normally be expected at the game and would have hit Celtic hard in the pocket.

The next few games passed without serious incident, although there were numerous disputed goals and penalty claims on both sides, which presumably contributed to the unfortunate events at Ibrox in August 1949 when the teams met in the League Cup.

Half an hour into the match, Rangers' Sammy Cox put in a strong challenge on Charlie Tully, which the Celtic players and fans claimed was a foul but the referee considered a fair tackle. The reaction from the visiting support was furious. As the play raged on, bottles rained down from the west terracing and fighting broke out, forcing police to intervene. According to the *Herald*, had the officers not stepped in promptly 'a riot would have taken place'.

As the fighting continued, Rangers took the lead, which did not improve the mood of the hooligan element within the Celtic support. There were further disturbances at half-time, and violence erupted again ten minutes into the second half when the home team were awarded a penalty.

Two weeks later, on the day that a delegation from the SFA met with Glasgow magistrates to discuss the Ibrox trouble, the two clubs met again in the Glasgow Cup. Once again, there was controversy, with a disputed foul leading to a Rangers goal with three minutes to go. The *Herald* reported, 'Celtic's chagrin knew no bounds then, and to the horror of those who have the interests of the game at heart, Tully was quite clearly seen to be urging his teammates to leave the field.' The more level-headed among them wisely decided to continue playing, thus probably avoiding widespread disorder on the terraces. As it was, dozens of police officers were deployed around the pitch and on the Parkhead slopes to keep the peace.

The latest incident prompted the *Herald*, probably Scotland's most respected newspaper at the time, to publish the startling headline 'Celtic v. Rangers Matches Should Be Stopped'. The article said no further derbies should be allowed that season, a view, the writer claimed, that was shared by Celtic, if 'referees who can completely control play and players are not available to handle such games'.

Of course, banning Old Firm games was never a realistic option. In fact, on 24 September, just 11 days later, a quirk of the fixture list meant that the rivals would meet again at Ibrox. To say the authorities were concerned about what might happen would be putting it mildly.

In an attempt to defuse the tensions between the rival sets of supporters, flags and banners were banned from the ground, and to lessen the chances of missiles being hurled, bottles were also prohibited. Notices issued by the Rangers board went up around the turnstiles warning that police action would be taken against anyone trying to break the rules: 'Admission will be refused to any person found carrying flags, bottles or any other missiles. Any persons found inside the ground in possession of flags, bottles or any other missiles will be removed from the premises and may be prosecuted.'

The authorities would have been somewhat relieved to learn that the Celtic Supporters Association had organised a boycott of the game over their complaint that their team had been discriminated against by referees. As a result, the crowd of 64,000 was much lower than usual, with an estimated 35,000 Celtic fans staying away. The London-based *Picture Post* magazine reported, 'The terraces at Ibrox's West End, where Celtic supporters traditionally gather, were half-heartedly empty a few minutes before the game began, whilst the East End terraces, the Rangers' spiritual home, seethed and heaved like a towering ant heap.'

PLUS ÇA CHANGE ...

According to the *Glasgow Herald*, the atmosphere inside Ibrox was 'like a cemetery' and Celtic's arrival on the pitch saw 'no more than a few dozen pairs of hands clapped'. The smattering of green-and-white-clad fans who turned out 'made violent gestures' towards photographers who might have been tempted to expose their presence on the terraces.

Despite the smaller crowd, the policing of the match was as rigorous as ever. Ten mounted police and one hundred and fifty on foot took their positions before the match, with a walkie-talkie squad coordinating the operation from the press-box. The only message sent out over the airwaves throughout the afternoon was a half-time score update for the officers stationed outside the stadium.

The police's only other major task was a futile attempt during the interval at trying to burst a large blue inflatable that was construed to have fallen foul of the prohibition on banners. The *Herald* reported that officers allowed the balloon to float off over the heads of 'men who sang "God Save the King", chanted of following on even to Dublin, and as a piece de resistance bellowed a concoction in which the words "no surrender" were distinguishable'.

But for all the commotion that surrounded the Old Firm games of the 1940s, it should not be forgotten that it was also the era of one of the great Rangers teams. Celtic were nowhere near the force they had been, and the Light Blues' results against them demonstrated their vast superiority.

Between the start of the 1945–46 season and the end of the 1949–50 campaign, Rangers were undefeated in ten league games against their ancient rivals, scoring twenty-six goals and conceding just seven in the process. Among the eight victories were three 4–0 wins and a run of five consecutive games in which Celtic failed to find the net.

This was the era of the much-celebrated 'Iron Curtain' defence, which provided the bedrock for all of Rangers' success in the post-war years. The famed back line was made up of goalkeeper Bobby Brown, George Young, Jock 'Tiger' Shaw, Ian McColl,

Willie Woodburn and Sammy Cox. The unit had a remarkable record of playing in virtually every game, and this consistency was a vital factor in Rangers securing three out of the four 'official' league titles played for in the decade. In the 1948–49 season, they had been almost ever-present as the Ibrox men landed their first 'triple crown' of the league championship, the Scottish Cup and the recently created League Cup.

But it wasn't all about defence. In Willie Waddell, Rangers had one of the finest wingers ever to play the game, and his talents on the right side of the attack were complemented by inside-forward Torry Gillick. Centre-forward Willie Thornton had signed for the club as a schoolboy in 1936 and went on to make more than 430 appearances. He was the first post-war Rangers player to score 100 goals and, in an Ibrox career that spanned 17 years, scored a total of 255 times. Jimmy Duncanson was a prolific striker, with a scoring rate of one goal every two games. He also netted 22 times against Celtic, putting him third in the all-time list of Rangers' Old Firm scorers, behind R.C. Hamilton and Ally McCoist.

Thornton and Duncanson were both absent as Rangers took to the field against Celtic on that tense Saturday afternoon in late September 1949. Once the game was under way, it was a muted affair by Old Firm standards, unsurprisingly, perhaps, given recent events. Both teams seemed to be so worried about igniting trouble among spectators that they appeared not to be approaching the game in quite as full-blooded a manner as they normally would. Even an early goal from Rangers – outside-left Eddie Rutherford shot them into the lead in just five minutes – failed to stir up the passions of the supporters, and the first half was an insipid affair. But three minutes before half-time, Willie Waddell suddenly burst into action.

He picked up the ball on the right before rounding two Celtic defenders and offering the ball on a plate to Willie Findlay, who slotted it past Miller into the away team's goal. Yet even the celebrations were understated, as if the players were fearful of showing too much emotion lest they were blamed for sparking a negative reaction on the terraces.

PLUS ÇA CHANGE...

The second half was a much more interesting contest, even though Rangers were never in any danger of seeing their lead eroded. Waddell was on top form, giving his opposite number, Roy Milne, a torrid time, prompting newspapers to compare his swerves and ball control to those of the legendary England winger Stanley Matthews.

As a player, a manager and then an administrator, 'Deedle', as Waddell was known to the fans, made a massive contribution to the progress and development of Rangers Football Club over five decades. His playing career, which he began as a 17 year old, was phenomenal – he appeared almost 300 times in official peacetime matches, scoring 56 goals. In addition to the honours he won during the war, he collected four league championship medals, two Scottish Cups and three League Cups. For a winger, he was strongly built, and his power complemented his incredible pace, leaving opposition full-backs trailing in his wake. But his real strength was the pinpoint accuracy with which he could deliver crosses with his right foot. Invariably, they would find the head of his friend Willie Thornton, who more often than not would turn the chance into a goal.

After retiring as a player, Waddell became manager of Kilmarnock, where he had remarkable success, leading the Ayrshire club to an unlikely league championship in 1965. Having achieved as much as he could ever have been expected to at Rugby Park, Waddell retired from the game to become a football journalist.

In 1969, he was tempted back into the game when he was appointed manager of Rangers, and while he didn't manage to break Celtic's stranglehold on the game at that time, he led the club to their only European trophy to date and laid the foundations for success in the 1970s. Waddell also took responsibility as the public face of the club in the aftermath of the Ibrox Disaster of 1971. It was his decision that Rangers players should attend the funerals of the victims, and he also organised hospital visits by the squad to meet the injured. He later said that the players had been 'upset and moved' at what they had heard from the survivors.

FOLLOW, FOLLOW

Following the European Cup-Winners' Cup triumph in 1972, Waddell moved into a new administrative role as general manager, his first achievement being to successfully appeal against the two-year ban from European football imposed on Rangers because of crowd trouble after the final. He believed that if supporters were treated well they would behave well, and the 1971 disaster demonstrated just how unsafe British football grounds were. Waddell devoted much of the next decade to rebuilding Ibrox and turning it into the safest, most comfortable stadium in Europe.

But it was as a flying winger that Deedle made his reputation, and his second-half performance against Celtic in 1949 was typical of what he was capable of. As well as consistently setting up goals for others, he was also a regular scorer in his own right, and it appeared he'd added another to his impressive goal tally midway through the second half. The goal was disallowed after a debatable offside decision, but it was only a matter of time before Waddell would put Rangers three ahead.

The goal came from the penalty spot after Jock Shaw – who had been moved to outside-left after he picked up an injury – was brought down in the area. Waddell made no mistake with his spot kick, and he capped a fine individual performance by laying on the cross that allowed Billy Williamson to seal a 4–0 win.

In the wake of the trouble at the earlier games, the *Picture Post* had sent one of its writers from London to dispatch a report from the front line, but he left disappointed. 'Not a banner has floated on bloodstained air. Not a bottle. Not a battle,' the author wrote. Likewise, for all its previous hand-wringing and navel-gazing, the *Herald* was scathing about this watered-down version of the Old Firm. 'A Rangers v. Celtic match used to be the greatest club game in the world,' the paper stated; 'now it is an anaemic, lustreless fixture – just another fixture.'

And this is the Old Firm paradox. For all the words written in condemnation of the fixture and everything that surrounds it, the match remains the most important on the Scottish football calendar. All those who make a living out of covering the game rely on the controversy generated by meetings between the two clubs, however distasteful they may claim they find it. Games that pass without incident are dismissed as anodyne; without the baggage, they are 'just another fixture'.

8

THE GREATEST TEAM?

RANGERS 3 CELTIC 0
SCOTTISH CUP FINAL REPLAY
PLAYED AT HAMPDEN PARK, GLASGOW
15 MAY 1963

Rangers team: Ritchie, Shearer, Provan, Greig, McKinnon, Baxter, Henderson, McMillan, Millar, Brand, Wilson

Rangers scorers: Brand (2), Wilson

It was the year the '60s really started to swing. Beatlemania was sweeping the country, as screaming teenage girls swooned at John, Paul, George and Ringo's every move and the Fab Four fought it out with the Stones at the top of the pop charts. Women's skirts were getting shorter while men's hair was getting longer, and across the world social change was in the air.

If 1963 was the beginning of an exciting new cultural era, it was an equally exciting time to be a Rangers supporter. The swaggering Jim Baxter was Scotland's first 'pop star' footballer and he was the focal point of what many supporters believe to be the greatest Ibrox team of all time.

The classic line-up of the era is one that many old-time supporters still know off by heart: Billy Ritchie, Bobby Shearer, Eric Caldow, John Greig, Ronnie McKinnon, Jim Baxter, Willie Henderson, Ian McMillan, Jimmy Millar, Ralph Brand and Davie Wilson. Ten of that eleven played in the 1963 Scottish Cup final replay, David Provan replacing Caldow, who had suffered a broken leg a few weeks before.

The 1963 final replay is considered by many to be Baxter's finest performance in a light-blue shirt. Others have described it as the most embarrassingly one-sided Scottish Cup final of all time.

The mass exodus of Celtic fans from the Hampden slopes began the moment the ball hit the net for the third time. With 25 minutes to go, Ralph Brand's second goal ensured that Rangers would be lifting the Scottish Cup. It was only a three-goal difference, but it might as well have been seven or eight, such was the gulf between the teams. And the Celtic fans knew it. They may have declared themselves in song to be 'faithful through and through' but that evening they weren't hanging around to share in their team's pain. In their thousands, they streamed towards the Hampden exits, with the triumphal songs of the Rangers fans ringing in their ears. By the time the final whistle blew, the east terracing was virtually empty.

At the other end of the stadium, the Ibrox faithful celebrated, their only disappointment being that their heroes hadn't turned the screw in the closing minutes and inflicted a real humiliation on their deadly rivals. The 7–1 League Cup final defeat of 1957 was still painfully fresh in the minds of the Rangers fans, and many saw this as an opportunity to cancel out that embarrassment. There's little doubt that Celtic were lucky to concede only three goals.

In April 1954, Symon had taken over as manager from Bill Struth, who finally resigned at the age of 79, after a series of health setbacks. In September 1956, on the eve of an Old Firm game, he died at his home in the South Side of Glasgow.

Struth was the most successful manager in Scottish football history, but in the last few years of his tenure Rangers had begun to slip from their position of dominance. Symon had a major rebuilding task on his hands. However, with the introduction of youngsters like Shearer, Caldow and Alex Scott alongside some of the great names from the Struth era, Rangers were soon back at the top of the pile.

Symon continued the rebuilding process into the new decade and by the start of the 1960s had assembled one of the great Rangers teams of all time. The team was a classic combination of defensive steel, provided by the likes of Shearer, Greig and McKinnon, and the attacking flair of Henderson, Wilson, Millar and Brand.

The undoubted star was, of course, midfield supremo Baxter. He was Scotland's original playboy footballer, almost as well known for his off-field antics as his performances on the pitch. He invariably saved his best for the big stage, and in Scotland it doesn't get any bigger than an Old Firm cup final.

It had been a magnificent season for Rangers. They had stormed to a league championship win, losing just two of their thirty-four games and eventually finishing nine points clear of second-placed Kilmarnock. Celtic, who came in 13 points behind the champions, were beaten home and away, including a 4–0 New Year game at Ibrox.

A 3–2 defeat to Kilmarnock in the League Cup final came as a disappointment, as did a heavy defeat to Tottenham Hotspur in Europe, but normal service was resumed in the Scottish Cup. Airdrie, East Stirlingshire, Dundee and Dundee United were all defeated as Rangers reached the final, where they would face Celtic. It was their twelfth final since 1930 but, incredibly, the first Old Firm final since the hoodoo-busting game of 1928.

With Baxter in his pomp, Rangers went into the match as overwhelming favourites, but, as so often happens when the Glasgow rivals meet, the game failed to live up to expectations. On a wet and windy afternoon, neither team produced much in the way of flowing football for the crowd of 129,643 to savour.

Celtic had their much-maligned goalkeeper to thank for keeping them in the game. Frank Haffey is best known for his hapless performance between the sticks when Scotland were crushed 9–3 by England at Wembley in 1961. But on this occasion he made the headlines for all the right reasons as he single-handedly defied Rangers. He pulled off a string of saves, the best of them stopping a powerful shot by Ralph Brand in the second half. In addition, Henderson hit the bar and another effort was cleared off the line by a defender. In the end, Brand managed to beat Haffey once, but his goal was negated by a Bobby Murdoch strike at the other end, so the game ended level.

The replay took place 11 days later and again drew a massive crowd, of 120,273. The combined attendance of 249,916 wasn't a record – the final and replay played between Rangers and Morton in 1948 were attended by 265,199 – but the gate receipts of £50,500 were the highest ever taken for a final.

This time, Rangers were determined to put their rivals to the sword and took the lead as early as the seventh minute. Jimmy Millar released Willie Henderson down the right-hand side and the winger sent in a perfect cross, which Brand swept past Haffey. The early goal further increased Rangers' confidence and it was one-way traffic from then on. Ian McMillan turned back the clock with a vintage performance and the Rangers defence comfortably coped with whatever Celtic had to throw at them.

Shearer, Wilson, McMillan and Millar were all singled out for praise for their performances, but it was Baxter who was head and shoulders above everyone else. He swept the ball about the pitch with ease, dictating the play and leaving his opponents chasing shadows. Rangers dominated the first half, with only the strident defensive work of Billy McNeill preventing them running up a cricket score.

With a minute to go before half-time, the Light Blues finally got the breakthrough their play deserved. Jimmy Millar passed to his strike partner Brand, whose low shot was only parried away by Haffey, allowing Davie Wilson to net an easy rebound.

The timing of the goal effectively put an end to any hopes Celtic might have had of retrieving something from the game. In the second half, they looked dispirited and offered little resistance, and when Brand's dipping shot from 25 yards bounced past Haffey into the net, the outcome was sealed.

Having been the hero of the first match, Haffey had turned villain, being given the blame for Rangers' second and third goals. The criticism was somewhat harsh. There would have been no replay were it not for his heroics in the drawn game, and Rangers were so superior in the replay that they surely would have won it regardless.

After the third goal went in, there was no doubt where the cup was going, and from then on Rangers toyed with their opponents. Not surprisingly, Baxter, the man who later played keepie-uppie on the Wembley turf against world champions England, was tormentor-in-chief. At one point, it is said, he sat on the ball while it was in play, goading the Celtic players into trying to retrieve it. Wisely, they chose not to. It was too much for the Celtic fans to bear. When Bobby Shearer lifted the trophy, it was against the backdrop of a half-empty stadium.

Baxter left the pitch with the match ball shoved up his jersey. He later presented it to Ian McMillan to mark his third cup final win, although the SFA took a dim view, writing to Rangers to demand the ball's immediate return.

Amid the praise for Baxter, it would be unfair to ignore the contribution of two-goal hero Ralph Brand to the win. Brand was first spotted by Bill Struth playing for Scotland schoolboys against England at Wembley in 1952. The match was shown live on television and the Rangers manager had been tipped off by former Rangers player Bob McAulay, one of his network of scouts, to keep an eye on the young boy from Edinburgh.

'When I got back home after the game, I got a telegram from Mr Struth, which I still have, asking me to phone him at Ibrox,' Brand recalls. 'I called him and he asked if I would like to go through and see him at Ibrox.'

As a promising schoolboy footballer, Brand had previously been courted by his home-town teams Hearts and Hibs and had visited their grounds at Tynecastle and Easter Road on many occasions. But this was different. 'We went in the main entrance, where there was a commissionaire who ushered you in and sat you down. Then there was the marble staircase with the oak banisters and the portrait of Alan Morton hanging on the wall. In those days, to be allowed in that front door, and especially to be allowed up that staircase, you had to be someone special.'

Having signed as an amateur, Brand spent the next year travelling through to Ibrox one night a week for training, before signing up as a professional in 1953. By then, he'd already made his first-team debut against Kilmarnock and was beginning to establish himself alongside boyhood heroes like Young, McColl and Shaw.

By the start of the next decade, a new and equally dominant Rangers team had been created and Brand, who formed a prolific strike partnership with Jimmy Millar, was an integral member. He remembers, 'After I had got into the team in the early 1960s, when we had a really good side, being able to walk into the Ibrox dressing-room before a game and knowing that the number 10 shirt hanging up in the corner was my shirt was really something else.

'You didn't have to look at the team sheet because the team practically picked itself in those days. We were expected to win every game we played at that time, so the possibility of losing to Celtic was never considered.'

Brand was in some ways a player ahead of his time. During his daily train commute to Glasgow with fellow Edinburgh resident Millar, he would discuss tactics and go over incidents from games. He would also stay behind after the morning training session to work on moves with his strike partner, something that is rare even today. And long before sports nutritionists became part of a football club's backroom team, Brand understood the importance of diet and eschewed the usual steak and chips preferred by his teammates. All this made him seem like something of a maverick, or even a troublemaker, but he stuck by his principles and was rewarded with a hugely successful career.

The league and cup double of 1962–63 laid the foundations for the following season's clean sweep. Led on the pitch by 'Captain Cutlass' Shearer and inspired by the genius of Baxter, Symon's men swept the board to claim a magnificent treble.

9

KING KAI RULES

RANGERS 1 CELTIC 0
SCOTTISH CUP FINAL REPLAY
PLAYED AT HAMPDEN PARK, GLASGOW
27 APRIL 1966

Rangers team: Ritchie, Johansen, Provan, Greig, McKinnon, Millar,
Henderson, Watson, McLean, Johnston, Wilson

Rangers scorer: Johansen

The Old Firm derby is a match that can make or break careers. As players like Fernando Ricksen and Anton Rogan can testify, a single moment of madness in the white heat of battle is something that can be impossible to live down. No matter what else you might go on to achieve, you will always be the guy who was substituted after 20 minutes in your first Old Firm game or the hapless defender who inexplicably threw his hand in the air to give away a penalty.

On the other hand, an inspired piece of skill is enough to give new life to the most stagnant of careers. Just ask Bert Konterman, who went from figure of fun to cult hero after his spectacular 30-yard League Cup semi-final winner against Celtic in 2002.

There can be few better examples of a player turning his whole career around on the back of an Old Firm performance than that of Kai Johansen, the hero of the 1966 Scottish Cup final. The Dane was one of several Scandinavians brought to Morton in the mid-'60s by the Greenock club's legendary manager Hal Stewart, and he quickly gained a reputation at Cappielow as a dangerous attacking right-back.

His performances tempted Scot Symon to pay £25,000 to bring him to Ibrox in the summer of 1965, but by his own admission he initially found it difficult to settle at the bigger club. Football history is littered with talented players who have failed at the Old Firm clubs simply because they found the unique demands of playing for Rangers or Celtic too much to cope with, and for a while it looked like Johansen might be another.

It didn't help that he arrived at Rangers at the beginning of one of the most difficult periods in their history. The previous season, they had finished fifth in the league, behind champions Kilmarnock, Hearts, Dunfermline and Hibs. If there was any consolation for the Rangers fans, it was that Celtic had been even worse, coming in eighth. But after years of mediocrity, Celtic's fortunes were about to dramatically improve with the arrival of Jock Stein as manager.

The first half of the decade had belonged to Rangers, but Celtic were undoubtedly in the ascendancy in the second half. If 1963 was the year the '60s began to swing, then 1966 was arguably the one in which the decade reached its high point, for music, fashion and sport.

The Beatles were at the peak of their powers, having led the British Invasion of America. John Lennon infamously declared in a newspaper interview in March 1966, 'We're more popular than Jesus now.' The landmark album *Revolver* was released later in the same year and was followed by the group's last-ever live concert in San Francisco. Meanwhile, pirate radio stations were beginning to broadcast US-style pop shows to young music fans fed up with the stodgy, out-of-touch BBC.

Carnaby Street in London was the fashion capital of the world, with Mary Quant the undisputed queen of design. Her shop Bazaar was a regular haunt of the Beatles, who would often drop in to buy one of her designs for their girlfriends. Her greatest claim to fame, though, was the creation of the miniskirt, the look that defined the

'60s. By 1966, hemlines had crept higher and higher, with some daring women wearing skirts seven or eight inches above the knee.

London was swinging for another reason in the summer of '66 as England won the World Cup for the first (and so far only) time. A 4–2 victory over West Germany at Wembley saw Bobby Moore lift the Jules Rimet Trophy and sparked off celebrations throughout the country.

Scots were forced to grin and bear it – until, of course, they declared themselves the new world champions after defeating England at Wembley the following year. The game was possibly Jim Baxter's finest in a Scotland shirt, taunting the English in much the same way as he had the Celtic players in the 1963 cup final replay.

The most tragic news story of the year was that of the Aberfan disaster in October. A coal slag heap in the South Wales village collapsed and swept into a primary school, killing 144 people, including 116 children.

In politics, Labour won the general election under Harold Wilson with a majority of ninety-six, having previously had a majority of just one seat.

Justice of sorts was finally served in the decade's two most notorious crimes. In May, the Moors Murderers, Ian Brady and Myra Hindley, were sentenced to life in prison for three child murders in and around Manchester between 1963 and 1965. The pair later confessed to killing two other children and burying their bodies on Saddleworth Moor. Hindley died in prison in 2002, but Glasgow-born Brady remains in a secure psychiatric hospital, the longest-serving prisoner in the English legal system. Ronald 'Buster' Edwards was arrested in September 1966 in connection with the Great Train Robbery three years earlier. He was later jailed for 15 years for his part in the robbery.

The biggest television hits of the year were the game show *It's a Knockout* and the sitcom *Till Death Us Do Part*. But the programme to have the biggest impact was the docudrama *Cathy Come Home*, about a young couple who lost their home – and eventually their children – after falling into unemployment and poverty. The programme, watched by 12 million people, is credited with changing the British public's attitudes towards homelessness and may even have had an influence on government policy.

Rangers started the 1965–66 season well but came off the rails spectacularly at New Year, when they were hammered 5–1 at Celtic Park despite taking the lead in the first minute. Celtic eventually went on to win the league by two points from Rangers, their first title in twelve years.

Having also lost the League Cup final to Celtic in October, Rangers had the chance to redeem themselves in the Scottish Cup, where they would again face their city rivals in the final. However, the previous results, especially the crushing New Year defeat, made Celtic huge favourites to come out on top at Hampden.

On a bright afternoon in late April, a massive crowd of 126,600 packed into the national stadium for the final. Any hopes that they would witness an exhibition of free-flowing, attacking football were soon dashed as it became clear that both Symon and Stein were adopting a safety-first policy. It may seem surprising that, with 197 goals between them in the league, both teams were so cautious, but such is the pressure in these games to avoid defeat at all costs that a defensive approach is inevitable.

The result was that the two teams cancelled each other out and the final ended in stalemate. However, Rangers came out of the match with more credit and demonstrated that they were not the pushovers most pundits had predicted. Nevertheless, it was widely assumed that they had missed their chance and that Celtic would come out on top in the replay four days later. The *Glasgow Herald* declared, 'Celtic will still be expected to retain the trophy on the grounds, no doubt, that the reserves of match winning potential at their disposal are stronger than Rangers.'

One of the key features of the first match was the battle between Kai Johansen and Celtic's winger John Hughes. The Dane had been given a torrid time by Hughes in the League Cup final and Celtic had clearly identified him as a potential weak link, setting out early to put as much pressure on him as possible. This time, Johansen was more than up to the task and not only subdued

Hughes but was able to provide an attacking threat of his own.

In an interview with Johansen in 2003, he told me that he had been determined in the Scottish Cup final to lay the ghosts of the 5–1 game to rest. 'That day, I was more determined than I have ever been in a football game because I had such a hard time in the past,' he recalled. 'I had struggled against John Hughes and that had made things difficult for me. In fact, things got so bad I told Scot Symon I wanted to go back home to Denmark. At the start of my Rangers career, I really felt I didn't belong there. But the cup final changed all that.'

Despite again being dismissed as underdogs, Rangers – having kept Celtic at bay in the first game – went into the replay with great confidence. The only change from the first game was the replacement of Jim Forrest with George McLean in attack.

Again Rangers adopted a defensive approach, with Jimmy Millar used in a protective role in front of the back line. His presence was invaluable in helping John Greig and Ronnie McKinnon to snuff out the threat of Celtic's forwards Chalmers and McBride. Jimmy Johnstone was proving a handful for Rangers left-back David Provan, but on the other wing Johansen was again able to keep Hughes under control.

The first half was typical Old Firm fare – punctuated by hard, and sometimes rash, tackling and frequent stoppages for free kicks. Rangers struggled to get into any sort of attacking rhythm and, as is so often the case on these occasions, the tension meant good football was at a premium. The Light Blues managed only two half-chances in the first period: a dipping shot from Greig that went over the bar and another from Bobby Watson that was deflected wide. Celtic were marginally more of a threat, but they struggled to break down the Rangers defence and, when they did make a breakthrough, found goalkeeper Billy Ritchie in good form.

A similar pattern followed after the break, with Celtic using the wind to their advantage as they tried to get what would surely be the winning goal. Numerous chances to break the stalemate were passed up and the game appeared to be heading inexorably towards extra time.

Then, with 20 minutes to go, came the decisive moment.

Willie Henderson picked the ball up on the right touchline just inside the Celtic half and passed it inside to Greig. The captain drove forward and released Willie Johnston on the left-hand side. He jinked past three defenders and reached the byline before cutting it back towards McLean. From six yards out, he fluffed his effort, but the ball ran through to Henderson at the back post. He fired in a shot that was cleared off the line by Bobby Murdoch.

The ball rebounded out of the penalty area and straight into the path of Johansen, who was coming in from the right. He took one touch to bring the ball under control, a second to take him to the edge of the 18-yard box and with his third let fly with a tremendous shot that flew into the net despite the desperate efforts of the Celtic defenders to stop it.

'The place just exploded, and the next thing I knew all the players had jumped on top of me,' Johansen recalled. 'It was such an emotional moment and as I was lying there under all the players, wee Willie Henderson said to me, "Now you'll know what it is like to be a Ranger." I didn't pay much attention to that at the time, but from that moment on it all changed for me.'

Johansen's goal won Rangers the cup for a record 19th time in their history and sparked huge celebrations on the terraces. As the match drifted towards its conclusion and the Celtic supporters drifted towards the exits, the Ibrox faithful in the 97,000 crowd cheered themselves hoarse, and the party continued long into the night.

After the final whistle, Johansen was carried from the pitch above the heads of his teammates, tears streaming down his face. He wasn't the only emotional Ranger that night. Captain John Greig described it as the 'greatest moment of my career', telling reporters, 'On the two previous occasions I played in a cup final Rangers were favourites. But this time we were the underdogs and victory gave me tremendous satisfaction.'

Fans lined the route from Mount Florida to the centre of Glasgow, where Rangers had set up base at the St Enoch Hotel. The team bus had to edge its way through some 5,000 supporters who had packed into St Enoch Square, despite the late hour, to catch a glimpse of the trophy and the goalscoring hero. Eventually, the shy, retiring Dane appeared on the hotel balcony to take a bow.

'I didn't realise but I really didn't know what it meant to be a Ranger – but I soon found out,' Johansen told me. 'We went to the hotel in St Enoch Square after the game and I came out onto the balcony like a king to see the crowds. It was embarrassing, but never before in the history of Rangers was something like that needed. It was in the heat of Celtic's period of dominance. We needed this.'

It wasn't just the team as a whole that benefited from the last-gasp goal. Johansen himself never looked back. He said, 'The fans had taken to me and I had taken to them. The fear I played with was gone and I could play my natural game. My career changed through that goal. It was my greatest-ever moment in football.' The goal ensured Johansen a permanent place in the hearts of Rangers fans and there was widespread sadness when he died in 2007, after a battle with cancer.

The cup final win was a last hurrah for Rangers. Players like Ritchie, Shearer, Caldow, Millar, Brand and Wilson had either gone or were moving towards the end of their Ibrox careers and for the most part their replacements were nowhere near up to standard.

The following season, Celtic won their first treble and, even more depressingly for the Ibrox fans, Stein took Celtic to a European Cup triumph. Symon found himself under increasing pressure, with critics claiming his austere management style was outdated and not suited to the modern game. In January 1967, a humiliating Scottish Cup defeat to Second Division Berwick Rangers heaped further pressure on the manager and even a narrow defeat to Bayern Munich in the European Cup-Winners' Cup final failed to lift the mood.

Six months later, with Rangers at the top of the league, Symon's thirteen-year tenure as manager ended when he was sacked. His assistant Davie White, a young, modern 'tracksuit manager', took over in November 1967. He came close to winning the league title at the end of the season, but his reign as manager lasted only until November 1969, a trophyless two years.

It had become a depressing time to be a Rangers supporter. Surely not one of the crowd who hailed King Kai outside the St Enoch Hotel in 1966 would have imagined it would be four years before Rangers would lift another trophy.

10

. . . .

OUT OF THE WILDERNESS

RANGERS 1 CELTIC 0
LEAGUE CUP FINAL
PLAYED AT HAMPDEN PARK, GLASGOW
24 OCTOBER 1970

*Rangers team: McCloy, Jardine, Miller, Jackson, McKinnon, Conn,
MacDonald, Henderson, W. Johnston, Stein, D. Johnstone*

Rangers scorer: Johnstone

It was a story that the writers of *Roy of the Rovers* would have been proud of. A lanky 16 year old is plucked from the reserves and thrown into the starting line-up for the cup final, replacing the club captain, who has a career-threatening injury. A team that hasn't won a trophy for four years takes on its deadliest rivals at the national stadium. Minutes before half-time, the teenager leaps above the defenders and heads the ball into the net. His team holds out for the rest of the game and wins the trophy. The scorer of the winning goal instantly attains hero status and goes on to become one of the club's greatest-ever strikers.

It may sound like the stuff of comic-strip fiction, but for Derek Johnstone this was a true-life story. He was the 16 year old in question, barely old enough to be out of school and thrust into the spotlight after captain John Greig was declared unfit just days before the 1970 League Cup final.

FOLLOW, FOLLOW

After the unfortunate Davie White era, Rangers were in desperate need of a leader, and the board turned to Willie Waddell, who had been a wonderful servant for the club as a player under Bill Struth. When he was named as the new Rangers manager in 1969, his appointment was met with almost universal acclaim. He immediately set about clearing out what he saw as dead wood and attempted to rebuild the Rangers team.

It was no surprise that, as someone who had been given his chance in the Rangers first team as a raw 17 year old, he put a heavy emphasis on youth, making players like Sandy Jardine, Alex MacDonald, Colin Jackson and Alfie Conn regulars.

Dundee-born Johnstone was another to benefit from Waddell's youth policy. He had signed up at Ibrox as a schoolboy in 1968 and just weeks after turning professional made his first-team debut, against Cowdenbeath in September 1970. He made an instant impact, scoring twice in a 5–0 victory.

The win was a rare high point in the early part of Waddell's first full season. Despite all his changes, Rangers had made a stuttering start and by October they were a distant fifth in the league. They had shown better form in the League Cup, though, and battled their way past Dunfermline, Morton, Motherwell, Hibs and Cowdenbeath to reach the final and yet another Old Firm showdown at Hampden.

It had been four long years since Kai Johansen's Scottish Cup winner in 1966, the last time the Rangers fans had seen their team lift silverware. For most clubs, such a trophy drought would barely raise an eyebrow, but for Rangers it was almost unthinkable. For the support, victory against Celtic was more than just desirable: it was a must.

Despite his team being considered underdogs by just about everyone, Waddell exuded a quiet confidence as the final approached, and this rubbed off on the fans. Even a 2–0 defeat to Aberdeen at Ibrox a week before the final failed to dampen the enthusiasm. However, had the supporters known the drama that was developing behind the scenes, they might have been a little more worried.

OUT OF THE WILDERNESS

Captain John Greig woke up on the Monday morning before the final to discover his shin was badly swollen. During the game against Aberdeen, he had suffered a gash on his leg. It hadn't seemed particularly serious at first, but infection had set in, possibly because the chemicals used to treat the Ibrox pitch had got into his bloodstream.

A specialist who examined the injury immediately told Greig he would not be able to take part in the final. In fact, he went so far as to warn the stunned player that he would be risking his career if he was to play – and if complications set in, he could even face having the leg amputated!

If Greig himself was devastated by the diagnosis, it also came as a major shock to Willie Waddell. The presence of his talismanic captain as both a player and a leader was vital to his plans for overcoming Celtic, and Greig's absence left a gaping hole.

Centre-back Ronnie McKinnon was the obvious choice to be given the role of stand-in captain, but deciding who would take Greig's place on the pitch required some more thought. Waddell's decision to reshuffle his team and play Johnstone came as a surprise to everyone, not least the player himself.

The news was broken to him in the Ibrox boot room by the manager and his assistant Jock Wallace on the eve of the match. Johnstone recalls, 'I will never forget the Friday before the game. He and Jock took me in and he said, "Look, son, don't be nervous. Here's half a dozen tickets. Bring your family to the game. You're playing. And have a good night's sleep." The thing is that I did have a good night's sleep because I never got nervous. I was never the nervous type.'

His selection was undoubtedly a gamble. Johnstone was tall and powerful and had shown signs in his brief first-team appearances as well as in his second-eleven performances that he had a talent. But this was a player who had never even seen a game at Hampden, never mind played in one. Here was Waddell handing him the Rangers number 9 shirt for what was arguably the club's most important game in years. 'Celtic were in the midst of nine in a row and, to be honest, Rangers were toiling,' says Johnstone. 'I was fortunate as we had a bad start to the season and I was scoring a lot of goals for the reserves.

Colin Stein wasn't firing on all cylinders and the team were struggling for goals and results. But it was a chance that Willie Waddell took in playing me.'

As the two giants of Scottish football went head to head in front of 106,000 fans, Rangers started the better team and had Celtic on the back foot for much of the first half. The team ethic instilled during Wallace's gruelling training sessions at Gullane Sands paid dividends, as Rangers demonstrated an urgency and determination that Stein's team simply couldn't cope with.

Fittingly for a man who had been a flying winger in his playing days, Waddell also made great use of the flanks. With Willie Henderson causing chaos on one wing and Willie Johnston on the other, Celtic were stretched. The not-inconsiderable presence of Derek Johnstone in the traditional centre-forward role alongside Colin Stein gave the defenders even more to worry about.

Five minutes before half-time, Waddell's gamble paid off. Alex MacDonald played a 30-yard pass from the halfway line, releasing Willie Johnston on the right. He brought it under control with his left foot, then swung a right-footed cross into the penalty area. The ball looped high into the box, where Johnstone was waiting to pounce eight yards out. He timed his leap to perfection, outjumping defenders Billy McNeill and Jim Craig to get his header in. Half of Hampden erupted as the ball ended up in the bottom left corner of the net, beyond the despairing dive of the yellow-shirted Celtic goalkeeper, Evan Williams.

Johnstone says, 'Obviously the goal was great. It was a tremendous move. For the header, I got in between McNeill and Craig. I just timed it well and it went into the corner.'

It was the only goal of the game. Rangers managed to hold on to their lead, although Celtic pressure in the second half meant there were nervy moments for the fans and players. Sandy Jardine recalls, 'That was the first time I was going to win a trophy and I always remember for the last five or ten minutes I was really nervous and wanting the final whistle to be blown so we could get up and lift the trophy.'

OUT OF THE WILDERNESS

When Ronnie McKinnon collected the cup, it was a moment of joy and relief for the supporters. The victory had long-term implications, both for Johnstone and for Rangers as a team. The goal ensured the player would always have a place in the hearts of the Ibrox supporters. 'It was a game I will never forget because it was the making of me,' he says. 'It meant the fans took to me right away.'

Despite his goal heroics, Johnstone didn't get the chance to take part in the post-match celebrations with the rest of the squad, and he almost lost a memento of his first cup final. After Hampden, the 16 year old was taken back to his digs at the home of John Greig's uncle just outside Glasgow. He was flying out to Iceland the next day with the Scotland Under-18 team – including Graeme Souness – and because he hadn't been home, he had to take his winner's medal with him.

For safety, he hid the medal away in a drawer in his hotel room – then promptly forgot all about it until he was on board the return flight to Scotland. In a panic, he went straight to Ibrox from Glasgow Airport and sought help from Willie Waddell. The Rangers boss immediately called in the SFA and, after a series of frantic phone calls, the medal was found and returned.

Johnstone went on to score 210 goals for Rangers, including what was at the time a post-war league record of 132, an achievement that is even more impressive when you consider he played a large percentage of his games at centre-half and in midfield.

During his first spell at Ibrox, between 1970 and 1983, he won the European Cup-Winners' Cup and two trebles, along with numerous other league and cup honours. He also captained the side for three years, before being transferred to Chelsea in 1983. He returned in 1985 and played out the last two seasons of his career at the club where he had first made his name as a teenager.

The cup win was seen as a new beginning by the club's fans, who had endured a miserable time in the second half of the '60s. The new decade coincided with the end of the flower-power age, the official splitting-up of the Beatles symbolising the end of an era. While the

'60s had been a decade of social change, the '70s was a time of great technological advancement. The first jumbo jet landed at Heathrow airport in January 1971, while in the same year computer giant IBM launched floppy disks.

The confidence the cup win gave Rangers cannot be overstated. The club was back on form and the victory paved the way for even greater triumphs. A European trophy and two trebles would come in the next few years, as Rangers finally broke Celtic's dominance and regained their position as the best team in the country.

Jardine says, 'Willie Waddell, when he became manager, set about restoring some of the traditions of the club. A lot of personnel left and new players came in, and we had a much younger team. Initially, we started off in the league terribly, but we did fantastically in Europe, going all the way to win the European Cup–Winners' Cup. But from that he laid the foundations for the team that won two trebles and became the dominant team in Scotland of the '70s.'

11

A CENTENARY CELEBRATION

RANGERS 3 CELTIC 2
SCOTTISH CUP FINAL
PLAYED AT HAMPDEN PARK, GLASGOW
5 MAY 1973

Rangers team: McCloy, Jardine, Mathieson, Forsyth, Johnstone, Greig, MacDonald, Conn, McLean, Parlane, Young

Rangers scorers: Parlane, Conn, Forsyth

Tom Forsyth's goal in the centenary Scottish Cup final ranks among the most memorable in Rangers' illustrious history.

Some goals find their way into the hall of fame thanks to a sublime piece of skill, while others live long in the memory because of the sheer quality of the strike. The winner in the 1973 Scottish Cup final was neither a dazzling Cooperesque solo run nor a Wilkins-style 25-yard piledriver. But Forsyth's sclaff from three inches is remembered just as fondly by the Rangers fans as anything produced by those two legends.

What the goal lacked in quality, it made up for in significance. That Scottish Cup final meant so much to Rangers and their legions of fans. It had been seven years since the old cup had last rested in the oak-panelled trophy room at Ibrox. The League Cup win of 1970 was starting to feel like a long time ago, and Rangers seemed no closer to wresting the league flag away from Celtic Park, where it had flown every season since 1966.

But now they had the chance to celebrate their official centenary year by triumphing in Scottish football's showpiece occasion and at the same time strike a blow against their biggest rivals. In front of 120,000 at Hampden, they did exactly that, Forsyth's goal proving to be the difference between the teams in a classic final.

In the seven years that had passed since the last Scottish Cup final triumph, much had changed, not least fashions. The '60s were well and truly over and the traditional, clean-cut image of players like Eric Caldow, Bobby Shearer and Jimmy Millar was long gone. Long hair and massive sideburns were now de rigueur on the pitch, just as they were on the terraces.

It was the year of glam rock, with the Birmingham band Slade scoring three number ones, including the Christmas classic 'Merry Xmas Everybody'. Gary Glitter reached the top of the charts with 'Leader of the Gang' and Sweet's 'Blockbuster' was number one for five weeks, while T-Rex and David Bowie were also at the peak of their powers. Dawn's 'Tie a Yellow Ribbon Round the Old Oak Tree' was at the head of the Top 40 on the week of the cup final.

For movie lovers, 1973 was also a big year, *The Exorcist*, *American Graffiti*, *The Sting*, *Enter the Dragon*, *Papillon*, *The Wicker Man*, *Serpico*, *Live and Let Die*, *The Way We Were*, *Magnum Force* and *Mean Streets* all hitting the cinemas. It was a less than vintage year for television, though, with the most notable small-screen event being the broadcast of the pilot episode of the longest-running comedy series in the world, *Last of the Summer Wine*.

The year also marked the end of the Vietnam War but saw the Watergate scandal grip America, eventually leading to the resignation of President Richard Nixon. At home, coal shortages caused by industrial action resulted in the three-day week coming into force on 31 December in a bid to reduce electricity consumption. Petrol prices were already sky-high thanks to the oil embargo imposed by Arab countries in protest at the US's backing of Israel in the Yom Kippur War.

If it was a momentous year in politics and popular culture, so it was in football for Rangers. Their cup final performance was full of the sort of spirit and energy demanded by the manager Jock Wallace. He had stepped up to take over as boss following the surprise resignation of Willie Waddell in the immediate aftermath of the European Cup-Winners' Cup triumph in Barcelona at the end of the previous season.

Wallace had been Waddell's assistant and was credited with transforming the fitness of the players in the squad. The notoriously gruelling pre-season sessions he oversaw on the sand dunes of Gullane were just a part – albeit the most publicised part – of the regime he introduced.

Largely as a result of the newspaper coverage of those sessions at 'Murder Hill', Wallace had a fearsome reputation, and this was only enhanced by his gruff demeanour. But contrary to the public's perception, he was not a ranter by nature, and while describing him as a gentle giant might be going a bit far, his former players insist he had a much mellower nature than many on the outside would suspect.

He was undoubtedly a man of the people, and when he became manager in the summer of 1972 the Rangers fans were delighted that one of their own – a man who as an eight year old would blag his way onto the local Rangers supporters bus so he could get to Ibrox – had been given the job. Wallace had a connection with the people on the terraces, because he was a fan himself.

Unfortunately, his first season in charge saw Celtic win their eighth consecutive title, but there were signs in the second half of the season that Wallace was creating a team that could finally break Jock Stein's stranglehold on the Scottish League.

The climax of the season was yet another Old Firm cup final. Not only was it Rangers' centenary year, it was also the 100th anniversary of the Scottish Football Association, and while Old Firm games so often fail to live up to the pre-match hype, this time the teams delivered a match befitting the occasion.

As usual on such occasions, the atmosphere inside the vast Hampden bowl was febrile, the noise generated by the massive crowd likened by one reporter to the sound of Concorde landing.

But it was Celtic who got off to a supersonic start, taking the lead through Kenny Dalglish in the 24th minute.

Rangers fought their way back into the game and ten minutes later were on level terms. Alex MacDonald picked up a pass from Willie Mathieson on the left and chipped a cross towards the near post. Derek Parlane escaped the attentions of his marker and headed the ball past Ally Hunter in the Celtic goal.

The tempo was unrelenting, both teams carving out more chances before the half-time whistle brought some respite. But just 17 seconds after the restart, Hampden erupted again as Rangers took the lead. Parlane flicked a pass from Quentin Young into the path of Alfie Conn, who left a gasping Billy McNeill in his wake as he bore down on goal. Hunter raced out to meet the Rangers midfielder, but Conn coolly shot past him into the net.

The Rangers fans were delirious, but their joy was short-lived, as Celtic were soon back level. John Greig, with a dive that goalkeeper Peter McCloy would have been proud of, leaped across the goalmouth to punch away a shot from Dixie Deans and deny Celtic a certain goal. Nowadays, the Rangers captain would have been guaranteed a red card, but in the '70s a penalty was considered punishment enough. The deafening whistles of the Rangers fans massed behind the goal failed to put off George Connelly, who slotted home the kick from 12 yards.

The blow of losing the lead might have sunk previous Rangers teams, but this was a Jock Wallace team, and it was instilled with a 'no surrender' spirit. Rather than retreating into defence, Rangers pushed forward and were soon rewarded for their adventure.

Tommy McLean floated a free kick in from the left, which was met magnificently by Derek Johnstone. His header beat Hunter and it looked like Johnstone had repeated his heroics of three years earlier. But this time the ball struck the left-hand post before bouncing agonisingly along the goal line and hitting the other post.

For a moment, time seemed to stand still and Hampden fell silent as 120,000 fans held their breath. The ball bobbled off the post into the path of Tom Forsyth. He was standing on his own, less than a foot from goal, the empty net gaping in front of him. He wasn't exactly renowned as a penalty-box predator, but he couldn't possibly miss. Could he?

He stuck out his right foot and aimed it at the ball. Just for a moment, it looked like he had missed it completely, but his studs made contact and the ball rolled over the line and into the net. Forsyth turned and, with an expression on his face that showed he was just as surprised by what had happened as everyone else, raced off in celebration.

Nicknamed 'Jaws' for his no-nonsense style and ferocious tackling, Forsyth was brought to Rangers from Motherwell by Wallace in 1972 and stayed at Ibrox for the rest of his career. He played an important role in Scotland's famous 1978 World Cup win over Holland in Argentina, one of his twenty-two international appearances. His other big moment for the national team came in 1976, when his perfectly timed last-ditch tackle on England's Mick Channon denied the striker an almost certain goal and ensured Scotland a 2–1 victory over the auld enemy.

But it was his cup final goal that he will always be remembered for, even though he personally thought the ball had already crossed the line before he got his famous touch. In a *Daily Record* interview many years later, he said:

> Being a defender, I hardly ever crossed the halfway line, so nobody could believe I was up there when big Derek's header hit the post and rolled along the line.
>
> To this day, I still think it was in. I thought Derek's header had crossed the line after it hit the first post and rolled along to hit the other one before I put it in. But everyone says it was my goal and I'm happy to take it. It wasn't exactly a 30-yarder but it didn't matter to me how far out it was – I just had to make sure it crossed the line.
>
> But the reaction to the goal astonishes me even now. I still get people coming up to me to talk about it. If I

had scored a 'normal' goal from 15 yards or nodded in a header, people probably wouldn't remember it.

With just five goals in a long and illustrious career, Forsyth was certainly an unexpected scorer – especially as far as his teammates were concerned. Captain John Greig was as shocked as anyone else to see the big defender claim the goal. 'Big Tam couldn't even score at training,' Greig told *The Sun* in 2003. 'At shooting practice he put it all over the place. He was the last guy we expected to score in a cup final. I think he scored from about three inches. We kidded him on that if he hadn't fitted his long studs to his boots he would have missed it.'

From then on, Rangers were in complete control of the match and could have increased their lead, both Conn and Young coming close. When referee John Gordon blew the final whistle, the players embraced, Greig even shedding a tear or two. For a player who had been at Ibrox throughout the tough years, it was an emotional moment.

Despite his own cup-winning performance three years earlier, Derek Johnstone feels the 1973 Scottish Cup final is the greatest Old Firm clash ever. 'It had everything, including Tam's winner, and was the best game I've ever played in,' he says. 'Other games were exciting, but this one was pure football, with both teams on top of their game. I remember playing at centre-half and Kenny Dalglish trying to turn me with that big backside of his.'

George Ritchie, who has been an Ibrox regular since 1962, was one of the thousands of jubilant Rangers fans crammed onto the Hampden terraces. 'This was actually my first cup final, so it holds so many fond memories for me,' he says. 'I was right up at the back of the Rangers end and wasn't wearing my glasses, so when the goal went in I couldn't see what was going on. The first thing I remember is big Tam Forsyth running away with his arms in the air, and from that moment on he was my hero.

'The thing I remember most is the way the crowd moved. Whenever there was a goal or some major incident, you would just get swept away and you'd end up miles from where you started. Ibrox was mainly terracing at the time, so we were used to standing at games, but this was something else. I'd never been in a crowd that size before and I'm certain I never will again. It was frightening in some ways but still an exhilarating experience.'

Also standing on Hampden's dusty ash terraces that afternoon was a young boy who would go on to become an Ibrox legend. Ally McCoist was just ten years old when he and a pal sneaked off on a bus from East Kilbride to the South Side of Glasgow to sample the big-match atmosphere. The two youngsters, unaccompanied by adults, stood among the 122,000 crowd, watched the game, then made their way home.

It's hard to imagine a ten year old nowadays being allowed to take public transport anywhere, let alone disappear unnoticed for hours on end on a Saturday afternoon. But this was a different era, a time when children went out to play in the morning and wouldn't be seen again until they were dragged in at teatime. It was almost three decades before McCoist's mother, Jessie, knew where her son had been that day.

At the end of the match, Jock Wallace, the architect of the victory, immediately made his way to Celtic's Bobby Murdoch. The Rangers boss had inadvertently snubbed the player's offer of a handshake after the League Cup win in 1970 and he was determined to make it right this time, particularly as it had earned him a ticking-off. Wallace said afterwards: 'I didn't mean [to walk past him]. I was just carried away. That night I got a row from my mother who saw it on television. I remembered it.'

To mark the fact that it was the SFA's centenary Scottish Cup final, a member of the Royal Family, Princess Alexandra, made the presentation of the old trophy for the first and only time. As he prepared to receive the cup, Rangers captain John Greig spruced himself up for his royal encounter, using a method that is unlikely to find its way into any etiquette books. 'I was going up the steps to get the cup from the Princess and I looked down and saw my hands were filthy,' he remembered in an interview with *The Sun*.

'I thought I'd better clean up quickly so I spat on them and wiped my hands on my jersey so I wouldn't shake her hand with a big dirty paw.'

After the presentation, Greig thrust the trophy towards his manager and shouted, 'You asked for the cup – here it is!' The action demonstrated just how important a role Wallace had played. Typically, though, he was determined to shift the focus of any praise for the victory away from him and onto the players. The day after the victory, Wallace held court at Ibrox. 'No one knows how hard they have worked,' he told reporters. 'They were down. They picked themselves up. They're the men.'

Wallace's team finally broke Celtic's league domination in 1975 when 30,000 travelling fans descended on Easter Road to see Rangers beat Hibs and finally win the title. The championship was part of a treble – one of two the Ibrox club secured in the second half of the '70s under Wallace.

Derek Johnstone judges Wallace as the best manager he served under during his career. 'He wasn't the greatest coach, but he was a marvellous motivator and his man-management was great,' he says. 'He knew if you needed a kick up the backside or a pat on the head. The proof of his success was the Cup-Winners' Cup and two trebles in seven or eight years.'

Tom Forsyth was also in awe of Wallace's managerial talents, telling the *Record*, 'Jock was a superb motivator and he had us really up for the game. He always made us feel we had to win these games.'

Wallace's resignation in 1978, after the second clean sweep, came as a massive shock to players and fans alike. Loyal to the end, Wallace never disclosed his reasons for walking out on the club he loved. He returned five years later when duty called but was unable to recreate the magic of his first period in charge.

With the departure of Wallace and many of the players who had served the club so well for so long, Rangers experienced a slump in fortunes. Despite being an inspirational captain, John Greig found the move into management a difficult one to make.

A CENTENARY CELEBRATION

Occasional victories against Celtic and in cup finals failed to mask his team's major deficiencies, and with the rise of Aberdeen and Dundee United, Rangers found themselves in the unprecedented position of being Scotland's fourth-best team – an unacceptable state of affairs for everyone associated with the club.

12

BATTLE FEVER

RANGERS 3 CELTIC 2
LEAGUE CUP FINAL
PLAYED AT HAMPDEN PARK, GLASGOW
25 MARCH 1984

*Rangers team: McCloy, Nicholl, Dawson, McLelland, Paterson,
McPherson, Russell, McCoist, Clark, MacDonald, Cooper*

Rangers scorer: McCoist (3)

Jock Wallace's words as he stood outside Hampden before the 1984
League Cup final summed up everything about the man. Briefly
breaking away from signing autographs for young fans, he turned to a
television camera and delivered his pre-match prediction. 'I fancy us
very strongly,' he told the interviewer. 'I've got the battle fever on. I
fancy Rangers to win today.'

This was no hubristic boast; it was simply a case of Wallace calling
it as he saw it. From any other manager, it could have come across as
arrogance or mind games. From Wallace, it was nothing more than
honesty and plain speaking. He knew what frame of mind his players
were in. It was a national cup final against Celtic, he was up for it and
he had made sure his players were too.

Four months after returning to the Ibrox manager's post, Wallace
was taking a patchwork team into a final that few expected them to win.
But under their new manager Rangers were a different proposition

from the shambles that he had inherited. The Light Blues had turned to the jungle fighter as a replacement for John Greig after Scotland's two brightest young managers, Alex Ferguson and Jim McLean, had turned them down.

Greig had gone straight from player to manager when Wallace had resigned in 1978 immediately after securing the second of two trebles. His appointment as manager without any prior experience turned out to be a mistake, and Rangers suffered several lean years when they were not only trailing Celtic but also found themselves left behind Ferguson's Aberdeen and McLean's Dundee United. Ibrox had undergone a transformation prompted by the 1971 disaster, but the magnificent new stands were rarely full. Poor performances led to dwindling crowds and eventually Greig's departure.

In October 1983, after the club failed to land Ferguson or McLean, Wallace answered the emergency call and immediately set about trying to restore pride in the team. If nothing else, a Wallace team was guaranteed to be full of fight, and that was just one of the qualities that had been missing in the dying days of the Greig reign. Wallace enjoyed a good start to his second spell as manager and improved morale and fitness, helping the team put together a long unbeaten streak.

Even with his motivational abilities, Wallace faced a difficult task thanks to a lack of strength in depth in his squad. Too many of his team were ordinary at best, although Rangers did undoubtedly have some good players in that era. The best of them – Bobby Russell, Davie Cooper and John McClelland – would almost certainly have found a place in many of the most successful Ibrox teams throughout history.

Others, like Jimmy Nicholl, Robert Prytz and Davie McPherson, were already or would go on to become established internationals, playing at the highest level of the game. And the Rangers youth system had also thrown up a couple of promising youngsters in the shape of Ian Durrant and Derek Ferguson, who would go on to become mainstays of the Rangers midfield.

But one man Wallace had at his disposal would play a more important part in the final than anyone else – and would eventually become a Rangers legend. Ally McCoist's signing from Sunderland by John Greig in the summer of 1983 was not universally welcomed by the fans, not least because he had previously turned down a chance to move to Ibrox from St Johnstone, instead choosing to try his luck down south. His time in the north-east of England had not been particularly successful, leading many supporters to have serious misgivings about his arrival.

McCoist's early performances were hardly inspiring, although it should be pointed out that he was often used in midfield. Nonetheless, without managing to overcome many of the doubters, he still scored an impressive 35 goals in his first season. And three of them came in one of the most thrilling Old Firm finals ever seen.

Rangers had won their way to Hampden by defeating Dundee United 3–1 on aggregate in a two-legged semi-final. Going into the final, Wallace was missing regular starters Prytz, Ian Redford and Bobby Williamson, and most experts expected Celtic to come out on top.

The match appeared to hold little appeal for the Celtic fans, with large spaces on the Hampden terraces in the sections reserved for those in green and white. The Rangers end, however, was packed and the Ibrox supporters among the 66,000 crowd were in vociferous mood. The improvements seen under Wallace had given new hope to the beleaguered Rangers followers and this was seen as an opportunity to prove that it was not a false dawn.

Away from football, the mid-'80s was a period of dramatic events both at home and abroad, and 1984 was no exception. On 6 March, a strike began in the coal-mining industry that would become one of the longest and most bitter in the history of UK industrial relations. The action lasted a year, with both the unions and Margaret Thatcher's government refusing to back down. The dispute led to angry and violent confrontations between strikers and police at picket lines on a daily basis.

If the TV images of picket-line clashes were dramatic, they were nothing compared to the pictures of the famine in Ethiopia broadcast by the BBC in October. Moving news reports by Michael Buerk told how thousands had already died of starvation in the country and that the lives of many millions were at risk. The reports had an immediate impact, leading to fund-raising efforts around the UK. Most notable was Band Aid, which saw dozens of the biggest names in pop music brought together by Bob Geldof and Midge Ure to record a charity single. The record went on to become the biggest-selling UK single of all time and led to the 1985 Live Aid concert, which raised millions for the starving Africans.

In October, the IRA attempted to assassinate Margaret Thatcher and the Cabinet by blowing up the Grand Hotel in Brighton, where they were staying during the Tory party conference. Just over two weeks later, Indian prime minister Indira Ghandi was assassinated by two security guards, leading to rioting in Delhi.

The year's League Cup final was a typically scrappy affair, the tone set by a wild lunge by Celtic defender Mark Reid on Davie Cooper and a kung-fu-style flying kick by Sandy Clark on Roy Aitken, both of which resulted in yellow cards. Rangers had the better opportunities in the early part of the first half, John McClelland twice coming close with a snap shot and then a glancing header from a magnificent Cooper cross. Celtic then enjoyed a period of dominance themselves, without ever seriously troubling Peter McCloy in the Rangers goal.

Cooper and Russell, veterans of the glory days of Wallace's first period in charge, were Rangers' best performers and it was their combination play on the left that led to the first goal. Just a minute before half-time, Cooper played an inch-perfect pass with the outside of his left foot to Russell, who had made an intelligent run into the penalty area. The midfielder nutmegged Murdo McLeod, who scythed him down as he headed towards goal. It looked a stonewall penalty and referee Bob Valentine agreed, despite Roy Aitken's angry protests.

Ally McCoist, never one lacking in confidence, stepped forward and slammed the ball into the bottom right corner of the net, sending Pat Bonner the wrong way. It was a perfect time to score, especially as it came against the run of play, and the Rangers fans were in jubilant mood as the half-time whistle blew.

Celtic continued to protest the penalty decision, although former manager Billy McNeill, who was in the commentary box for STV, was convinced the referee had called it right. McNeill, who claimed in 2010 that Celtic had been the victims of refereeing injustices in Old Firm games for 50 years, told viewers, 'I'll be honest: had it been my team, I'd have been looking for a penalty kick.'

Fifteen minutes into the second half, Rangers extended their lead, and again it was McCoist who struck. Celtic's defence failed to deal with a huge kick from McCloy, and Aitken was outmuscled by Sandy Clark, who managed to head the ball into McCoist's path. He slid in and, from six yards out, prodded it under the onrushing Pat Bonner.

At that point, Celtic looked down and out. As the Rangers players and fans celebrated, the finger-pointing began in the Celtic defence, with Bonner and Aitken apparently arguing over who was to blame. Meanwhile, television viewers saw Jock Wallace leaning out of the Rangers dugout, fist clenched, exhorting his players to 'f***ing come on!'

A third goal would have finished the game, and it almost came when Sandy Clark stretched to reach a Bobby Russell cross and played it into McCoist's path. Just as he was about to pull the trigger, Dave McPherson tried a somewhat ambitious overhead kick, succeeding only in putting the striker off.

A few minutes later, a well-worked set piece saw Brian McClair pull a goal back, but as the game approached injury time it looked like Rangers had done enough. Then, in the last minute, came the dramatic finale. Having been the hero with his two goals, McCoist turned villain when he tripped McLeod in the penalty box. Again Valentine had no hesitation in pointing to the spot, and Mark Reid blasted the kick past McCloy.

The final whistle blew before there could be any more action and the shattered Rangers players collapsed to the turf, knowing that they might have blown their only chance of silverware that season. Having fought back from two goals down, Celtic were now overwhelming favourites going into extra time. But Wallace's never-say-die spirit came to the fore and he rallied his troops during the short break.

A minute before the end of the first period, Wallace and Rangers got their reward when Aitken bundled McCoist over in the penalty area. The striker got back to his feet and again took the kick, but this time Bonner managed to stop it. McCoist, the arch-predator, was first to react and he struck the rebound into the net to complete his hat-trick.

It marked a major turnaround in fortunes for the striker. His status as an Ibrox legend is now unquestioned, but in the mid-'80s there were real doubts over his future at Rangers. His Hampden hat-trick helped win over the critics.

Speaking to *The Sun* in 2009, Peter McCloy said:

> Ally had been booed earlier in the year when Dundee knocked us out of the Scottish Cup and he'd missed a few chances. I remember speaking to him after the game and telling him to keep his head up.
>
> All strikers miss chances but fortunately things changed spectacularly for Ally after that League Cup final. Some say he's a lucky boy, but he was also a great goalscorer and it's been nice to see him do so well over the years.

This time, Rangers were able to hang on to their lead, and when Bob Valentine blew the final whistle, players, fans and backroom staff alike celebrated. Wallace leapt from the dugout waving a fist in the air in triumph, before running onto the pitch to congratulate his players. He had done what he had been brought back to do, and although there was still a long hard road ahead, he savoured the moment.

The win was the fourth League Cup triumph for McCloy, his first coming 14 years earlier. His record in the competition could actually have been even better if he had not suffered two pieces of bad luck. 'I played in four League Cup finals and got four winner's medals,' the goalkeeper told *The Sun*. 'But I also missed two after being injured just a few days before the games. I broke a finger in St Etienne and missed one final, then I got hurt against Celtic and missed out on another.'

BATTLE FEVER

For the fans, it was a glorious afternoon. John White was among the 40,000 Rangers supporters in the crowd. 'It was my first Old Firm cup final and I was stood with a group of friends right beside the Celtic supporters through the fence, in the old north enclosure,' he remembers. 'I don't recall there being any police presence. Both sets of supporters goaded each other and a fair amount of coins were thrown from either side of the fence.

'It was the first time I'd been so close to the Celtic supporters that I could see their faces. The Rangers supporters started singing, "You never sold all your tickets," which was what the newspapers had been reporting. This brought a laugh around the terracing, and as me and my friends joined in we could pick out individual Celtic fans to sing the song to, personally.

'When the final whistle went and we'd won, there was this mass outpouring of joy. What a great feeling! We all sang and danced as the Celtic end emptied. I remember shouting something like "the ref was a Tim" at this Celtic supporter through the fence and him going mental back at me, jumping up on the fence and trying to get at me. I genuinely thought he'd be waiting for me outside. He wasn't and we sang loud and proud as we left Hampden to head home on the supporters bus to Renfrew.

'I'd started following Rangers on a supporters bus in the early '80s and it was generally a depressing experience. So to win a cup, especially against Celtic, with big Jock Wallace back, felt like we were finally going to return to the good times. However, my loyalty to the Gers didn't blind me to the fact that we still had a long way to go to match a rampant Aberdeen or Dundee United, who were a good team at that time too. Looking back, it was a false dawn, but a happy day nonetheless.'

13

GOALS GALORE

RANGERS 4 CELTIC 4
SCOTTISH PREMIER DIVISION
PLAYED AT IBROX PARK, GLASGOW
22 MARCH 1986

Rangers team: Walker, Burns, Munro, McPherson, McKinnon, Durrant, McMinn, Russell, Fleck, Fraser, McCoist

Rangers scorers: Fraser (2), McCoist, Fleck

Football is sometimes capable of serving up something so extraordinary that it completely exceeds everyone's expectations. This was one of those occasions.

It is rare indeed for both sets of supporters to leave an Old Firm match satisfied with the outcome, but when the players trooped off the rain-sodden Ibrox pitch after this epic contest they received a standing ovation from all four stands.

It had been a classic game, the initiative swinging back and forth between the teams. There wasn't much in the way of silky football on display, but there was plenty of drama as Rangers fought back from 3–1 down to take a 4–3 lead, only to concede a late equaliser.

For once, controversy was nowhere to be seen. It was all about the football, and while purists would have had palpitations at some of the defending, it would have been impossible to argue that this was anything other than entertainment of the highest order.

Afterwards, both managers sang the praises of their own team – and the opposition. And, in the most bizarre twist of all, even the referee was commended for his performance – truly proof that this was no ordinary Old Firm encounter.

The defensive blunders that led to the cornucopia of goals were painfully obvious to anyone, as was the general lack of quality, but analysis of what had gone wrong was for another day. In the immediate aftermath, it was enough for the 44,000-strong crowd to simply savour what they had just witnessed.

This was the dark depths of the second Jock Wallace era, a time when Rangers were reduced to scrapping it out with the likes of Dundee and St Mirren for fifth place in the league while the New Firm of Aberdeen and Dundee United were challenging with Celtic and Hearts for the title.

It was the fourth Old Firm match of the season, and although Rangers had struggled generally throughout the campaign, they had already beaten Celtic 3–0 in the first Ibrox encounter in November and drawn 1–1 at Parkhead back in August.

Wallace's team had enjoyed a good start to the season, but a 2–0 defeat to Celtic on New Year's Day came in the midst of a desperate run that had seen them record just two victories in a dozen games. By the time the final derby came around in March, they were well out of the title race and involved in a battle for the final UEFA Cup place.

The big news for Rangers fans was that Davie Cooper had been dropped to the bench, with Wallace preferring to go with a youthful front pairing of Ally McCoist and Robert Fleck. He also gave a place to the promising young midfielder Ian Durrant, who had scored in the November victory over Celtic.

Amid torrential rain, Rangers started the game well and were much the better side for the first 20 minutes. Ally McCoist went close early on when his left-foot volley was saved by Pat Bonner. The opening was created through good work by Durrant and Ted McMinn, who was already proving to be a nuisance to the Celtic defence.

But as is often the way in Old Firm clashes, Rangers paid the penalty for failing to take advantage of their early dominance. In the

21st minute, Maurice Johnston was the first to react when Brian McClair sliced his shot following a cross from Owen Archdeacon on the left. Eight minutes later, another Archdeacon cross managed to squeeze through to McClair, and this time he was able to steer the ball past Nicky Walker.

At 2–0 down, even the most optimistic Rangers supporter must have doubted they were going to get anything from the game. But just four minutes after McClair's goal, the home team were handed a major boost when Celtic's right-back Willie McStay was sent off. Having been warned for a foul on McMinn, then booked for scything down the same player, it was no surprise when he was red-carded for another wild lunge on the Rangers winger.

Dumfries-born McMinn had joined Rangers from his home-town team Queen of the South and despite his less than glamorous background quickly became a big favourite with the Rangers supporters. His ungainly running style earned him the nickname 'the Tin Man', and while his technique was somewhat unorthodox, this was part of what made him so effective. Opposition defenders genuinely didn't know what he was going to do next – although there was a feeling that McMinn himself wasn't entirely sure either.

'Willie and I had been having a real battle and both of us had been booked,' McMinn recalls. 'Not long after their second goal, I got the ball to stop it going out for a goal kick and I saw Willie coming at me. As his feet left the ground, I saw a gap between his legs and poked the ball through. He clattered into me and sent me flying.

'The referee had no choice but to send him off, and as I was being treated on the pitch, the Celtic fans were pelting me with coins. In the end, I had to go off injured and watched the rest of what was an amazing game from the bench.'

It was a key moment. Celtic were still regrouping when Rangers pulled a goal back, less than two minutes after the sending-off. Durrant played McCoist through on the left and for once he was the goal provider, sending a perfect cross to the back post, where Cammy Fraser rose to head home.

By half-time, the fans had been treated to three goals and a sending-off, but there was much more to come after the interval. While Rangers had been on the ascendancy before the break, it took Celtic just three minutes from the restart to stretch their lead again. Johnston cut open the Rangers defence with an excellent pass to Tommy Burns, and the Celtic midfielder made no mistake with a cool finish inside Walker's left-hand post.

It should have been a fatal blow to Rangers' hopes, but Wallace's team refused to give up without a fight and, in a devastating 11-minute spell, turned the game on its head. Five minutes after going further behind, they closed the gap to a single goal again. This time, McCoist, who had supplied Fraser for the first goal, was the man who put the ball in the net.

A long kick-out from Walker bounced through to McCoist around 25 yards out. He cut inside one defender before hitting a low shot beyond Bonner into the bottom right corner of the net. Moments later, Durrant almost equalised with a trademark burst forward from midfield, followed by a shot from the edge of the penalty area that went inches wide.

The leveller was not long in coming, though. Hugh Burns, who had been pushed forward into midfield from right-back, played a pass into the path of Dave McPherson, who thundered forward down the right before sending a low cross into the Celtic penalty box. The defenders failed to clear and the ball broke to Fleck, whose deflected shot looped past Bonner into the net.

Now Rangers were flying. As they piled on the pressure, a fourth goal looked inevitable, and it came in the 63rd minute. Davie Cooper, who had come on to replace McMinn, swung in a corner from the right that was punched away by Bonner. The goalkeeper's clearance went only as far as Davie McKinnon at the edge of the penalty area and he headed the ball straight back into the goalmouth, where Fraser nodded it over the line into the unguarded net.

By rights, that should have been that. Down to ten men and having just seen their 3–1 lead overturned, Celtic should have been mentally and physically drained, but they managed to find the wherewithal to go looking for an equaliser. When Murdo McLeod picked up a pass 30 yards from the Rangers goal, there seemed no danger, but, from nowhere, he let fly with a spectacular drive that flew into the net. Against all the odds, the visitors were now level.

It wasn't quite over yet. With seconds remaining and the rain coming down even harder, Rangers came within inches of securing victory. A forward run by Tommy Burns was halted by Bobby Russell, who immediately launched Rangers on the counter-attack. Fleck used his strength to shake off a challenge, then powered into the penalty area before cutting the ball back to McCoist, whose first-time shot was saved at point-blank range by Pat Bonner.

It was the last serious action of the game. A few minutes later, David Syme blew the final whistle on one of the most remarkable Old Firm games of all time. Players, managers, fans and pundits alike were in agreement that this had been something special.

McMinn says, 'This was certainly up there with the best Old Firm games of all time. I still tell my kids I played a major role in the match and I suppose I did, because I tempted one of their defenders into getting sent off and that helped changed the game, even if my own game ended at the same time.'

Ally McCoist later described it as 'the most incredible game I've ever played in'. He recalled, 'We came back and scored three goals on the trot and we're 4–3 in front. We think we're home and dry but Murdo McLeod hit a screamer from the edge of the box, right into the top corner. I think I can safely say it's the only Old Firm game when the two sets of fans went home happy.'

George Ritchie, who was among the 44,000 who witnessed the match, takes issue with McCoist's view: 'I know I'm probably just an old whinger, but I can honestly say I did not go home happy. It was a great game and I'm really pleased I was there to see it, but I really felt we blew it. I was totally gutted when the final whistle went and we had drawn. Against ten men, Rangers should have been able to see the game out. But I suppose I'm just hard to please. To be honest, I'm never happy after an Old Firm game unless we have won, and this game was no different.'

George may have been in the minority, but if one story is to be believed, there was at least one other man inside Ibrox that afternoon who was less than impressed by the reaction to the result. In fact, there is a theory that the match prompted – or at least hastened – major changes at Ibrox that would alter the face of Scottish football.

David Holmes had been appointed to the post of chief executive in 1985 by the John Lawrence construction group, which now had a controlling interest in the club. His job was to stop the rot and reverse what was threatening to become a terminal decline in fortunes. The story goes that, listening to the celebrations that followed the 4–4 game, he decided there and then that urgent action was needed. Holmes seemingly felt that it was demeaning for fans and players of a club of Rangers' stature to be rejoicing in such a result. There may be some truth in the tale, but it would be astonishing if Holmes had not already recognised that a major shake-up was required. Fifth place in the league, no trophies and plummeting attendances told their own story.

The dramatic changes came less than two weeks later. Wallace was removed as manager, and, to the shock of the football world, Graeme Souness was named as the new player-manager. He swept into Ibrox tasked with helping to drag the club into the modern era while creating a team befitting its history.

14

COME THE REVOLUTION

RANGERS 2 CELTIC 1
LEAGUE CUP FINAL
PLAYED AT HAMPDEN PARK, GLASGOW
26 OCTOBER 1986

Rangers team: Woods, Nicholl, Munro, Dawson, Butcher, Fraser,
Ferguson, McMinn, McCoist, Durrant, Cooper

Rangers scorers: Durrant, Cooper

Even for jaded veterans of the Old Firm derby, the 1986 League Cup final was something out of the ordinary. With one sending-off, another red card shown then rescinded, ten bookings, a sectarian controversy, two superb goals and a disputed penalty with only a few minutes to go, it was, to put it mildly, more than just another day at the office.

But even without the on-field drama and controversy, this was always going to be an attention-grabbing Glasgow derby as a result of the astonishing off-field moves made by Rangers the previous summer.

The arrival of Scotland captain and former Liverpool star Graeme Souness at Ibrox as player-manager made headlines around the world. His job was to breathe new life into a club that was seemingly in terminal decline. The League Cup final would be the first major test of the new regime, and the fact that it was Rangers v. Celtic, the Challengers v. the Champions, made it all the more intriguing.

FOLLOW, FOLLOW

Souness wanted to win trophies, and, to help him fulfil his task, he was given unprecedented resources to lure some of British football's biggest names north. On his appointment, rumours about who he would be signing immediately began to circulate, with speculation intensifying during the World Cup in Mexico. In the end, two of the stars of the England squad – goalkeeper Chris Woods and centre-half Terry Butcher – joined the Souness revolution.

The long-suffering Rangers support were in an optimistic mood as the new season got under way, but it wasn't until the Old Firm game at Ibrox at the end of August that the revolution really got going. The 1–0 victory, the first Scottish League game to be broadcast live on television, was secured by a fine goal from Ian Durrant, set up by a piece of sublime skill from Davie Cooper. Both players would be key figures when the new Rangers collected their first piece of silverware.

When he came to Rangers, Souness infamously declared that he would happily lose four times a season to Celtic if his team still won the league. It didn't take him long to have a rethink. Once he had sampled the Old Firm experience and seen at first hand what it meant to the supporters, he understood that it was more than a game, although he remained convinced that trophies were what mattered in the end. If beating Celtic could be combined with winning competitions, he'd be delighted.

Terry Butcher was someone who instantly grasped the significance of the derby. He had played at the highest level in domestic, European and international football, including a World Cup and a European final, but even so, nothing prepared him for the fervour of an Old Firm final in front of almost 75,000 fans.

As Rangers captain, Butcher understood that he was walking in the footsteps of giants and had decades of tradition to live up to. The players prepared for the game by viewing video clips of past finals. Seeing the old footage heightened the sense of responsibility felt by the new captain, and he revelled in the occasion. Butcher said at the time:

COME THE REVOLUTION

It was a great day. I had my family up for the first time to watch me in a domestic final. We saw all the clips beforehand, John Greig leading the team to triumph. I felt that tradition and felt we had to do well as a result. It was also unique that there was all the Englishmen playing and that it would be the first time an Englishman would lift the trophy. That's all going through your mind when you line up.

The players were nervous as the team bus wound its way through the crowds outside Hampden. Those who could stomach it played cards; the rest sat in silence as they contemplated the match ahead.

It was something of a makeshift Rangers team that walked out at Hampden to a cacophony of noise. Dave McPherson, a mainstay of the defence, was suspended, meaning a rare start for former captain Ally Dawson. Normally a full-back, he lined up alongside Butcher in the centre of defence.

An injury to Graeme Souness meant there was also a place in the team for Cammy Fraser, who had fallen out with the fans when he directed a two-fingered salute at the Ibrox stands during the darkest days of the Jock Wallace regime. The absence of Souness also gave Derek Ferguson the chance to shine. The 19 year old was given the central midfield role that his manager revelled in, and he grabbed the opportunity with both hands.

For Souness, the pre-match nerves were made worse by the fact that he wouldn't be on the pitch to influence the game. In an interview at the time, he said:

> It was tense for me. I can remember going up the stairs [from the dressing-room] and I got to the swing doors at Hampden and I stopped as the whistle blew for the start of the game. I had to push myself through those doors. I'd much rather have been playing in that game.

The manager's late arrival meant he missed out on a bizarre piece of pre-match entertainment courtesy of the sponsors, Skol. In an attempt to add some razzmatazz to the occasion, a horse-drawn carriage circled the pitch with glamour girls on board throwing footballs into the crowd. The stunt backfired somewhat when they were met with an inevitable chorus of 'Get yer tits oot for the boys' from the terraces, the embarrassment compounded by the fact that it was all captured by TV cameras and broadcast around the country.

Once this sideshow was over, the main event could finally get under way. For those who remembered the 1984 League Cup final between the teams, there was a sense of déjà vu in the early moments when Davie Cooper was cynically chopped down in full flight by Roy Aitken. From the resulting free kick, Fraser hit the post with a fierce low shot that skidded past Bonner. Celtic had clearly identified Cooper as the danger man; within a few minutes, both Aitken and Alan McInally were booked for fouls on the winger.

Although Celtic just shaded the first half, Cooper and Ted McMinn were causing huge problems for their full-backs. McMinn, who had only just recovered from a broken foot, came close with a long-range drive that went narrowly wide of Bonner's left-hand post. In Souness's absence, Ferguson was dominant in the middle of the park, while Ian Durrant was an attacking threat alongside Ally McCoist. Dawson was performing admirably in central defence, although Souness would have been alarmed shortly before half-time when Maurice Johnston hit the post for Celtic.

Despite that scare, Rangers dictated the game in the early part of the second half. Cooper continued to taunt the Celtic defence and in the 62nd minute he was upended for the umpteenth time, on this occasion by Peter Grant. Fraser's free kick from wide on the right evaded everyone, before falling for Durrant at the back post. He brought it down on his chest before turning away from his marker and blasting low past Bonner to put Rangers into a deserved lead.

It was a superbly taken goal, and further evidence of the massive talent Durrant possessed, a talent that was cruelly diminished when Aberdeen's Neil Simpson inflicted a career-threatening injury on him a couple of years later.

His goal brought Celtic to life, and for the first time in the match they exerted some serious pressure on the Rangers defence. First, Brian McClair hit the bar with a free kick, then the same player blasted a right-footed shot past Woods into the top right corner of the net.

As Rangers fought back, tempers were getting frayed. Whyte received a yellow card for yet another cynical foul on Cooper, just moments after McMinn was elbowed in the face by Grant. The Celtic defender was himself later booked for a crude challenge on McCoist as the crime count continued to rise.

Then, with just six minutes to go, the game erupted in the way that only Old Firm matches can. Cooper was once again hacked down as he took on McLeod on the right. Ferguson swung the resulting free kick high towards Terry Butcher at the back post, but as the Englishman attempted to reach the ball, he was hauled to the ground by Aitken and David Syme pointed to the spot.

In a second consecutive Old Firm final, Aitken had given away a crucial penalty in the closing moments of the game. Two Celtic players were booked during the inevitable protests, but amid the melee the coolest man on the pitch was Davie Cooper. Once the commotion had died down, he calmly stepped forward and sent Bonner the wrong way. After the abuse dished out to him by the Celtic defenders throughout the match, it was fitting that he should score the winning goal.

Rangers were prepared for an onslaught in the closing moments, but instead of trying to turn their sense of injustice into something positive, Celtic lost the plot, and in doing so lost any chance of saving the game. Striker Maurice Johnston was shown a red card by referee David Syme for head-butting Stuart Munro in an off-the-ball incident.

During the resulting fracas, the Celtic defender Tony Shepherd was also sent off after Syme thought he'd been struck by the player. In extraordinary scenes, the linesman stepped in to point out that the referee had actually been hit by a coin thrown by the Celtic fans and Shepherd was allowed to remain on the pitch. Amid the chaos, the Parkhead manager Davie Hay came onto the pitch to remonstrate, for which he was later fined.

Meanwhile, Johnston trudged off the pitch to a chorus of 'Cheerio, cheerio' from the Rangers end. He chose to retaliate by making the sign of the cross as he headed for the tunnel, an act apparently intended to wind up the Rangers fans further. Years later, his teammate Tommy Burns wrote about the incident in his autobiography *Twists and Turns*: 'Maurice may have his own privately held religious beliefs but in any word-association test, faith is not what you would automatically put after his name.' Johnston, of course, ended up as a Rangers player in 1989, although his actions that Sunday afternoon were not forgotten by some fans.

Johnston was fined by Celtic for his sending-off, although the club also issued a statement in which they said they were 'aggrieved' at 'some aspects' of the final. Looking back at the TV footage, it's difficult to see why they felt so hard done by.

The only major contentious occurrence in the match was the penalty incident, and pictures clearly show Aitken clambering over Butcher as they both went for the ball. Had the roles been reversed, it is a certainty that Celtic would have felt 'aggrieved' had they not been awarded a penalty themselves. Furthermore, Syme showed a remarkable tolerance for the fouls committed by a succession of Celtic players, on Cooper in particular. On another day, another referee might well have sent more than one defender off for repeatedly hacking down the winger.

Celtic also praised the 'exemplary conduct' of their fans at Hampden, with no mention, let alone condemnation, of the fact that one of their number had hit the referee with a missile – and almost got one of their own players sent off as a result.

The statement concluded with a doom-laden warning that the events at Hampden would strengthen the resolve of the board to create a team good enough to 'overcome all obstacles to our ambitions'. Quite what those 'obstacles' were was not specified, although the fans were in no doubt that the club were the victims of a terrible miscarriage of justice. It wasn't the first time, and by no means the last, that complaints about refereeing decisions emerged after a Celtic defeat in an important Old Firm game.

COME THE REVOLUTION

The controversial end to the game and the post-match fallout failed to take any of the shine off the win for Rangers. Following the final whistle, Terry Butcher led the players over to the supporters to thank them for their backing before walking up the steps to collect the trophy. As he lifted the cup above his head – the first Englishman ever to do so – the fans were full of belief that the good times had finally returned to Ibrox.

For Ted McMinn, who had been at Ibrox during the darkest days, the transformation of the club's fortunes under Souness was remarkable, even if he didn't see eye to eye with his new boss. McMinn felt his face didn't fit in the new regime, but he still played an important role in the first few months of the Souness era.

'Because of my injury, I was just really happy to have made the starting 11 and to win my first cup final with the club was absolutely amazing,' he says. 'I don't think my contribution was that stunning but it was the best feeling in the world to celebrate with your own fans knowing that the terracing at the other end was completely empty.

'The supporters deserved their day in the sun after being starved of success for so long. It was a sweet moment as the scarves and hats flew down from the terracing onto the pitch as we paraded the cup. In the dressing-room afterwards, I had to pinch myself when I sat looking at my medal. It was a day when it was great to be alive.'

McMinn celebrated the cup win with a night on the town with his pals, while the rest of the Rangers squad enjoyed an official bash at Ibrox. His already shaky relationship with Souness deteriorated further after an off-the-field incident and he was soon on his way – signed by former boss Jock Wallace, who was now the manager of Sevilla in Spain.

Lifelong fan Duncan Stewart was a teenager at the time but had already suffered years of misery as a supporter. He recalls, 'All through the dark days, me and my dad used to go to every home game, rain or shine. It could be a soul-destroying experience but suddenly, when Souness arrived with these England internationals, we had hope.

'I'll always remember the Skol Cup final because it was the first time I'd come out of a game feeling like it was the start of something big. We'd beaten Celtic before and even won cup finals but they always seemed like one-off victories. You never really had any confidence that you wouldn't go out the next week and lose to Clydebank or someone. Now it was different.

'My favourite player was Ian Durrant, so when he scored in the final I was totally over the moon. It was right in front of the Rangers end and I can remember it clearly to this day. The way he took the ball down and then hit the shot almost in the same move was a different class and to top it off the players celebrated right in front of us.

'At the end they all came over again and you could see what it meant to guys like Butcher. He really seemed to have made a connection with the fans. I know some guys don't like him now because of some of the things he's said over the years, and I can understand that, but I'll never forget what he did that season.'

For Souness, securing a trophy within the first six months of his arrival was a bonus and he was especially pleased that the win had come against Celtic. 'To win any trophy is a special feeling, but to win against our Old Firm rivals was even more special,' he said in an interview at the time. 'I don't think anybody could put into words what winning a cup final against your oldest rivals actually means.'

The final was seen as a major test of Rangers' championship credentials, and although the manager was delighted to land his first piece of silverware, he knew that his team wasn't quite the finished article. Among the Hampden crowd that Sunday afternoon was a certain Graham Roberts, who had travelled north to sample the Old Firm atmosphere. Within weeks, the Tottenham and England defender signed up to the Souness revolution, and he proved to be the final piece in the jigsaw.

In the New Year's Day derby at Ibrox, Rangers won 2–0, with Graeme Souness at his strutting, arrogant best, pulling the strings in the middle of the park. The victory was enough to convince fans and pundits alike that Souness's team had what it took to finally regain the championship. A 19-match unbeaten run helped them to the verge of the title, and it finally came at Aberdeen, when Terry Butcher

The first Rangers team to win the Scottish Cup; they defeated Celtic 3–1 in the final in February 1894. Back row (left to right): H. McCreadie, J. Steel, N. Smith, J. Taylor (trainer), D. Haddow, D. Mitchell. Middle row: A. McCreadie, D. Boyd, W. Wilton (secretary), J. Drummond, J. McPherson, J. Barker. Front row: R. Marshall, J. Gray.
(courtesy of the Daily Record and Sunday Mail Ltd)

Goalmouth action from the 1928 Scottish Cup final, when Rangers finally broke the hoodoo that had seen them go 25 years without lifting the trophy. (courtesy of the Daily Record and Sunday Mail Ltd)

Jim Baxter leaves the pitch with the ball up his shirt after his virtuoso performance against Celtic in the 1963 Scottish Cup final replay. (courtesy of the Daily Record and Sunday Mail Ltd)

Winning goalscorer Kai Johansen is carried from the Hampden pitch by teammates after the goal that defeated Celtic in the 1966 Scottish Cup final replay. (courtesy of the Daily Record and Sunday Mail Ltd)

A 16-year-old Derek Johnstone rises above defenders Billy McNeill and Jim Craig to head the winning goal for Rangers in the 1970 League Cup final. (courtesy of the Daily Record and Sunday Mail Ltd)

Tom Forsyth prods home the winning goal in the centenary Scottish Cup final of 1973. (courtesy of the Daily Record and Sunday Mail Ltd)

Princess Alexandra meets the Rangers players ahead of the 1973 Scottish Cup final. She later presented the trophy to the winning captain, John Greig. (courtesy of the Daily Record and Sunday Mail Ltd)

Rangers players including Ally McCoist, Ted McMinn and Derek Ferguson celebrate their victory in the 1986 League Cup final, the first trophy won under Graeme Souness. (courtesy of the Daily Record and Sunday Mail Ltd)

Rangers captain Terry Butcher, goalkeeper Chris Woods and Celtic striker Frank McAvennie clash during a fiery Old Firm match in October 1987. (courtesy of the Daily Record and Sunday Mail Ltd)

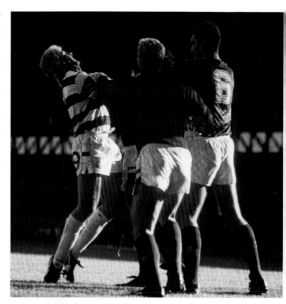

Chris Woods, Terry Butcher and Graham Roberts arrive for their trial at Glasgow Sheriff Court following the decision to prosecute them over their actions during the Old Firm derby in October 1987. (courtesy of the Daily Record and Sunday Mail Ltd)

Mark Walters pounces to score Rangers' fifth goal in the 5–1 victory over Celtic at Ibrox in August 1988. (courtesy of the Daily Record and Sunday Mail Ltd)

At Ibrox in July 1989, former Celtic star Maurice Johnston is sensationally unveiled as a Rangers player by Graeme Souness. Months later, Johnston scored a last-minute winner against his old club. (courtesy of the Daily Record and Sunday Mail Ltd)

The Rangers team celebrate their crucial 1–0 win at Celtic Park in 1997 with a controversial Celtic-style 'huddle'. (courtesy of the Daily Record and Sunday Mail Ltd)

Neil McCann, Rod Wallace and Gabriel Amato celebrate as Rangers defeat Celtic 3–0 to win the league at Parkhead in May 1999.
(courtesy of the Daily Record and Sunday Mail Ltd)

Mayhem breaks out at Celtic Park. Blood poured from the head of referee Hugh Dallas after he was struck by a coin during the 1999 'Shame Game'.
(courtesy of the Daily Record and Sunday Mail Ltd)

Jubilant Rangers players stage another celebratory huddle after winning the league in 1999.
(courtesy of the Daily Record and Sunday Mail Ltd)

Captain Barry Ferguson slots home Rangers' first goal in a 5–1 rout of Celtic in November 2000. (courtesy of the Daily Record and Sunday Mail Ltd)

Danish star Peter Løvenkrands rushes off to receive the adulation of the Rangers fans after his last-minute diving header to win the 2002 Scottish Cup. (courtesy of the Daily Record and Sunday Mail Ltd)

Nacho Novo celebrates his goal at Celtic Park in February 2005. It helped Rangers to their first victory at Celtic's ground in five years. (courtesy of the Daily Record and Sunday Mail Ltd)

Kenny Miller celebrates in front of the Rangers fans at Celtic Park after one of his two goals in a 4–2 victory in August 2008.
(courtesy of the Daily Record and Sunday Mail Ltd)

Maurice Edu scrambles home a last-minute winner at Ibrox in February 2010, a goal that went a long way towards securing the league title.
(courtesy of the Daily Record and Sunday Mail Ltd)

scored in a 1–1 draw, while Celtic suffered a shock 2–1 defeat at home to Falkirk. After nine barren years, Rangers were finally champions again, with a team that lived up to the splendid surroundings of Ibrox Stadium.

For a while, the goings-on at Rangers pushed other news off the front pages, but 1986 was a year of major events. In April, the world's worst nuclear disaster struck in Chernobyl in the Soviet Union, expelling 190 tonnes of highly radioactive uranium into the atmosphere. Contamination from the explosions spread all over the world and large areas of Ukraine, Belarus and Russia had to be evacuated. It is estimated that the disaster could ultimately have caused up to 4,000 deaths from cancer over the years.

Millions watched on TV as Prince Andrew and Sarah Ferguson were married at Westminster Abbey on 23 July, but it wasn't the most watched programme of 1986. That title went to *EastEnders*, which recorded huge viewing figures throughout the year, culminating in the Christmas Day episode, which had the second-highest audience of all time on British television. More than 30 million viewers tuned in to see Den Watts serve divorce papers on his wife, Angie, after discovering that she had feigned a terminal illness to try to stop him from leaving her.

To the delight of housewives and students across the country, daytime TV finally arrived in Britain in 1986, its biggest success being the Australian soap *Neighbours*. The story of life on Ramsay Street in the fictional town of Erinsborough was a surprise hit, making stars of Kylie Minogue and Jason Donovan. On the big screen, there was an Aussie theme as well, with Paul Hogan's *Crocodile Dundee* a surprise box-office success alongside the Tom Cruise blockbuster *Top Gun*.

Graeme Souness and David Holmes had turned Rangers into a big box office team again and, at the same time, dragged the club into the modern era. The game in Scotland would never be the same again.

15

. . . .

FOOTBALL IN THE DOCK

RANGERS 2 CELTIC 2
SCOTTISH PREMIER DIVISION
PLAYED AT IBROX STADIUM, GLASGOW
17 OCTOBER 1987

*Rangers team: Woods, Gough, Phillips, Roberts, Butcher, D. Ferguson,
Francis, Durrant, McGregor, Falco, McCoist*

Rangers scorers: McCoist, Gough

It should be remembered as one of the most dramatic and exciting
Old Firm clashes ever. Instead, the 2–2 draw at Ibrox in October 1987
takes pride of place in Scotland's footballing hall of infamy.

Following the unprecedented intervention of the Glasgow
procurator fiscal, four players found themselves in court – and two
were saddled with criminal records – in connection with an on-field
skirmish that would nowadays be described as nothing more than
'handbags'.

Terry Butcher, Chris Woods, Graham Roberts and Frank
McAvennie were the unfortunate quartet who found themselves
hauled over the coals in what appeared to be a concerted effort by the
legal authorities to make an example of sinning footballers.

Their 'crime' was to get involved in the sort of scuffle that features
in matches up and down the country every week. In the 17th minute
of what had already been a fiery match, Woods collected a Stuart

Munro pass back and as he prepared to clear the ball downfield, McAvennie blocked him. As the pair went toe to toe and exchanged slaps, Butcher stepped in to protect his teammate, giving McAvennie a hefty shove in the chest. Roberts also got involved before Woods appeared to make contact with the striker with his forearm, prompting McAvennie to collapse dramatically to the ground, holding his face in apparent agony.

It was school-playground stuff, but unsurprisingly Woods and McAvennie were both ordered off while Butcher was booked for his part in the dust-up, and as far as most observers were concerned, that was the end of it. Procurator Fiscal Sandy Jessop had other ideas, though. He considered that the players' actions amounted to a breach of the peace and ordered a police investigation before taking them to court.

Following a trial at Glasgow Sheriff Court, Woods and Butcher were both found guilty and fined while McAvennie and Roberts were cleared, the latter on a not-proven verdict. But more than 20 years later, the decision to prosecute the players remains one of the most extraordinary episodes Scottish football has ever seen, and is still a source of bafflement and anger for those involved.

Thanks to the pantomime that followed, the details of the actual game are often forgotten, which is a pity, as it was as fine an example of a 'blood and snotters' Old Firm clash as you could hope to see. Despite the presence of players like Derek Ferguson, Trevor Francis, Ian Durrant and Paul McStay on the Ibrox pitch, there was little in the way of cultured football on display, but for sheer visceral entertainment it was hard to beat.

The tone was set in the early minutes when McAvennie barged into Woods as he tipped a cross over the bar. Veteran former England international Francis, who had joined Rangers from Serie A side Atalanta and still showed fleeting glimpses of the quality that had made him Britain's first £1-million player, then had a shot parried away by Celtic goalkeeper Allen McKnight.

Then came the moment when it all kicked off. Both teams were reduced to ten men, but Rangers, having lost their goalkeeper, were clearly at a major disadvantage, especially as Roberts, one of their two centre-halfs, took over as emergency goalkeeper. Moments after pulling on the red jersey, Roberts was called into action, turning a Peter Grant shot round the post. Thirty-three minutes in, the gaps in the Rangers defence were exposed when Derek Whyte fired a long, hopeful pass in the direction of Andy Walker, who outpaced Butcher and fired it under the temporary keeper into the net.

When Butcher hooked the ball into his own goal under pressure from Grant two minutes later, it looked like Rangers were in danger of suffering a severe drubbing. Grant celebrated the goal by running towards the Celtic fans, sinking to his knees and blessing himself. At half-time, with his team two goals ahead, Billy McNeill told his players they could only throw it away. Little did he realise that was exactly what they would do.

Instead of being forced onto the back foot to protect their temporary goalkeeper, it was Rangers who looked the more dangerous team. The sending-off of Butcher in the 62nd minute should have ended Rangers' resistance. He received the red card after a shove on McKnight, which the goalkeeper made the most of.

But the sending-off invigorated the Rangers support and the noise that poured down from the stands seemed to fill the remaining nine men on the pitch with a new spirit. Three minutes after Butcher went off, Rangers were back in the match. Ferguson showed great determination and skill in the middle of the park to beat two opponents before feeding a pass to Richard Gough. The defender, who had been pushed into a forward position alongside Ally McCoist, touched it on to his strike partner, who showed great composure to shoot left-footed past McKnight into the net.

Despite their numerical superiority, Celtic still failed to put any serious pressure on Roberts; the Englishman dealt easily with a couple of tame shots from Walker and Tommy Burns and a header from Billy Stark that rebounded back off the crossbar. Other than that, the closest the visitors came to extending their lead was a sliced clearance by Rangers substitute Avi Cohen that almost looped under the bar.

A single-goal lead was always going to be precarious, but as the game moved towards full-time it looked like Celtic were going to survive. As the clock approached ninety minutes, Rangers gave it one last effort. A Roberts goal kick fell short, but Ferguson was first to react and won it deep inside his own half before sending a perfect reverse pass out to Durrant on the right.

Digging deep into his reserves, with one last burst of energy the midfielder drove across the halfway line and beat Celtic defender Anton Rogan before crossing to McCoist. Instead of sending the ball towards goal, the striker intelligently cushioned a header back out to Durrant, who had continued his forward movement. He crossed first time into the penalty area, but the ball evaded both McCoist and McKnight, who came flying out of his goal to punch clear and missed the ball completely.

Even so, with several Celtic defenders in the box, it looked like the chance had gone, but the first person to react was the improvised forward Richard Gough. As the defenders dallied, he stuck out a leg and prodded the ball into the unguarded net. The goal sparked wild celebrations on the pitch and in the stands. The way the game had gone, the last-minute equaliser felt like a winner to the home fans.

There was still time for one last controversial incident before the game was finally brought to an end. Celtic substitute Owen Archdeacon needlessly barged into Roberts as he collected a pass back, prompting the keeper to collapse theatrically to the ground. As he prepared to take the resulting free kick, the crowd burst into 'The Billy Boys', and Roberts milked the moment by conducting the choir. It was a fittingly daft way for such a crazy match to end. In an admirable piece of understatement, Rangers manager Graeme Souness commented afterwards, 'It was an eventful game and I'm glad we got something from it.'

Rangers failed to capitalise on the psychological effects of their comeback, eventually finishing in third place in the league, well behind champions Celtic. But the off-field implications of what happened that Saturday afternoon were enormous.

FOOTBALL IN THE DOCK

Two weeks after the game, Woods, Roberts and McAvennie were summoned to Govan police station, where they were charged with behaviour likely to cause a breach of the peace. The two Rangers players spent seventeen minutes in the station, accompanied by their solicitor, before departing through a crowd of photographers and television cameramen. An hour later, McAvennie went through the same process. Butcher was later charged with the same offence.

Given the high profiles of the players involved – they were arguably the four biggest names playing in Scotland at the time – the decision to go ahead with legal action was sensational and sparked a media frenzy, not only at home but in England and abroad.

Len Murray, a renowned Glasgow lawyer, recalled how he was listening to Beethoven at home with his wife when he became embroiled in the case. First, McAvennie's agent, Bill McMurdo, phoned to ask if he would represent his client in court. He had barely replaced the handset when a lawyer acting for Rangers came to his door and made a similar request on behalf of Butcher, Woods and Roberts.

Murray agreed to represent all four players and immediately set about trying to have the case dropped completely. He believes it was a 'terrible error of judgment' for the trial to go ahead, particularly in the powder-keg atmosphere of Glasgow. In 2002, he told the *Evening Times*:

> The public interest would have been sufficiently served had Sandy Jessop told the players, 'A report has been made to me. Behave yourself – watch it.' Glasgow being Glasgow, the risk of there being some kind of reaction in Scotland if the trial went ahead was horrendous. I think it was by the grace of God that nothing did happen, to be quite honest.

The charges were later amended to accuse the players of conducting themselves in a disorderly way and of committing a breach of the peace. On 12 April 1988, the trial finally went ahead, amid huge publicity. Police argued in court that the players' actions could have caused a riot. One senior officer referred to the 'unbridled hatred on the faces of some of the fans when they were shouting obscenities and insults at each other'.

After the verdicts were delivered, Sheriff Archibald McKay told all four defendants, 'A large percentage of supporters are readily converted by breaches of the peace into two rival mobs. That they were not so transformed is no credit to you. You must have been aware of your wider responsibilities and you failed to discharge them.'

Woods and Butcher both appealed against the verdict but failed to have their convictions overturned. However, the appeal court judges were divided two to one over the case. Lord Murray, the appeal judge who held the minority opinion, criticised the players' behaviour but said it should have been considered in the context of a physical contact sport governed by its own rules. He also warned against prosecutors bringing breach of the peace charges in 'marginal or sensitive' cases.

Rangers fan Paul Dunnachie was 12 years old at the time and followed the drama on the radio. He says: 'Back in the '80s and '90s, the Old Firm games tended to be played on a Saturday at 3 p.m., with radio commentary for the last five minutes or so of the first half and the whole of the second. I remember listening to the match on the radio and it sounded hectic stuff.

'The following day, the newspapers and television were full of the incident where Frank McAvennie and Chris Woods were sent off and then Terry Butcher followed them with a red card. But my memories of the game are mostly of the actions of Peter Grant and Graham Roberts.

'My parents had brought me up not to think of Protestant and Catholic. For better or worse, they pretty much ignored the subject completely. So when the highlights were shown on TV the next day, I was a bit puzzled about just what was going on when Terry Butcher blasted the ball past Graham Roberts in the Rangers goal and Peter Grant slid onto his knees and started to bless himself.

'I'd seen players doing this in the World Cup on TV in the past, mostly when they were about to take or face a penalty kick, but I must admit that I was a bit confused about why a Celtic player was celebrating a goal against Rangers – an own goal at that – in this way. Although it was easy to work out that it was something that someone who didn't like Rangers much might do! A valuable life lesson learned watching *Scotsport* on a Sunday afternoon.

'Later in the game, Graham Roberts started to conduct the Rangers crowd blasting out "The Billy Boys". For something written so deeply into the folklore of the fixture, it was a blink-and-you'll-miss-it moment. As a 12-year-old kid, this was a song that I did recognise, albeit I had no idea who or what a Billy Boy was, and I thought it was a great laugh. After all, if a guy at one end could do something to appeal to his followers then why couldn't the Rangers player do likewise up at the other end?

'Looking back at it with the benefit of 20 years' hindsight, I can see an argument that Grant and Roberts should have been the only ones in court. McAvennie, Woods and Butcher all committed fouls on the pitch, but Grant and Roberts played to the crowd and milked the situation.

'The emotions around the Old Firm ran high on match day, and players who choose to do something to add to that are playing with fire. Grant grew up in the environment and Roberts had been in Glasgow for the best part of a year – they knew exactly what they were doing.

'Of course, there's an ongoing responsibility for the media to be consistent in dealing with such incidents. You can't ignore one and slaughter the other. In more recent times, Paul Gascoigne was criticised roundly for miming the playing of a flute as he warmed up at Parkhead, while Artur Boruc stripped off his goalkeeper top and ran around the pitch with a T-shirt bearing the slogan 'God Bless the Pope' after a match at Parkhead in 2008 to very little media criticism.

'Boruc's supporters and apologists might point to the player's religious beliefs as a justification for his actions, but there's a time and place for religious observance, and the minutes after the final whistle of the final Old Firm game of the season in a close title race are as far removed from the appropriate time and place as you'll find. The faces might have changed, and the methods might have changed, but the themes of the Old Firm game remain the same as always.'

....

16

FIVE-STAR RANGERS

RANGERS 5 CELTIC 1
SCOTTISH PREMIER DIVISION
PLAYED AT IBROX STADIUM, GLASGOW
27 AUGUST 1988

Rangers team: Woods, Stevens, Brown, Gough, Butcher, Wilkins,
I. Ferguson, Durrant, Drinkell, McCoist, Walters

Rangers scorers: McCoist (2), Wilkins, Drinkell, Walters

Victory in an Old Firm game can often have far-reaching consequences
that are not immediately obvious at the time. A big win can have a
major psychological effect on the triumphant team, setting the tone
for an entire season or giving a boost to a flagging squad late in the
campaign.

In the case of Rangers' 5–1 win over Celtic in August 1988, it
marked the start of ten years of dominance by the Ibrox club and dealt
a mental blow to Celtic that they almost didn't recover from.

Having seen his team fail to beat their city rivals in the league
the season before, Graeme Souness now knew just how important
the Old Firm derby could be. In an interview leading up to the first
clash of the 1988–89 season, he admitted he'd been wrong in his first
analysis that the derby was just another game. 'The longer I'm with
Rangers, the more I realise just how important the games against

Celtic are,' he said. 'In particular, they are vital to the supporters. But they also figure prominently in the minds and hearts of the players.'

The manager also spoke confidently about his team's prospects going into the game, one which he admitted he was looking forward to with relish. As it turned out, his optimism was well placed, but no one could have predicted what was to come when Celtic took the lead in just five minutes. A shot from Peter Grant hit the post and Frank McAvennie was alert enough to steer the rebound home past Chris Woods. As a rainstorm swept across Ibrox, the Celtic fans celebrated, blissfully unaware that their team was about to be swamped.

Celtic had taken seven points out of a possible eight in the previous season's Old Firm games, and statistics show that the team that scores first in these derbies rarely goes on to lose, so in those circumstances the visiting supporters could have been forgiven for thinking this was going to be their day. How wrong they were. The rainstorm passed over and the sun broke through. It remained shining on the Rangers fans, literally and metaphorically, for the rest of the match.

Five minutes after celebrating taking the lead, the Celtic supporters were silenced when the Old Firm master Ally McCoist equalised in typical style. He steered the ball past Celtic goalkeeper Ian Andrews from 16 yards, after seeing a shot by John Brown blocked. It was McCoist's 201st goal for Rangers in all competitions since signing five years earlier, and most of those who had doubted the wisdom of bringing him to Ibrox in 1983 had long since changed their point of view.

The equaliser gave Rangers a boost and suddenly they were the team making all the running and creating all the chances. With Celtic increasingly on the back foot, it was no surprise when Rangers took the lead nine minutes before half-time, with one of the all-time great Old Firm strikes.

It was a goal made in England. A long throw from Gary Stevens found the head of Terry Butcher, and he flicked it on. A Celtic defender managed to head it out of the penalty area, but from 20 yards Ray Wilkins met it perfectly and crashed an unstoppable volley past Andrews into the top corner. Even at the age of almost 32 and in the twilight of his career, Wilkins had already proved a shrewd signing by Graeme Souness. His vision and the quality of his passing were head and shoulders above those of anyone else in the Scottish Premier Division, apart from the manager himself.

He thoroughly dominated the midfield on this occasion, ably assisted by Ian Durrant and Ian Ferguson. The three of them completely overwhelmed Paul McStay, on whom Celtic relied so much. With his threat negated, the Rangers midfield trio could stamp their authority on the game, providing the ammunition for the front three of McCoist, Kevin Drinkell and Mark Walters.

By half-time, Rangers were already well on top and any hopes Celtic had of retrieving the situation were erased a minute into the second half. The second strike had been a thing of beauty, but the goal that put Rangers 3–1 up was a personal disaster for the Celtic goalkeeper.

The move began with a Stevens free kick that picked out Durrant on the left. He whipped in a right-footed cross, which was met by McCoist, and his back-header looped towards the goal. It looked like an easy take for Andrews under the crossbar, but he seemed to be distracted by the presence of Drinkell and lost track of the ball. He desperately flapped at it but only succeeded in helping it into the net.

Celtic defenders raced to the referee to protest, but the dejected reaction of the goalkeeper as he retrieved the ball from the back of the net suggested he knew it was a mistake on his part that had caused the goal, rather than an infringement by a forward.

Rangers were now cruising, with Mark Walters in particular causing mayhem in the Celtic defence. He made a vital contribution to both the fourth and fifth goals, and it would have been a sweet moment for him after the abuse he had suffered the previous season on his debut for Rangers.

Remarkably, Walters, a £500,000 signing from Aston Villa, was the first black player ever to play in the Scottish Premier Division, and his arrival provoked a sadly predictable reaction from Neanderthal elements among opposition fans. The worst abuse came on his debut, which just happened to be against Celtic at Parkhead. In scenes that shamed Scotland, home fans dressed in monkey suits and hurled bananas at the player. At one point, the game was held up as the fruit was removed.

What made the abuse even more objectionable was its premeditated nature. The idea of a football supporter going to the trouble of hiring a fancy-dress suit for the purpose of racist abuse quite frankly turns the stomach.

In 2007, Gerry Britton, who was a youth player with Celtic at the time and went on to play for numerous Scottish clubs, told *Scotland on Sunday* how he was instructed to remove the fruit from the track around the pitch the following day. 'It was one of the very few days I fell out with fans of the club I grew up loving,' he said. 'It was bad enough having to hear it, and hearing that a fruit shop near the ground sold out of bananas, but it was truly sickening when our job the day after the game was to clear them away. There were dozens of them, scattered everywhere.'

The abuse, probably the single worst example of racism at a Scottish football match, was compounded by the lack of condemnation from the media and the football authorities. Television coverage gave little more than a passing mention, while one newspaper pointed out that only a 'handful' of fans threw fruit. Most other press coverage completely ignored the issue. In the circumstances, Walters might well have been wondering what he had let himself in for by moving north of the border.

But to his credit he shrugged it off and quickly proved that he was a very talented footballer, in the tradition of great Rangers wingers. By the start of the next season, he was a key figure in the Rangers team assembled by Graeme Souness to regain the title they had lost last time around. Against Celtic at Ibrox, he was outstanding and, with the England manager Bobby Robson watching from the stands, there was speculation he might even force his way into the international team.

A typical piece of Walters trickery created Rangers' fourth goal in 58 minutes. He picked up the ball on the right and, after a quick shimmy and step-over, left the defender for dead and sent a perfect cross to Kevin Drinkell, whose diving header bulleted into the net. As the scorer was mobbed by his teammates, Walters famously celebrated with a forward roll in front of the Copland Road stand.

The fifth goal came just four minutes later. McCoist pounced on a blunder by Aitken and as he charged towards goal the Celtic captain fouled him in the penalty area. It would have been a certain penalty, but the ball broke to Walters, who slotted it home.

With almost half an hour to go, Rangers could easily have gone on to score several more, but they seemed to ease off, much to the annoyance of the supporters, who once again wanted to see the 7–1 League Cup final defeat being avenged. Even the players recognised that they could have scored more. In an interview a few years after the game, Ally McCoist said:

> From a personal point of view, I honestly believe we should have gone on and beaten them more, because at 5–1 I looked up at the clock and I think there was about 20 minutes to go, and I thought, 'Here we go, this is going to be a real trouncing.'

There might not have been the seven or eight goals that the fans would have loved to see, but the 5–1 scoreline was still a trouncing, and if there was any sense of disappointment among the supporters, they didn't show it.

Douglas Connery believes he was always destined to be a Rangers fan, as he was born on 27 April 1966, the day of Rangers' famous Scottish Cup victory over Celtic. 'My dad was going to call me Kai after the famous Kai Johansen, after his glorious winning goal that night,' he recalls.

'The one game that really sticks out for me would have to be that 5–1 drubbing in 1988. What a day that was. I had been looking forward to the game all week at work and had my ticket for the east enclosure. I was in the ground an hour before kick-off and the atmosphere was absolutely electric.

FOLLOW, FOLLOW

'Celtic scored first in a frantic start to the game in glorious August sunshine, then I witnessed the best volley I have seen in my life, from Ray Wilkins. There was a second's delay before every Rangers fan realised it had hit the back of the net, then the noise was unbelievable. I thought the main stand roof was going to blow off – it was brilliant.

'Rangers seemed to kick in from there, and gave Celtic an absolute hiding. Mark Walters was tearing them apart down the wing and he was man of the match for me. But I had to pinch myself – we were 5–1 up with 20 minutes still to play and took the foot off the gas. If we had kept going, I would have witnessed the biggest drubbing of Celtic ever in an Old Firm match. Anyway, I was in heaven and still recall the Wilkins strike as if it were yesterday.'

Among those who watched the highlights of the game on *Scotsport* was a ten-year-old boy in Lanarkshire whose dream was to play for Rangers and Scotland. Young Lee McCulloch went on to fulfil his ambition, and even scored for Rangers against Celtic, but he still has fond memories of that sunny day in August 1988.

Like many other young fans, he went to all the home games with his father, until it came to Old Firm day, when he had to stay at home. 'My dad wouldn't let me go to the games against Celtic, but of course that's exactly the game you want to go to. And when you're told you can't go, it just makes you want to even more.

'That 5–1 game is the one I remember most. Even watching it on TV, you could tell how good the atmosphere was. Rangers had an amazing team at that time, and on that day it all came together.'

The result is seen by many as the moment the nine-in-a-row era truly began. A player who would later have a major part to play in the quest to achieve the record had hit the headlines earlier in the summer. Future Rangers star Paul Gascoigne became the UK's first £2-million player when he moved from Newcastle United to Spurs.

Scottish golfer Sandy Lyle also hit the back pages when in April he became the first British player to don the famous green jacket after winning the US Masters. A month later, Wimbledon shocked the world of football when they beat Liverpool 1–0 at Wembley to win the FA Cup in May.

FIVE-STAR RANGERS

The news in Scotland was dominated by two major disasters, which resulted in more than four hundred deaths. In July, the Piper Alpha oil rig in the North Sea exploded and burst into flames, killing 167 workers. In December, a New York-bound Pan Am flight was blown up over the town of Lockerbie, killing a total of 270 people, including 11 on the ground. Libyan agent Abdelbaset Ali Mohmed Al Megrahi was jailed in 2001 after being convicted of the Lockerbie bombing by a Scottish court sitting in the Netherlands. In August 2009, the Scottish government released him on compassionate grounds, allowing him to return to Libya as he was suffering from terminal prostate cancer.

The ongoing Troubles in Northern Ireland continued to claim many lives, and 1988 was one of the bloodiest years for some time. In March, the SAS shot dead three IRA members in Gibraltar as they prepared to launch a bomb attack on a British military band. At their funeral in Belfast ten days later, UDA gunman Michael Stone attacked the crowd with grenades and pistols, killing six mourners. As he fled on foot, he was captured and beaten by members of the crowd before being bundled into a car to be shot by the IRA. However, the Royal Ulster Constabulary intercepted the vehicle and arrested Stone, who was eventually given sentences totalling 682 years.

This was also the year in which Tory health minister Edwina Currie angered farmers and sparked a public health scare when she claimed that most of Britain's eggs were affected by salmonella. She was forced to quit as egg sales plummeted following her 'highly irresponsible' comments.

Harry Enfield burst onto the television scene with his comedy characters Stavros and Loadsamoney on Channel 4's *Friday Night Live*. The first Red Nose Day raised loadsamoney – £15 million, to be exact – for charity. For a few months in 1988, pop trio Bros threatened to become the new Beatles – or at least the new Bay City Rollers. Hundreds of obsessed fans, known as Brosettes, followed their every move, and at their concerts the music was drowned out by the screaming of the hysterical teenage girls who made up most of the audience.

In 1988, the tabloids were reporting on what they saw as an

alarming new phenomenon known as acid house. Young people across the country were dancing the night away at illegal warehouse raves, high on the drug Ecstasy. These were the days of smiley-face T-shirts, gaudy hooded tops, baggy jeans and bandanas. But for national newspapers and politicians, raves were a threat to the nation's youth, and they spent much time and effort exposing what went on at these events.

The year's 5–1 win over Celtic might have been only the third league game of the season, but such was Rangers' superiority that they were already being tipped as runaway title winners. Celtic did win the next Old Firm game 3–1, but in the New Year's Day match Rangers again ran up a big win, this time 4–1. For the next decade, Celtic remained firmly in their rivals' shadow as Rangers went from strength to strength and eventually equalled Celtic's record of winning nine successive league titles.

17

PUBLIC ENEMY

RANGERS 1 CELTIC 0
SCOTTISH PREMIER DIVISION
PLAYED AT IBROX STADIUM, GLASGOW
4 NOVEMBER 1989

Rangers team: Woods, Stevens, Munro, Brown, Butcher, Wilkins, Steven,
I. Ferguson, McCoist, Johnston, Walters

Rangers scorer: Johnston

It was the moment Celtic supporters had been dreading since the day
Maurice Johnston had first been paraded as a Rangers player.

With a swing of his right foot, the man they called 'Judas'
cemented his position as Public Enemy No. 1 among the green half
of Glasgow – and simultaneously won over the remaining doubters
on the other side.

Johnston's first goal for Rangers against his old team was as
inevitable as it was dramatic. Two minutes remained of what had been
a relatively uneventful derby when Gary Stevens sent a hopeful cross
into the Celtic penalty area. It should have been easy enough to deal
with, but defender Chris Morris snatched at his clearance and played
it straight to Johnston at the edge of the penalty area.

The striker took one touch to tee the ball up, then struck it with
pinpoint accuracy into the bottom right corner of Pat Bonner's net.
A huge roar erupted from three of the Ibrox stands as the home fans

celebrated wildly. In the Broomloan Road end, the Celtic supporters sat silently in a state of shock.

Johnston celebrated the goal as if it was the moment his entire career had been building up to and, given the torrent of abuse he had suffered in both his appearances against Celtic for his new club, it was hardly surprising. A huge smile spread across his face as he ran from the pitch to salute the Rangers fans in the Copland Road stand. They in turn cheered, danced and generally revelled in the moment.

If there were any dissenters among the Rangers support refusing to celebrate the goal because of their antipathy towards the scorer, they were keeping a low profile. A few red-white-and-blue scarves did fly onto the track, but this was more likely to do with over-exuberance than some form of protest.

Six months earlier, anyone who had suggested such a scenario was even remotely possible would have been laughed out of town and more than likely advised to seek urgent medical attention. Johnston, who had moved from Celtic to Nantes in 1987, had been unveiled in May as a Celtic player, the prodigal son returning to his spiritual home after going off to seek his fortune in foreign lands. When the deal to take him back to Parkhead collapsed, it appeared he would be remaining in France. No one anticipated the news that broke on 10 July: that Johnston would instead be joining Rangers.

More than 20 years on, it is hard to overstate the enormity of the signing. Not only was Johnston an ex-Celtic player (one with a track record of antagonising the Rangers support) and not only had he been on the verge of rejoining his former club, but he was also a Roman Catholic. To say that he was an unlikely signing target for Graeme Souness would be something of an understatement.

For Rangers fans of a certain age, the Johnston signing is their JFK moment. Like thousands of others, Duncan Stewart will always remember where he was when he heard the news. 'I was 17 and had just left school, so I was lounging around in the house all summer. I can remember I'd just got up and the eleven o'clock news came on the radio and it was the lead item.

'I just couldn't believe it. I was so shocked I had to tell someone, so I ran downstairs to tell my mum, who wasn't remotely interested in football. Even she understood that this was big. I wasn't particularly bothered that he was a Catholic, but this was Mo Johnston we were talking about. The guy who blessed himself to wind up the Rangers fans when he was sent off in the Skol Cup final! I always got the impression that he was a guy who hated Rangers and would never even consider playing for us.

'Once I got over the initial shock, I got to thinking about it and was actually quite pleased. It was only a few weeks earlier that Celtic had been showing him off as their new star signing, and now he was playing for us. It was the ultimate kick in the teeth to our biggest rivals, and as a supporter that's the sort of thing you love.

'Also, the club was getting stick all the time for not signing Catholics, so that was something that we couldn't have thrown at us any more. There was always going to be a backlash from some fans about signing a Catholic, but overall I think most people felt that it was probably something that had to happen eventually. I just don't think they expected it to happen this way!

'The funny thing is that when he played for Celtic, Johnston used to live near us and all the local kids used to hang around his house to catch a glimpse of him getting into his Porsche. The Rangers player Ian Ferguson moved into the same house later; they had the same agent. But I don't think anyone in their right mind imagined they'd ever be teammates at Ibrox.'

Johnston began his career in the early 1980s with Partick Thistle, where his prolific scoring record made him one of the hottest properties in British football. He moved south to Watford in 1983 and helped them beat relegation from the First Division and reach their first-ever FA Cup final. Nine games into his second season at Vicarage Road, Johnston moved back to Scotland and signed for Celtic, where he enjoyed three successful seasons before leaving for Nantes.

During his time in France, Johnston improved as a player and seemed to mature as a person. Along with players like Frank McAvennie and

Charlie Nicholas, he had once had a reputation as a champagne-swilling playboy and he was regularly the subject of lurid tabloid stories about his love life.

He claimed the constant pressure of being a high-profile Celtic player had forced him to quit Scotland for France. But after insisting he would never return, Johnston changed his mind and in May 1989 appeared at a press conference in Glasgow to announce that he was signing for Celtic. Wearing the green and white hoops and standing alongside a beaming Billy McNeill, he told reporters he'd had offers from England and the Continent but declared he 'wanted to wear the green and white again'. Moving back to Parkhead was a dream, he said. 'Deep down I've always wanted to be back with Celtic.'

The dream quickly turned into a nightmare, though, as a financial wrangle hit the deal and Johnston told Celtic he would not be signing after all. The club was understandably miffed at this turn of events and persuaded world governing body FIFA that Johnston was now their player. On 29 June, he obtained a court order preventing Celtic from holding on to his registration and the following day Parkhead chiefs finally gave up on the deal.

By now, rumours were already circulating in Glasgow that Johnston might be signing for Rangers. The nature of the city is that there is always gossip flying around relating to the Old Firm, 99 per cent of which turns out to be completely untrue, and the denials from Johnston seemed to indicate that this was just another crazy story.

However, despite the repeated rebuttals – agent Bill McMurdo was quoted in one newspaper as saying, 'You can run that story for ten years and it still wouldn't be true' – the rumours wouldn't go away. Finally, on 10 July, the truth was revealed. Johnston and his people had been in talks with Ibrox bosses and now a deal had been done. Mo Johnston was a Rangers player.

On the surface, it was scarcely believable. In his autobiography, *Mo: The Maurice Johnston Story*, published just a year earlier, Johnston had been scathing about Rangers and their signing policy. He wrote:

> I am a Celtic man through and through and so I dislike
> Rangers because they are a force in Scottish football and
> therefore a threat to the club I love. But more than that,
> I hate the religious policy they maintain. Why won't they
> sign a Roman Catholic?

But closer examination of the facts could have provided some hint that Johnston might just have been tempted to move to Ibrox. Although he was raised as a Catholic, his father was actually a Protestant who supported Rangers. And from his time with the Scotland international squad, Johnston had friends at Ibrox, such as Richard Gough, Ian Durrant and, in particular, Ally McCoist. Perhaps most significant of all was his admiration for Rangers boss Graeme Souness. In his book, he described him as the 'best midfield player I have ever played with or against' and 'a great guy to have on your side'. Johnston also revealed that he had gone to Ibrox to see Rangers play Dundee the previous season: 'I was shown all the hospitality in the world and didn't get any hassle from Rangers fans. I felt I would have taken more stick if I had gone to see Celtic.'

In what was seen at the time as a joke, Johnston had also declared in his book, 'I might even agree to become Rangers' first Catholic if they paid me £1 million cash and bought me Stirling Castle.' The castle might not have been part of the deal, but his move to Rangers certainly made Johnston a wealthy man.

He was unveiled at a press conference in the Blue Room at Ibrox, accompanied by Souness, club owner David Murray and other directors. Dressed in a dark-blue blazer, white shirt and club tie, Johnston spoke in glowing terms about his new employers and the man who had signed him. 'I am an admirer of Graeme Souness and feel I am joining one of the biggest, probably *the* biggest club in Europe,' he told reporters. He also revealed that, not surprisingly, he wouldn't be returning to live in Glasgow.

Outside Ibrox, around 100 fans had gathered, most of whom told reporters they welcomed the signing. Of course, there were some who were trenchant in their criticism of Souness and the Ibrox board, and needless to say it was their comments that were given greater prominence in the following day's newspaper coverage, particularly in the popular tabloids.

One small group of fans turned up at the main entrance to the stadium carrying a wreath bearing the message '116 years of tradition ended', while in another incident two supporters set scarves and strips alight.

However, despite a few calls to the club demanding refunds on season tickets, there was no evidence of the mass protests many predicted. Most fans seemed to take a pragmatic view: Johnston was a quality player who could improve the Rangers team. His religion was, for many, a side issue. The fact that he had been snatched from under the noses of their greatest rivals was seen as the ultimate in one-upmanship.

The real anger came from the other side of the city, where Celtic fans saw Johnston's actions as the ultimate betrayal. Almost immediately, all eyes turned to the first Old Firm game of the season, which was to take place at Parkhead in August.

Inevitably, Johnston would face the wrath of the supporters who had once idolised him, and there were genuine fears for his safety. He already required the services of bodyguards to protect him as he went about his daily business. There was some speculation, scotched by Graeme Souness, that he would be left out of the derby.

The eyes of the world were on Scotland as Johnston prepared to enter the lions' den, and Celtic fans were paying huge sums to make sure they were part of the reception committee. One supporter told the *Glasgow Herald* he had paid £20 for a £4 ticket on the Saturday morning and by lunchtime had been offered £40 for it. His friend told the paper that they had turned down the offer, adding, 'We hate Johnston and we're gonnae show the bastard.'

For 90 minutes, Johnston was subjected to a tirade of invective from the home fans, who made up the majority of the 53,000 crowd, but thankfully the anger didn't spill over into anything more than verbal abuse. Johnston missed two decent second-half chances that in other circumstances he might have been expected to score from, and in the end Rangers left with a 1–1 draw.

The biggest concern for the visiting fans was the league table. By the end of the evening, Rangers were bottom of the Premier Division, with just one point and one goal from their opening three games. But by the time the second Old Firm game came around in November, the champions had put aside their early wobbles and were getting into their stride.

McCoist and Johnston had the makings of a prolific striking partnership, with 17 goals between them already, and a victory would take them over Celtic to the top of the league. With Mark Walters in superb form after returning from injury, Rangers were dominant as Celtic chose to play a defensive formation in a bid to soak up the home attacks and hit on the break.

Walters tormented Morris throughout the game and he also had a strong claim for a penalty rejected by the referee in the second half when he was brought down by Paul Elliott inside the box. But for all Rangers' supremacy, they struggled to make much in the way of clear chances, and when Johnston did get a couple of opportunities he failed to take advantage.

Again he was a target for the 7,500 Celtic fans in the Broomloan Road stand, and this time the booing and chanting were accompanied by a hail of missiles, including a meat pie hurled in his direction when he ventured a bit too close to the visiting supporters. But as the game appeared to be drifting towards a goalless conclusion, Johnston had the last laugh.

In any circumstances, a winning goal with three minutes to go in an Old Firm derby would be met with wild celebrations. As Johnston punched the air in front of the delirious Rangers supporters, he was engulfed by teammates before running along the track behind the goal. So exuberant were his celebrations that he received a yellow card. Any doubts over his commitment to the Rangers cause were dispelled in that moment.

The win took Rangers to the top of the league, ahead of Aberdeen on goal difference, and in the end they finished seven points clear of their northern rivals to take their second successive title. Celtic, meanwhile, suffered a monumental collapse and ended up in fifth place, seventeen points behind Rangers at a time when a win secured only two points.

In purely footballing terms, Johnston's signing couldn't be considered anything other than a success, his forty-six goals – including a total of three against Celtic – helping Rangers to two league titles. By the time he left to join Everton for £1.75 million in 1991, his powers were on the wane and it was widely considered to be a good piece of business by Rangers.

In terms of the wider implications of the signing, there's no doubt that it changed everything. A Rubicon had been crossed and it allowed Rangers to move forward without the continual attacks that the signing policy brought. Of course, since Rangers are Scotland's biggest and most successful football club, there are those who will always seek out new ways to criticise them, but the issue that had the potential to cause most damage was now gone.

While there are some who still deeply regret the move, the majority of the fans were supportive of Johnston's signing and accepted that refusing to play Catholics was no longer a realistic position for the club to take.

Souness insisted that damaging Celtic was not the motivation behind the deal, but he must have been well aware that it would be one of the consequences. From the moment Johnston put pen to paper at Ibrox, it was almost nine years before Celtic won the league again. The signing was obviously not the only factor, but the psychological blow it delivered to a club already swaying on its feet was enormous.

Johnston is now living in North America, where his career eventually took him in the late '90s. It's doubtful that he will ever come back to Scottish football, unwilling to expose his family to the inevitable storm that would surround his return.

The wounds caused by his 'betrayal' still run deep. His proposed participation in an Old Firm veterans charity match in Glasgow in 2005 caused such outrage among Celtic supporters that he was eventually forced to pull out to allow the event to go ahead. After more than 20 years, their hatred of Johnston shows no sign of abating.

18

HAPPY NEW YEAR

CELTIC 2 RANGERS 4
SCOTTISH PREMIER DIVISION
PLAYED AT CELTIC PARK, GLASGOW
1 JANUARY 1994

*Rangers team: Maxwell, Stevens, Murray, Gough, Pressley, Brown,
Steven, McCall, Durie, Hateley, Mikhailichenko*

Rangers scorers: Hateley, Mikhailichenko (2), Kuznetsov (sub)

It's traditional that if a tall, dark stranger is the first person to cross your threshold in the New Year, they'll bring you 12 months of good fortune. Mark Hateley might have looked the part, but when he first-footed Celtic on the opening day of 1994, he brought them nothing but misery.

Less than a minute into the first match of the year, the Englishman breached a Celtic defence that appeared to be suffering from the effects of another Scottish New Year tradition: the stinking hangover.

As a contest, this Old Firm clash was over almost before it had begun. Thousands of Rangers fans were still filing into Parkhead when they heard not one but two massive cheers. If any of them feared the worst, their concerns were soon allayed when they arrived at the top of the terraces to find their fellow fans in a state of delirium.

Four minutes into the game and Rangers were already two goals ahead. By the half-hour mark, it was 3–0 and Celtic were in meltdown, on and off the park. Fans, already in a permanent state of anger at the way their club was being run, went into apoplexy as the goals rained in. There were several pitch invasions, including one interloper who went for the Rangers goalkeeper, and in the stands numerous supporters hurled coins, abuse and even confectionery at club directors.

The fury of the Celtic supporters had been building for years. Rangers had been transformed by the Ibrox revolution of 1986 and the arrival of Graeme Souness. The good times had continued under new owner David Murray, who took over in 1988, and even the departure of Souness to Liverpool three years later failed to have an impact on Rangers' dominance.

Assistant boss Walter Smith had moved into the hot seat and carried on the policy of bringing some of the biggest names in British and European football to Ibrox. He took Rangers to the verge of a European Cup final in 1993, and the following season saw them pursuing a sixth consecutive league title.

Souness meanwhile, had suffered a tough time of things at Liverpool, where he had been such a success as a player. He guided them to FA Cup glory in 1992 at the end of his first full season – weeks after undergoing major heart surgery – and was responsible for the breakthrough of youngsters Steve McManaman, Robbie Fowler and Jamie Redknapp into the first team. But his time in charge was marred by poor man-management, dressing-room squabbles and bad signings. His team struggled in the league and after a shock FA Cup defeat to Bristol City at the end of January 1994, he finally stepped down. On the day of Souness's departure from Ibrox, Rangers chairman David Murray had said the manager was making the biggest mistake of his career by joining Liverpool, and so it turned out.

While one high-profile manager was losing his job, another was starting in a new post. Former Spurs boss Terry Venables was appointed England coach in January 1994, succeeding Graham Taylor. A fly-on-the-wall documentary charting Taylor's turbulent time as manager was broadcast by Channel 4 later in the year and proved to be one of the television highlights of the year, with Taylor's 'Do I not like that!' exclamation becoming a national catchphrase.

Catchphrases were a feature of the year's TV, with two of 1994's comedy hits relying heavily on their use. *Knowing Me, Knowing You* was a spoof chat show starring Alan Partridge, played by Steve Coogan. The title of the show, followed by the response 'Ahaaa!' was Partridge's attempt at a Bruce Forsyth-style catchphrase. The BBC's *Fast Show* was even more driven by catchphrases, with many, such as 'Suits you, sir', 'Does my bum look big in this?', 'Scorchio!' and 'Jumpers for goalposts', crossing over into everyday use.

The film of the year for critics was undoubtedly Quentin Tarantino's *Pulp Fiction*, while the British romantic comedy *Four Weddings and a Funeral*, starring Hugh Grant, was the big box-office smash. It also spawned a massive chart hit for Glasgow's Wet Wet Wet, who remained at number one for fifteen weeks with the movie's theme, 'Love Is All Around'. The music scene also saw the birth of Britpop, with rivals Oasis and Blur both releasing landmark albums in 1994.

In February 1994, police began excavation work at 25 Cromwell Street, Gloucester, the home of builder Fred West. Following the discovery of human remains, West was charged with the murders of twelve young women and girls – including his first wife and one of his daughters. He hanged himself in prison before going on trial. His wife, Rosemary, was convicted of ten killings and was sentenced to spend the rest of her life in prison.

The political world was rocked in May 1994 when Labour leader and Monklands East MP John Smith died of a heart attack. His sudden death led to a huge outpouring of grief, particularly in Scotland. Smith, who has been described as 'the best prime minister we never had', was succeeded later in the year by Tony Blair.

As the year began, Rangers fans were starting to seriously consider the possibility of emulating, even beating, Jock Stein's record nine titles in a row. Followers of their rivals in the East End of Glasgow were becoming increasingly frustrated and concerned at the lack of success on the pitch and the financial issues off it. While Rangers were signing big-money international players like Mark Hateley, Trevor

Steven, Alexei Mikhailichenko, Oleg Kuznetsov, Gordon Durie and Stuart McCall, Celtic were making do with embarrassing flops like Tony Cascarino, Stuart Slater, Gary Gillespie, Wayne Biggins, Lee Martin and Carl Muggleton.

Lou Macari had taken over as Celtic manager in October 1993 after the resignation of Liam Brady, who quit after a calamitous two-year reign. Macari's first game was a 2–1 win at Ibrox and by the time the New Year's Day game came around, Celtic were in contention with Rangers at the top of the league.

Off the pitch, things were less rosy. A £17-million takeover bid by a consortium led by the Canada-based businessman Fergus McCann had been rejected by the Celtic board. Protests took place before each game, organised by a fans' group aiming to oust the board.

Despite the financial turmoil behind the scenes, Macari was in bullish mood ahead of the festive derby. Preparing his players at Seamill, on the Ayrshire coast, he predicted, 'If it comes to a battle, a little bit of a war, I quite fancy us. Looking back at our victory at Ibrox the last time we met, I was pleasantly surprised at the way our players responded. These occasions are usually more physical than real football matches and I think we have 11 here who could win it.' There were some grounds for optimism in the Celtic camp. The team had suffered just one defeat in fourteen league matches and had not conceded a goal at home under Macari.

While Celtic had a full-strength squad, Rangers went into the match with injury woes; Ally McCoist, Andy Goram, Ian Ferguson, Duncan Ferguson, David Robertson and Dave McPherson were all out. Doubts over McCall, Durie and Richard Gough forced Walter Smith to name a larger than usual squad, although in the end all three made it.

On a freezing, gloomy New Year's Day, 48,500 souls dragged themselves from the warmth of their homes to the East End of Glasgow. The Rangers fans crammed into the section of terracing reserved for them were in a party mood from the outset, perhaps anticipating what was to come.

Many of them were still arriving at the ground as Rangers launched their first attack in the opening seconds of the game, when Trevor Steven passed through the heart of the Celtic defence into the path of Mikhailichenko. He burst past the static central defence and only the awareness of goalkeeper Pat Bonner prevented a clear goalscoring chance.

The ease with which Rangers carved open their defence should have served as a warning to the home team, but ten seconds later they were again torn apart by the simplest of passes, and this time there was nothing Bonner could do to prevent a goal.

Stuart McCall's pass found Hateley on his own in acres of space, with the Celtic central defenders Dariusz Wdowczyk and Gillespie nowhere to be seen. Having beaten the offside trap, Hateley bore down on goal and, as the keeper approached him, he coolly curled it into the back of the net.

Three minutes later, Rangers doubled their lead with a near carbon copy of the first goal. This time, Hateley was involved in the build-up, when he touched the ball back to Durie, who played a perfect pass through to Neil Murray. Again Celtic's defence was woefully flat, and Murray was able to stride through the gaping hole at its heart. His shot was saved by Bonner's feet, but Mikhailichenko followed up to side-foot it into the unguarded net.

Duncan Stewart was one of thousands of Rangers fans who missed both the goals because they were still making their way into the ground. He and a pal had arrived at Parkhead without tickets and, after failing to locate anyone selling outside the ground, decided to take a chance and try to get in without one.

'Outside the ground there was a line of police and stewards checking tickets and we figured that if you got past them, then you were certain to get in,' he recalls. 'So we got into the middle of a crowd, aimed for what we thought was the weakest bit of the police line, put our heads down and just kept walking. Once we got past the line, we went through a gate and we were inside the ground.

'The turnstiles were at the top of the stairs, so once you got up the stairs and into the booth there was no turning back. When I told the guy at the window that I didn't have a ticket or any money, he just shrugged his shoulders and let me go through for nothing. The funny thing is my mate who was at the next turnstile had to stump up a tenner – obviously his guy was a Celtic fan!

'When we were going up the stairs, we heard a huge cheer that sounded like it came from the Rangers end. We thought it might have been a goal, but it seemed too early. Then there was another cheer a few minutes later, so we were sure that it wasn't a goal, as there was no way there could have been two already. But when we actually got onto the terraces, the place was absolutely bouncing and we knew straight away that we were winning.'

A third Rangers goal came in the 28th minute, and again Mikhailichenko was the scorer, taking advantage of more slack defending. Gary Stevens' cross from the left was headed back across goal by Hateley; Durie miskicked, but the ball spun to Mikhailichenko, who prodded it over the line from six yards.

The goal sparked wild celebrations at the Rangers end, but the Celtic supporters didn't take it well. A fan who had been receiving first-aid treatment at the side of the pitch was so enraged he leaped up from his stretcher and ran onto the park, making a beeline for Rangers goalkeeper Ally Maxwell. The offender was apprehended by a combination of police, stewards and Rangers players and bundled away before he could inflict any damage on Maxwell, but it was an alarming moment. Meanwhile, fighting broke out on the terraces among the home supporters and missiles began to rain down on the pitch.

The Herald reported that a Catholic priest who was in the crowd was injured when he was hit by a coin thrown by a fellow Celtic fan moments after the third goal went in. Father Peter McBride, a Royal Navy chaplain, suffered a gash to his forehead from the flying coin and the following day based his sermon on the incident.

In the main stand, the Celtic directors were the target of angry supporters. Missiles were thrown in the direction of the board members seated in the directors' box, and at one point David Murray had to dodge a flying Mars bar aimed at one of his Parkhead counterparts.

Meanwhile, the elated visiting fans struck up a mocking chorus of 'Keep the board', satirising Celtic's 'Sack the board' chant, further maddening the home support. In the world of football rivalry, there's only one thing that comes close to matching the elation of seeing your own team win, and that's watching the opposition implode.

'When the third goal went in, the Celtic fans just went ballistic,' recalls Duncan Stewart. 'They were arguing with each other and started chucking their scarves onto the track and screaming abuse. I even saw a few punches thrown. It was mayhem. You expect to see hatred and anger at Old Firm games, but you don't expect fans to direct it at their own.

'Of course, we were loving it, and when the "Keep the board" chants started up it just seemed to wind them up even more. Half-time was brilliant because we really thought at that stage that we could run up any score.'

During the half-time break, Lou Macari somehow managed to rally his players and they came out fighting in the second period. Two minutes after the restart, they pulled a goal back, with a well-worked free kick by John Collins that went in off a post. From a crowd-control point of view, it was probably the best thing that could have happened, as another Rangers goal at that stage could have provoked even more trouble.

The goal sparked a mini-revival for Celtic, and they came close to scoring a second goal when Charlie Nicholas hit the crossbar with a long-range shot. But with 20 minutes to go, Rangers brought on the injury-plagued Kuznetsov, and it was his intervention that sealed the victory. A cross from Durie was scrambled away but only as far as the Ukrainian substitute, who controlled it with his chest before sending an unstoppable, dipping shot past Bonner.

Eight minutes from the end, Nicholas scored a consolation goal for Celtic, a strike that brought a bigger cheer from the Rangers end than it did from the home support. By then, many of the Celtic fans had already begun to trudge home, and those who remained were in no mood to celebrate a meaningless goal. *The Times* reported that towards the end of the game one fan in the Main Stand 'knotted his scarf into a noose and swung it slowly in front of the directors'. In the end, police made fifty-four arrests inside and outside the ground; three of those arrested were pitch invaders.

Despite strong evidence to the contrary, the Celtic directors insisted that the violence that had erupted at the game had nothing to do with supporters' unhappiness with the board and was entirely down to frustration at the way the match unfolded. Supporters saw it differently, putting the trouble down to a combination of both factors, with one fans' group member, Peter Rafferty, describing it as a 'disaster waiting to happen'.

For the Rangers fans, it was another opportunity to gloat over their rivals, something they had got quite used to in recent years. 'To go to their place on New Year's Day and give them a good tanking was just brilliant, and to top it all off they were in total chaos,' says Duncan Stewart. 'It was the first time I'd been to a Rangers v. Celtic game at Parkhead, and I'll always remember it as one of my favourite Old Firm matches of all time.'

The SFA immediately confirmed that there would be an inquiry into the violence, particularly the attempted assault on Ally Maxwell, although, surprisingly in the circumstances, chief executive Jim Farry called for a 'sense of balance and perspective'. He said, 'It will all be done with a view to trying to ensure that this kind of thing is not repeated. The stage is for the players and when you get audience participation the show is not the same.' Although Farry insisted he was not prejudging the inquiry, the SFA eventually took no action against Celtic, deciding that the club had ensured adequate policing and stewarding of the match.

Despite talk of a Rangers crisis in the run-up to the game, the win put Walter Smith's team back at the top of the league and at the same time delivered a fatal blow to Celtic's title aspirations. Rangers eventually won their sixth consecutive title by three points from Aberdeen, with Celtic finishing fourth.

It was not a vintage season for Rangers, despite the championship win. They managed to win only half of their forty-four league games and failed to get a victory in any of their last five matches. But in many ways, it was a triumph gained in adversity, with Walter Smith having to cope with an injury list that would have floored any other team. The depth and quality of the Rangers squad ensured that the league was won again nonetheless, and the quest for nine in a row gathered pace.

19

● ●

OUT-THOUGHT, OUTFOUGHT
. . . AND OUTFOXED

With Rangers having taken their league domination to eight consecutive titles, they went into the 1996–97 season with the much-coveted nine in a row firmly in their sights. Celtic, understandably, were desperate to stop them. The result was a season-long state of frenzy that went into overdrive every time the two teams met. With each passing Old Firm match, the hype and tension grew, until – predictably – it all came to an ugly head in the final clash between the two rivals in March 1997. This chapter looks back at two of the most memorable games from that most tumultuous of seasons.

CELTIC 0 RANGERS 1
SCOTTISH PREMIER DIVISION
PLAYED AT CELTIC PARK, GLASGOW
14 NOVEMBER 1996

Rangers team: Goram, Cleland, Robertson, Petric, Gough, Björklund,
Moore, Gascoigne, McInnes, Albertz, Laudrup

Rangers scorer: Laudrup

FOLLOW, FOLLOW

On a night of high drama, it was a derby that had just about everything. Two saved penalties, an unbelievable miss, countless other chances and a pitch invasion by a fox, who did a lap of honour before vanishing into the night.

In a match that was broadcast live to the world on Sky TV, Paul Gascoigne and Pierre van Hooijdonk were both guilty of missing from the spot. But their failures were nothing compared to the glaring opportunity spurned by Peter van Vossen late in the game. As one wag put it, even the fox would have scored that one.

In the end, it was a piece of clinical finishing by the ever-cool Brian Laudrup that settled one of the most hyped-up Old Firm matches ever.

Rangers were undefeated in the previous seven Old Firm clashes, including a 2–0 victory at Ibrox earlier in the season, a result that had put Rangers five points clear. However, Tommy Burns's team had clawed their way back into contention, and by the time the latest instalment came around the two teams were level on points, with Celtic just ahead by a single goal.

It was the first time in 14 months that Rangers had gone into an Old Firm game behind their rivals in the league. A Celtic win would have put them three points ahead and a victory could have been the start of a run that would have seen the Parkhead side go nine points clear of Rangers. The way the fixtures fell, Celtic would have two more games to play before Rangers returned to league duty. A nine-point cushion at this stage in the season would have given Celtic a real boost, even though Rangers would have had games in hand.

Celtic fans were optimistic going into the game, especially as their star forwards, van Hooijdonk, Andreas Thom and Jorge Cadete, were all returning from injury. Even the bookmakers had them as 6–4 favourites to win the game.

It was an unusual position for Rangers to find themselves in ahead of a clash with Celtic. For the last eight seasons, Rangers had been the team to beat, coming under severe pressure from a succession of rivals hoping to knock them off their perch at the top of the league.

OUT-THOUGHT, OUTFOUGHT... AND OUTFOXED

But now the tables were turned and Brian Laudrup, who had helped put Celtic to the sword so often in recent years, wondered if their rivals would be able to cope.

'It's our turn to be the hunters now,' he said in the build-up to the game. 'Celtic being at the top of the table makes things interesting. In the last few seasons we have been under all sorts of pressure at the top of the league and Celtic will now taste that as they try to stay top.

'But being up there is pressure we would love to be under once again, that's for sure. For the game tomorrow, Celtic know they are the hunted. We know we are the hunters. It is as simple as that.'

Laudrup, as always, would be a key player. Signed from AC Milan in the summer of 1994, he was one of the few among the foreigners who had flooded the Scottish game in recent years who could genuinely be described as world class. He was a player who thrived on confidence and who performed at his best when he was comfortable with life. The frenzied media attention and stifling tactics of Italian football were not to his liking and he failed to reach his potential at Milan, but in Scotland he found his spiritual home. Happy and settled off the field, he was devastating on the pitch and for four seasons was untouchable. His close control, vision and pace were simply too much for Scottish defenders to cope with, although he was often criticised for his performances in Europe.

With characteristic dry humour, Walter Smith summed up the frenzy surrounding the build-up. 'This game has been more hyped than the last,' he said. 'If we're still close, the next will be even worse and eventually we'll just blow each other up.'

The match, the first Old Firm derby since Celtic Park had been renovated, was a 50,000 sell-out, with millions more around the world watching live on TV. After a six-week absence through injury, Andy Goram was recalled to the Rangers goal while Laudrup also returned to the team after missing the previous match. Both would play major roles in the outcome of the game.

Walter Smith had decided to play without a recognised striker, instead deploying Laudrup as a lone forward, with the intention of using his pace and skills to exploit gaps in the Celtic defence. The tactic worked perfectly. Celtic, despite enjoying the great bulk of possession, had difficulty creating space and chances, and Rangers always looked dangerous when they took the ball towards their opponents.

Having weathered early Celtic pressure, Rangers silenced the noisy home crowd in the seventh minute with a classic counter-attack. Almost inevitably, it was Laudrup who delivered the blow. A clearance from Andy Goram was headed on by Derek McInnes, but the ball headed straight for defender Brian O'Neill, 40 yards out, and there seemed to be no danger to the home goal.

However, as he tried to bring it under control, O'Neill lost his footing and fell on his backside. Quick as a flash, Laudrup pounced on the error and sped towards goal. Surrounded by defenders, the Dane still had a lot to do, but there was never any doubt what the outcome would be. As he drove forward, he cut inside Alan Stubbs before firing an unstoppable shot from 25 yards past the Celtic goalkeeper, Stewart Kerr.

The goal forced Celtic to push forward, and while they managed to create some chances, they also left themselves open to the Rangers counter. Morten Wieghorst missed a glaring chance in the 15th minute before Peter Grant sent a long-range shot soaring over the bar.

At the other end, Laudrup brilliantly broke away down the right, evading the attentions of three defenders before sending in a perfect cross, which was met by Jörg Albertz. The German couldn't get enough power on his header, though, and it was easily collected by Kerr.

Then, in the 27th minute, after a foul by Derek McInnes on Paolo Di Canio, Goram produced a spectacular two-fisted save from a swerving van Hooijdonk free kick. Laudrup could have doubled Rangers' lead 12 minutes later, when he again seized upon a defensive mistake, this time from Stubbs, but was denied by Kerr, who parried the shot after narrowing the angle.

The second half started in much the same way as the first ended: with chances at both ends. Then, from beneath the temporary west stand, a fox emerged to add a surreal note to the evening's entertainment. The match was held up for more than two minutes by referee Hugh

Dallas as the animal ran up, down and across the pitch, its every move being cheered by the crowd, before it finally disappeared into one of the Parkhead stands.

The action continued unabated after this bizarre interlude. Albertz had a header saved by Kerr, before Goram smothered a dangerous cross from Thom. Then David Robertson had a 20-yard shot saved, before Richard Gough blocked a goal-bound shot by Wieghorst.

With 20 minutes to go, Rangers had the chance to seal the match when Kerr knocked Laudrup down in the box after a defence-splitting pass from Gascoigne. The Englishman, who'd had an uncharacteristically quiet game, took the kick, but it was a weak effort and Kerr saved easily to his left.

Rangers substitute Peter van Vossen then unwittingly wrote himself into the Old Firm history books with one of the most memorable misses ever seen. The Dutchman started the move with a perfectly weighted pass to release Albertz, who beat the offside trap and carried the ball into the Celtic penalty area. As Kerr came to close him down, he rolled it to the left, where van Vossen had carried on his run. From seven yards, and with an open goal in front of him, the former Ajax winger somehow managed to scoop the ball over the bar.

Sky summariser Andy Gray described the miss as 'inexcusable', and it could have turned out to be even more costly. A minute later, Simon Donnelly was fouled by Gough in the penalty area and Dallas again pointed to the spot. With five minutes to go, van Hooijdonk had the chance to salvage a draw, but again the penalty was missed. This time, Goram threw himself to his right to push the ball away. The man known to the fans simply as 'The Goalie', who had so often produced heroics in Old Firm ties, celebrated as if he had just scored a penalty rather than saved one. He took the plaudits of his teammates, although in truth it had been another poor spot kick.

There was time for one final Celtic chance, but Wieghorst missed from six yards when it had seemed certain he would score. Then van Vossen had the opportunity to atone for his earlier miss when he broke through two minutes into injury time, but this time he was thwarted by Kerr.

It was the last action of the game, and when Hugh Dallas blew the final whistle Rangers knew they had secured a win that would be vital in their efforts to secure nine in a row. Celtic boss Tommy Burns was left rueing a string of missed chances. 'You can't do that against Rangers,' he mused, 'as they are very good on the counter-attack.'

Laudrup, the match-winner, admitted Celtic had played the better football, but the reality was that Rangers had created enough chances to have won three or four nil. The win put the Light Blues in a strong position in the league; however, by the time the final Old Firm game of the season came around, Celtic were still within touching distance. A victory would have put them within two points of Rangers, while defeat would have stretched the gap to eight. It ensured that the clash at Parkhead would be one of the most eagerly awaited in years – and the most fiercely contested.

CELTIC 0 RANGERS 1
SCOTTISH PREMIER DIVISION
PLAYED AT CELTIC PARK, GLASGOW
16 MARCH 1997

Rangers team: Dibble, Cleland, McLaren, Gough, Björklund, Moore, Ferguson, Durrant, Albertz, Hateley, Laudrup

Rangers scorer: Laudrup

It was a team dismissed as 'Dad's Army', a motley crew of veterans, semi-invalids and journeymen who limped into war rather than marched. And when veteran striker Mark Hateley was conscripted to the creaking regiment on the eve of this crucial battle with Celtic, there were plenty among the Rangers support who thought, 'We're doomed.'

With Gordon Durie in hospital suffering from a stomach problem and fellow strikers Sebastián Rozental, Peter van Vossen and Erik

OUT-THOUGHT, OUTFOUGHT . . . AND OUTFOXED

Bo Andersen all injured, veteran Ally McCoist was the only forward available to Walter Smith. Rangers were in the midst of a crisis. Ten days earlier, they had lost to Celtic in the quarter-final of the Scottish Cup, before being beaten by Dundee United in the league. Few had expected Walter Smith to turn to Hateley to provide a solution to the problem, but in many ways it proved to be an inspired move.

The Englishman had enjoyed perhaps the best period of his career at Ibrox, and his striking partnership with McCoist was one of the most prolific in Rangers' history. Signed from Monaco for £1 million in 1990, he scored 115 goals before moving south to QPR in the autumn of 1995. But at the age of 35, his best years were well behind him, and, to some, his signing smacked of desperation.

Sometimes desperate times call for desperate measures, however, and Smith knew that there was a good chance the presence of Hateley would both unsettle the Celtic defence and galvanise his own team. For his part, the striker was delighted to be given a chance to play his part in history. 'It was just as if I'd never been away,' he said at the time. 'Ally was winding me up from the word go. I just can't wait to pull on the jersey again. The chance to contribute to nine in a row is what dreams are made of.'

Hateley's signing wasn't the only shock for the Ibrox fans in the lead-up to the Celtic game. Talismanic goalkeeper Andy Goram suffered a rib injury that would rule him out. In his place would be former Manchester City goalkeeper Andy Dibble, signed as cover only days earlier and now making his debut in the full glare of the biggest Old Firm game of the decade.

But as Brian Laudrup recalled in an interview with the *Daily Record* in 2008, the Welshman's new teammates were less than convinced after watching him in training ahead of the derby. Laudrup said:

> He didn't manage to catch one ball. All the boys were thinking 'oh my God' and laughing nervously because he was so bad. To be fair to him the whole thing came out of the blue and when he arrived in Glasgow things went so quickly for him. It was quite worrying because there was

so much at stake and we had to go to the toughest place there is to get a result. Dibble also had the impossible task of trying to fill The Goalie's boots – someone who had saved us many times before against Celtic.

As so often under Tommy Burns, Celtic went into the derby with high hopes, having ended their nine-match, twenty-two-month winless run against Rangers with a 2–0 victory in the Scottish Cup. Their optimism was boosted further by the visitors' injury problems.

In addition to their selection issues up front and in goal, Rangers had defensive difficulties, with Richard Gough not fully fit after missing the last three games and David Robertson failing to recover from injury.

Stuart McCall and Paul Gascoigne were also long-term absentees from the Rangers midfield, although inevitably Gazza was not far from the headlines in the run-up to the Old Firm game. Given two weeks off by the club, he headed to London, where he embarked on an infamous marathon party session with the broadcasters Chris Evans and Danny Baker, before flying to New York to carry on the revelry. The media frenzy that surrounded his antics led many to question the player's future at Ibrox, and although he did make a comeback from his ankle injury before the end of the season, his Rangers days were numbered.

In an attempt at damage limitation, Gascoigne issued a public apology for his behaviour. It stated:

> I was given a fortnight off by the club. I was grateful to them at the time and I'm grateful now. I accept that as a Rangers and England player I should not be giving papers the chance to write anything about me other than in respect of my performances on the pitch.
>
> I realise that as Paul Gascoigne, I have an added responsibility and I promise I will try my hardest. I have been injured for some time and that has been frustrating. It's never easy sitting and watching from the sidelines and

it's harder for me than most because I live football and I live and breathe Rangers.

Gascoigne's behaviour was a distraction but the least of Walter Smith's worries as he took his team to Parkhead for the crucial match. He knew victory would almost certainly secure his team nine in a row and even a draw would make it highly unlikely that Celtic would close the gap with six games left; defeat would hand the initiative to Celtic.

Smith sprang another surprise when he announced his team, choosing Ian Durrant, who had started only one league game that season, instead of McCoist. With Gough, Durrant, Hateley and Ian Ferguson all in the starting line-up, Rangers had a core of players who had been over the course in Old Firm games numerous times. And just as importantly, in Brian Laudrup they had the match-winner supreme.

For the second successive Old Firm league game at Celtic Park, the great Dane was the man who scored the winner. But while his goal in the first encounter was a typical piece of Laudrup skill and clinical finishing, his second strike couldn't have been more different.

The scrambled goal came on the stroke of half-time at a point in the match when Celtic might have thought they had weathered the Rangers storm. During previous derbies at Parkhead, Rangers had arrived with the clear intention of soaking up pressure and hitting Celtic on the break. This time, despite the depleted line-up, the approach was far more positive.

The first significant chance of the game came in the tenth minute, when Paolo Di Canio and Peter Grant made a mess of a free kick and passed it straight to Ian Ferguson. His pass released Laudrup on the counter-attack and the Dane ran half the length of the pitch before teeing it up for Durrant, whose shot from the edge of the area went wide.

Hateley's physical presence was proving a headache for Celtic and he came close with a header from an Albertz cross after 20 minutes. A minute later, Stewart Kerr was forced into a save from a Durrant header as Rangers started to impose themselves on the game. These were warning signs for the Celtic defence that they were struggling to cope with crosses into the box from wide.

Celtic's only significant chance of the first half came four minutes before the break, when Di Canio hit the crossbar with a twenty-five-yard volley after Tosh McKinlay had flicked a free kick into his path.

But when the deadlock was broken a few minutes later, it came at the other end and was the result of some awful Celtic defending. A long free kick by Jörg Albertz was missed by Celtic's Italian defender Enrico Annoni under pressure from Hateley, but when the ball bounced through to Stubbs, there seemed little danger, despite the presence of Durrant.

The defender's attempted header back to Kerr was short and wide, allowing Durrant to flick the ball high over the exposed goalie. As the ball looped towards the goal, Laudrup and Celtic defender Malky Mackay both went for it, with the Rangers forward apparently getting the final touch to take it over the line. Rangers fan Paul Dunnachie says, 'It was arguably the goal that pretty much sealed nine in a row, and I've never been certain who actually got it. To be honest, I couldn't care less – it won Rangers the match and all but sealed the title.'

The Rangers players themselves remain unsure who actually got the vital touch, although Brian Laudrup was in no doubt that Mark Hateley's presence was vital, telling the *Record*:

> It was an emotional homecoming for Mark. It was almost like he'd never been away. He knew exactly what was required in a game like this and I was delighted to see him, as I'd always enjoyed a good partnership with him. He could flick on long balls and I could get into dangerous one-on-one areas with their defenders. That's exactly what he was told to do and that's where our goal came from. He outjumped Enrico Annoni and got enough on the ball to let me score the winner.
>
> I know Ian Durrant still claims he got the final touch, and that's fine by me. I was just happy we'd won.

OUT-THOUGHT, OUTFOUGHT...AND OUTFOXED

From a Rangers point of view, the goal came at the perfect time. The 7,000 visiting fans spent the entire half-time interval taunting the home support, happy in the knowledge that they had been in this position many times before in the last nine seasons. For all their defiance, the Celtic fans must have feared the worst as Laudrup turned to celebrate the goal.

In the second half, Rangers looked the more likely side to score, but Celtic were given some hope in the 67th minute when Hateley was shown a red card following a flare-up with the home goalkeeper. After Laudrup was fouled by Mackay, Kerr raced 20 yards out of his goal to confront Hateley, who had already become embroiled in a confrontation with several Celtic players. Quite why Kerr got himself involved is anyone's guess, but the same could be said for Hateley's decision to head-butt him.

Referee Hugh Dallas, who was only yards away, showed the Englishman a straight red card before cautioning Mackay for the original foul and Kerr for his aggressive behaviour. The incident served only to stoke up the rancour even further and did little to help Celtic's chances of salvaging something from the game.

Although play raged from end to end, the home team managed to create only half-chances, while Rangers had several good opportunities at the other end. And any hopes Celtic might have had of taking advantage of their numerical superiority were dashed with ten minutes to go, when Mackay was sent off for a second bookable foul on Laudrup. From the resulting free kick, Albertz blasted one of his trademark powerful shots narrowly wide.

Celtic's only clear-cut chance of the second half came five minutes from time. Di Canio crossed from the left and Simon Donnelly knocked it back across for Annoni, who, with a free header, sent it wide.

Annoni was also involved in the last major drama of the 90 minutes, when he was booked for a wild lunge at Laudrup. His fellow countryman Di Canio then got involved in a shouting match with Ian Ferguson, during which the local boy appeared to offer the Italian the chance to 'step outside'. Di Canio, who had earlier been mouthing off at the Rangers fans, made a snapping gesture with his hands and mouthed some words, which appeared to suggest that he was threatening to try to break Ferguson's leg in a tackle.

Minutes later, Dallas blew the final whistle and the Rangers players celebrated a vital victory. Meanwhile, Di Canio continued his war of words with Ferguson as the teams left the pitch, the Rangers midfielder clearly finding it all too easy to wind up the volatile Italian. During the melee, Di Canio struck Ferguson, and after the match he was called to the referee's room where he was cautioned for a second time. His behaviour could easily have resulted in a straight red card.

Meanwhile, as the Rangers fans celebrated, the players briefly formed a huddle in front of them, mocking Celtic's own pre-match ritual and infuriating the remaining home fans inside the ground. Walter Smith later revealed he'd used as motivation to his players the fact that Celtic had formed a huddle after the previous week's Scottish Cup game, something he felt had been an attempt to humiliate Rangers. Clearly, his players felt they were entitled to show their own togetherness as a team in exactly the same way.

As usual with the Old Firm, hostilities didn't end with the final whistle. Police made 37 arrests at the game and said there were 'a number of disturbances' as fighting broke out afterwards. The SFA launched an inquiry into events, accusing some players of failing to live up to their responsibilities.

The arguments raged on in the media for several days, with Celtic accusing Rangers of a lack of dignity in victory, a charge that infuriated Walter Smith. He hit back, pointing out that after every Rangers Old Firm victory, the newspapers were full of negative headlines that diverted attention away from the result and focused on other issues. But when Celtic had won in the Scottish Cup, Smith said, there were no such negative stories. 'They were allowed the pleasure of reading the next day's papers, which said everything for them was wonderful,' the Rangers boss added.

Smith made another interesting comment, which summed up the pressures surrounding Old Firm managers, particularly during the nine-in-a-row era: 'The other day there was no great joy for me in winning, just a strong sense of relief it was over.'

Paul Dunnachie believes the pre-match hype contributed to the trouble that followed, and that the subsequent media outrage was hypocritical to say the least. 'This match was the most hyped, certainly to that point and possibly since, that I can remember,' he says. 'I seem to remember that Sky TV were promoting a boxing match around the same time with the tagline of "Judgement Night" and the Scottish tabloid press, showing a remarkable lack of originality, dubbed the 16 March match-up at Parkhead "Judgement Day".

'The Judgement Day line was rolled out for at least a week before the match, along with a host of articles and interviews with people who all pushed the story that the upcoming match was the most important Old Firm game that had ever been played.

'The aftermath of the match was chaotic, with reports of trouble all over Glasgow. In the following days, the media, having spent the previous weeks winding the punters up to fever pitch, did an about-turn and reacted with horror that the supporters had taken it all so seriously.

'It was another case of the media seeking to play off and add to the hype of the Old Firm but also wanting to back off and criticise the very emotions that they depend upon to sell newspapers and achieve listeners.'

Despite the controversy, Celtic had to face the stark truth that they had deservedly lost a match against a Rangers team that was way below strength. In a season that meant so much to their supporters, Tommy Burns's team had, for the first time since the formation of the Premier Division, lost all four of their league fixtures against their rivals.

Under Smith, Rangers had once again shown a strength of character that Celtic simply couldn't match. In the *Daily Record*, Brian Laudrup commented, 'I remember we were so nervous before the game because we had a few new faces in the side. But we were so determined to win as we knew that would clinch the title. And we did just that.'

FOLLOW, FOLLOW

The victory at Parkhead gave Rangers the impetus to go on and win the league. They eventually equalled Celtic's record of consecutive titles with a victory over Dundee United at Tannadice. Fittingly, it was Laudrup who scored the winner. Despite the adversity they faced, Dad's Army simply refused to put up the white flag, and they had managed to rouse themselves for one last momentous battle. This time, it was enough to win the war.

20

SHAME GAME

CELTIC 0 RANGERS 3
SCOTTISH PREMIER LEAGUE
PLAYED AT CELTIC PARK, GLASGOW
2 MAY 1999

Rangers team: Klos, Porrini, Vidmar, Amoruso, Hendry,
van Bronckhorst, Albertz, Reyna, McCann, Amato, Wallace

Rangers scorers: McCann (2), Wallace

For Rangers fans, it will be forever remembered as the day they clinched the title at the home of their fiercest rivals for the first time.

But for everyone else, 2 May 1999 was the day the chaos of the Old Firm descended into anarchy. The madness that visited Parkhead that evening went beyond anything seen in the fixture before, as the Celtic fans and players completely lost the plot.

Referee Hugh Dallas was left bloodied after being hit by a missile from the crowd, several Celtic fans invaded the pitch in an attempt to get at the official and another nosedived from the upper tier of the stand into the seats below before being stretchered away for treatment.

As chaos broke out in the stands, three players – two from Celtic and one from Rangers – were ordered off and seven were booked. After the match, violence erupted in the streets around Parkhead, and later in the evening the windows at the referee's home were smashed.

Amid all the mayhem, it was easy to forget that a championship had been won. Two goals from Neil McCann and one from Rod Wallace gave Rangers a 3–0 win and handed them their eleventh league title in thirteen seasons. For the Rangers supporters, the victory was made all the sweeter by the fact that it was secured on enemy soil, the first time in their history that they had won the league at Celtic Park.

It was the outcome that Celtic had feared most. After watching Rangers land nine in a row, they had finally won the Premier League title back the previous season under Wim Jansen. But amid arguments over finances, the Dutchman quit after winning the trophy and was replaced as manager by Dr Jo Vengloš.

After a stuttering season, the Celtic fans now faced the nightmare scenario of not only losing the title at the first time of asking but doing so in their own back yard. Much of the pre-match coverage focused on the potential embarrassment to Celtic of Rangers clinching the title at Parkhead, whipping up anxiety levels even further. Even the normally mild-mannered Dr Jo appeared to be feeling the tension during the build-up.

Asked if his players would be affected by knowing the Parkhead fans dreaded Rangers winning the title in front of them, he angrily responded, 'Don't talk about losing games before those games have been played. The supporters can think and say what they like. But players can't afford to be anything other than positive.'

Although alcohol was later identified as the main cause of the ensuing mayhem in the crowd, the pressure brought about by the terror of defeat surely played a significant part in what happened.

Another Dutchman, Dick Advocaat, had taken over at Ibrox after Walter Smith stepped down at the end of the previous season – the first trophyless campaign since 1985–86. Advocaat was handed a vast war chest to build a team and he set off on an unprecedented three-year spending spree that was to bring some of Europe's top players to Scotland but would eventually leave the club in deep financial trouble.

SHAME GAME

Advocaat's arrival coincided with the departure of most of the stalwarts of the nine-in-a-row team. Among others, Richard Gough, Ally McCoist, Ian Durrant, Stuart McCall, Andy Goram and Brian Laudrup all said their farewells at the end of the Smith era, while Paul Gascoigne had departed during the previous season.

With the quest for ten successive titles ultimately ending in failure and with so many big players leaving, Advocaat had no option but to revamp the team. French goalkeeper Lionel Charbonnier, Scotland captain Colin Hendry, Romanian international Daniel Prodan and Dutch left-back Arthur Numan were all recruited to bolster the defence. Fellow Dutchman Giovanni van Bronckhorst, ex-Manchester United star Andrei Kanchelskis, Argentine striker Gabriel Amato and Englishman Rod Wallace also joined the Advocaat revolution. Meanwhile, others who had been bit-part players under Smith suddenly flourished in the new regime, with Barry Ferguson and Craig Moore in particular playing significant roles in the season ahead.

After a disappointing defeat to Hearts on the opening day of the season, the new team soon got into its stride. A totally unexpected 5–1 defeat to Celtic at Parkhead was the only blip, and by the winter break they were four points clear of Kilmarnock at the top of the table and ten ahead of their Glasgow rivals.

The new team was playing brilliant passing football and had already won the League Cup and made significant progress in the UEFA Cup. Advocaat still wasn't satisfied, though, and there were more arrivals as the season progressed. Goalkeeper Stefan Klos was signed to replace the injured Charbonnier, Claudio Reyna, the US captain, was added to the midfield options and French World Cup winner Stéphane Guivarc'h was brought in to boost the attack.

Perhaps the most significant signing, though, came from closer to home. Advocaat paid Hearts £1.5 million for the services of winger Neil McCann, and he was to play a decisive role in the outcome of the season.

By the time the final Old Firm league clash of the season came around, Rangers were within touching distance of the title. A 3–1 victory over Aberdeen coupled with a 1–0 defeat for Celtic at St

Johnstone meant Advocaat's team could go to Parkhead and win the league.

It had been a beautiful spring Sunday in Glasgow, but as evening fell a dark cloud settled over one corner of the East End of the city. It brought with it a torrent of hatred and venom the like of which had rarely been seen at a football match in Scotland.

During the pre-match warm-up, Rangers captain Lorenzo Amoruso led his team over to the 7,500 visiting supporters crammed into one corner of Celtic Park. The clenched fists of the players showed their determination to get the job done.

By the time the teams emerged ahead of the 6.05 p.m. kick-off, the 60,000 crowd had worked itself into a frenzy. The noise was deafening and the atmosphere electric, but the poison in the air was palpable. For the first 12 minutes of the game, the 50,000 Celtic supporters roared on their team, with the small band of Rangers fans doing their best to make themselves heard above the din.

Then everything changed, with a goal of the utmost skill and simplicity. The move started with Gio van Bronckhorst, who found himself in acres of space on the left before sliding an inch-perfect pass into the path of Rod Wallace, who had burst into the penalty area. His first-time cross was volleyed into the net by a stretching Neil McCann from six yards out. The goal, typical of the brand of flowing football Rangers had been producing all season, instantly silenced the home supporters and sent the travelling fans into raptures.

The championship was closer than ever, and the more the Rangers supporters celebrated, the more the hostility levels increased among their opponents. Every decision against Celtic was contested on the pitch and was met with howls of disbelief from the stands. As the red mist descended, it was only a matter of time before things got out of hand.

Half an hour into the match, McCann fouled Celtic's Stéphane Mahé, who, for reasons best known to himself, immediately jumped to his feet to confront the Rangers goalscorer. With Mahé having already been booked for dissent, Hugh Dallas had no choice but to send him off. Astonishing scenes then followed, as Mahé seemed to take leave of his senses, refusing to leave the pitch, appearing to lunge at the referee and having to be restrained by teammates. He eventually left the pitch in tears as the home supporters directed their ire at Hugh Dallas.

The incident fanned the flames of hatred that were already smouldering in the Parkhead stands. And when Hugh Dallas awarded Rangers a free kick five minutes before half-time, those flames turned into a full-on inferno. As van Bronckhorst prepared to take the kick, a fan burst out of his seat and made for the referee. Only the efforts of two Celtic players prevented him reaching his target. But before the game could restart, Dallas was struck by one of the many missiles that were being hurled onto the pitch from the home support. Blood poured from a head wound and he had to undergo treatment from the Celtic and Rangers physios before they declared he was fit to carry on.

Something approaching calm appeared to have descended and van Bronckhorst was finally able to take the free kick. It didn't last long. As the ball floated to the back post, Celtic's Vidar Riseth bundled Tony Vidmar to the ground and Dallas immediately pointed to the spot. This was the cue for a furious reaction from the Celtic players, which inevitably led to more chaos in the stands.

Another fan tried to get to the referee before being huckled by stewards and dragged away. Amid the mayhem, the coolest man in the ground was Jörg Albertz. He ignored the cacophony of boos and whistles to send Stewart Kerr the wrong way and double Rangers' lead.

Finally, half-time arrived, but not before another two pitch invaders were apprehended. There was even more drama when a Celtic fan plunged 40 ft from the upper level of the Jock Stein Stand into the supporters seated below. Millions of television pictures saw him waving while being stretchered away by paramedics. In a newspaper interview, the supporter denied being drunk. He also insisted he hadn't been trying to get at Hugh Dallas and was actually just going for a half-time pie when he tumbled over the edge. Despite his protestations of innocence, he revealed, club officials had banned him from the stadium for life.

The match was being beamed live around Britain by Sky TV, and around the country there was stunned disbelief at the unfolding events. Dave Watson was based in England at the time and watched the game with fellow Rangers fans, Celtic supporters and bemused locals.

He recalls, 'Even in the traditionally white-hot atmosphere that surrounds any Old Firm encounter, the madness and mayhem that ensued on that day surely tops any clash before or since. I was living in Blackpool at the time, and, unable to secure a ticket for the hottest match in years, went to my local pub to watch the game.

'Given the importance of the match, there was a fair old mix of interested locals interspersed with supporters of each side. Even in a Blackpool pub, the supporters congregated at different ends of the bar. Anyway, given the dubious decision to kick off at five past six, and with drink having been taken for a few hours beforehand, the pre-match atmosphere in the pub was "interesting". Nobody could have guessed what was to come.

'Neil McCann's early goal opened the floodgates to a Sunday evening unlike any other in the history of Scottish football. All around us, the Lancashire locals were literally speechless on witnessing the events unfolding before their eyes: Celtic fans invading the pitch, the referee being hit by a coin from the Celtic support, Stéphane Mahé refusing to leave the pitch on being shown the red card, a penalty being expertly dispatched by Jörg Albertz – and, of course, the half-time entertainment came early when a Celtic supporter tried to bungee jump off the top tier without the aid of a rope!

'All of this combined to leave the Bears in the pub thinking, "Life just does not get any better," while at least one Celtic supporter was almost pleading for the game to be abandoned, shouting that the referee couldn't possibly continue due to his injury. Such a display of humanity in the midst of battle was so heart-warming that I offered to share my champagne with him.'

Half-time seemed to take some of the sting out of the game, but seven minutes into the second half Dallas found himself at the centre of more controversy. Celtic goalkeeper Stewart Kerr rolled the ball out of his box with the intention of launching it in the direction of his forwards. But as he hesitated over his clearance, Neil McCann pounced, forcing the harried keeper to pick the ball up a full yard outside the penalty area. As the last man, his deliberate handball had denied McCann a clear goalscoring opportunity, but instead of producing a red card, Dallas instead decided to let him off with a booking. To add insult to injury, from the resulting free kick Kerr turned Amato's shot over the bar.

Having been handed this reprieve, Celtic tried to work their way back into the game, but despite some chances they never seriously troubled Stefan Klos, and if anything Rangers looked the more dangerous on the break.

With 15 minutes to go, the victory was sealed when substitute Jonatan Johansson found McCann, who easily turned defender Scott Marshall and rounded Kerr to slot the ball calmly into the empty net.

The match was over as a contest, but tempers remained fraught. With five minutes to go, Rod Wallace reacted angrily to a heavy challenge from Riseth and was given a second yellow card. Celtic's Enrico Annoni could consider himself lucky not to have been punished when he violently shoved fellow countryman Sergio Porrini during the resulting melee. In the final minute, Riseth lost his head and dived into a crazy and totally unnecessary tackle on Claudio Reyna, for which he too was sent off. By the end of the game, just 19 players remained on the park, but had the referee chosen to apply the rules strictly to the letter of the law, it could easily have been even fewer.

Following the final whistle, the Rangers players celebrated the famous and historic victory in front of their delirious fans. Just as they had done two seasons earlier, the team staged a mock huddle, enraging the few remaining home fans, who bombarded them with missiles as they ran down the tunnel to the safety of the changing-room. In the context of what had gone before, the huddle might have been somewhat ill-advised, but it was small beer compared to the earlier mayhem.

FOLLOW, FOLLOW

Rangers skipper Lorenzo Amoruso denied that the players' huddle was designed to mock Celtic, insisting it was nothing more than 'a spontaneous expression of communal joy'. The commission appointed to investigate events on behalf of the SPL accepted there had been no malicious intent. Lord Mackay of Drumadoon, Lex Gold, director of the Scottish Chambers of Commerce, and Glasgow solicitor William Stewart cleared Rangers of any blame for what had happened. Celtic, meanwhile, were fined £45,000 and Mahé's behaviour was singled out as a major contributory factor in the off-field trouble.

Strathclyde Police Chief Constable John Orr described the events surrounding the match as 'wholly unacceptable' and said they caused him 'serious concern'. He added, 'The behaviour of a small minority of fans was appalling. The four people who entered the field of play and those who took part in throwing coins are a disgrace. Thankfully, they are not representative of the vast majority of supporters who attended the match.'

As is so often the case after a powder-keg Old Firm clash, trouble continued long into the night, far from the scene of the match. Mr Orr revealed that there were 'sporadic disturbances' in the city centre and beyond, involving both sets of supporters. In a number of cases, officers attending incidents came under attack from thugs throwing bottles, bricks and stones. Three officers were injured and seven police vehicles were damaged.

Significantly, Mr Orr said that the majority of those who had taken part in the disorder and violence were under the influence of alcohol and might have been drinking for some time before kick-off. He added, 'The late timing of the match may have provided some supporters with an opportunity to overindulge in alcohol.' The violence ensured that Old Firm games would no longer be allowed to kick off at 6.05 p.m. for the benefit of Sky. Furthermore, everything would be done to ensure that a derby match would never again be scheduled in such a way that the game could be a league decider.

Not only did Hugh Dallas come under attack during the game but his home was also violated. A neighbour of the referee was found guilty of smashing windows at the Dallas family home in Lanarkshire hours after the game. The referee and his wife, Jacqueline, were sitting watching highlights of the game when the attack took place. Despite his conviction, the offender, a Celtic season-ticket holder, was allowed to continue attending matches at Parkhead, although he was reportedly given a 'very stern warning' by club officials.

Dallas described it as the worst night of his career – indeed the worst of his life. However, to his credit, he continued as a top-class referee for several years. In fact, a few weeks later he put himself back in the firing line by taking charge of the Scottish Cup final at Hampden, inevitably between Rangers and Celtic. This time, it was a relatively uneventful match, Rangers winning 1–0 to secure their sixth domestic treble in Advocaat's first season.

Long after the dust had settled on the 'shame game', Dallas remained a hate figure for Celtic supporters, a situation not helped by the club's decision to make public sections of a psychologist's report on the game that they had commissioned. Celtic's chief executive at the time, Allan MacDonald, highlighted a single line in the report that drew attention to Dallas patting van Bronckhorst on the back as he prepared to take the free kick that resulted in the Rangers penalty.

MacDonald claimed the study of the referee's body language came to the conclusion that 'he was capable of provoking the kind of crowd reaction we don't want to see inside Celtic Park', and he went on, 'Was it purely coincidental that shortly after he was seen patting Gio van Bronckhorst a coin came onto the park and struck the referee? Not according to the careful scrutiny of the game carried out by a man trained to understand crowd reactions and the reasons for them.'

However, the full report, which was submitted to the SPL's disciplinary commission, actually cleared Dallas of any blame and pointed the finger specifically at the behaviour of certain Celtic players. Nevertheless, the damage was done and the impression remained in the minds of some of the more paranoid Celtic fans that Dallas was biased towards Rangers.

Despite the bitterness that surrounded the day, Rangers fans refuse to let the controversy spoil their memories, even though they still feel the club has been unfairly tarnished by the behaviour of others. Dave

FOLLOW, FOLLOW

Watson says, 'As a Rangers supporter, I have never been happier than that day, and all that remained was to celebrate and start thinking of excuses why work would be a non-starter the following day.

'You will have noticed that all the bedlam that had taken place lay firmly at the feet of Celtic supporters and employees. Not so, according to the Scottish press over the next few days, as the clash was given the tag of "Old Firm Shame Game", something that rankles with Bears to this day. Nonetheless, it was a day never to forget – the day we won the league at Parkhead.'

21

SWEET REVENGE

RANGERS 5 CELTIC 1
SCOTTISH PREMIER LEAGUE
PLAYED AT IBROX PARK, GLASGOW
26 NOVEMBER 2000

Rangers team: Klos, Konterman, Wilson, Amoruso, Numan, Ferguson, Reyna, de Boer, Albertz, Miller, Flo

Rangers scorers: Ferguson, Flo, de Boer, Amoruso, Mols (sub)

This was as comprehensive a beating as you are ever likely to see in an Old Firm match. And what made it so remarkable was that it came just weeks after Rangers were on the wrong end of an equally humiliating thrashing at the hands of their city rivals. Furthermore, they had gone into this match in fourth place in the league and 15 points behind leaders Celtic. It wasn't even December, and the title race was already effectively over.

After two seasons of dominance under Dick Advocaat, in which Rangers won five out of the six domestic trophies available, they were suddenly – and inexplicably – in a state of crisis. The flowing football that had characterised the last two campaigns had vanished, and the team that had swept everyone aside just a few months earlier had, without warning, become a pushover.

A 6–2 defeat at Parkhead in August was followed by three consecutive league defeats, to Hibs, St Johnstone and Kilmarnock, as well as draws at Dundee and Dunfermline. Advocaat had spent heavily again in the summer, most notably on Dutch international defenders Bert Konterman and Fernando Ricksen, who cost a combined total of almost £8 million.

The pair did not impress on the field, to say the least, and behind the scenes their arrival was causing tension within the squad, with talk of a 'Dutch clique'. Despite the poor performances of Konterman and Ricksen, Advocaat persisted in playing them, further adding to the feeling that they were getting special treatment.

Other summer signings Peter Løvenkrands, Allan Johnston, Paul Ritchie and Kenny Miller were less expensive but equally unimpressive. Indeed, Ritchie – a free signing from Hearts – lasted just ten weeks before being sold to Manchester City.

Contributing to the sense of turmoil surrounding the club, Lorenzo Amoruso was stripped of the captaincy after a series of poor performances and fallings-out with Advocaat. Barry Ferguson, at the age of 22, was given the armband.

Chairman David Murray's immediate reaction to the heavy defeat to Celtic was a sign of the times. He chose to spend yet more money, this time on the £4.5-million signing from Barcelona of another Dutchman, Ronald de Boer. Unlike his compatriots, the midfielder was a proven world-class player, but even his arrival failed to inspire the team.

By November, Rangers were out of the Champions League, despite a good start to the campaign, trailing badly in the league and seemingly deeply divided in the dressing-room. Given all that, and the fact that they had already been soundly beaten in the first Old Firm match of the season, few Rangers fans were looking forward to the visit to Ibrox of Martin O'Neill's team. The chances of avenging the 6–2 humiliation seemed slim.

Days before the match, Rangers plunged into the transfer market once again, this time in spectacular fashion. Advocaat paid £12 million to bring the Norwegian international striker Tore André Flo to Ibrox from Chelsea and in doing so shattered the record for a transfer fee paid by a Scottish club. The fee for the 27 year old was twice the amount paid by Celtic for another Chelsea striker, Chris Sutton, in the summer.

Flo flew from London to Glasgow on the Wednesday before the derby and was immediately taken by John Greig from the airport to hospital for a medical. He was later driven to Ibrox to discuss personal terms and the following day trained with his new teammates before being officially paraded at an afternoon press conference.

The player cited his failure to play regular first-team football at Stamford Bridge as the main reason for his move and said he was well aware of what faced him on his debut against Celtic the following Sunday. 'I've watched derby games on TV, and I understand it is very important for the people here,' he told reporters at his press conference.

Flo had been a less than prolific scorer in England, so the signing represented a huge gamble. Former Rangers star Mark Hateley expressed some doubts about the capture, particularly given the huge price tag, warning, 'I don't think his scoring record in England represents great value for money.'

Given the amount Advocaat had invested in Flo, it was no surprise that he pitched him straight into the starting line-up against Celtic. What was slightly more surprising was the fact that he chose to play Kenny Miller alongside him, meaning both the Rangers forwards would be Old Firm debutants.

Ronald de Boer was also making his first appearance against Celtic, but his fellow countryman Ricksen was left out, presumably as a consequence of his disastrous performance in the 6–2 game, when he was substituted after just 20 minutes.

Rangers started the game like a team with a point to prove, and their two biggest signings, Flo and de Boer, both had excellent chances to score in the first five minutes. First, the Norwegian was sent clear on goal by Jörg Albertz, following good work from Claudio Reyna. Rab Douglas came out of his goal to meet him and did enough to put him off, Flo stabbing the ball agonisingly wide. Douglas and Swedish defender Johann Mjällby then contrived to lay on a glorious opportunity for de Boer. Mjällby ducked out of the way of a long pass from Amoruso, and the surprised keeper could only flap it into de Boer's path. From 12 yards out, and with the goal gaping, the former Barça and Ajax man hit it first time on the turn, but his shot was an inch too high and the chance was spurned

Celtic had a couple of long-range efforts in the first half, but their attack of Henrik Larsson and Chris Sutton was well marshalled by Amoruso and his central defensive partner Scott Wilson. The Italian was involved in a titanic physical battle with Sutton and was playing like a man possessed, throwing himself into tackles, launching into last-ditch blocks and powering into headers. The deposed skipper clearly felt he had a personal point to prove to his critics both in the stands and in the dugout.

Rangers were by far the better team and in the 35th minute finally made their dominance count with a well-worked goal by captain Barry Ferguson. Rangers broke down a Celtic attack just inside their own half and held on to the ball for four or five passes, eventually working it across the pitch to the right flank. Reyna played a perfectly weighted pass into the path of Ferguson, who had come from deep to power into the penalty area. He carried the ball for two strides to steady himself before calmly slotting it beyond Douglas into the corner of the net.

Minutes later, Sutton had loud claims for a penalty waved away as Ferguson raised his hands to protect himself from a Stiliyan Petrov shot. Then, in the 40th minute, Rangers had a good opportunity to double their lead when Albertz broke clear on the left. His cutback was intercepted by Tom Boyd, but Douglas had to get down quickly to prevent the ball ending up in the net.

Alan Thompson was then booked for a late tackle on Ferguson, who was by now dominating the midfield. Amoruso came close from the resulting free kick, his curling shot going just wide of the far post.

Rangers went in at half-time a goal up but knew that they could have had a more comfortable lead. Celtic were not offering much as an attacking threat but would always be dangerous at set pieces, and so it proved. Celtic won a corner after a vital tackle from Arthur Numan ten minutes after the restart. Defending from the corner was woeful, and Larsson, who otherwise had a quiet game, was able to power a header unhindered past Stefan Klos.

Rather than knocking them out of their stride, the goal seemed to act as a spur for Rangers, and within two minutes they were back in front. Albertz headed a de Boer corner against the bar, but Flo was on hand to flick the ball into the net from less than a yard out. It was a dream start for the record signing, even if he appeared somewhat surprised as he celebrated the goal.

Rangers were back on top again and passing the ball around the pitch with aplomb. Five minutes after the goal, any doubts over the final outcome were dispelled when Thompson was red-carded for a second booking after another clattering challenge on Ferguson. Moments later, Ferguson ran half the length of the pitch before playing an excellent, delicate pass to Flo. His attempted chip was blocked by Douglas, but Celtic couldn't prevent the ball going behind for a corner on the right.

From the resulting Albertz kick, de Boer rose unchallenged at the back post to head it down into the net, giving Rangers a 3–1 lead. Never one to hide his light under a bushel, de Boer took the adulation of the fans, leaping into the front row of the Copland Road stand to share the moment with his people. At 3–1 and one man down, it looked like Celtic's efforts would now be devoted to keeping the scoreline low rather than trying to get back into the game.

Michael Mols was brought on to replace Kenny Miller after Rangers' second goal, and it was trademark trickery from the striker that led to Rangers' fourth goal. First, he cleverly dummied a pass from Reyna and then spun away from his marker as de Boer played him into the penalty area. He then twisted and turned away from two defenders before firing in a shot that Douglas had to turn away for a corner.

From the resulting kick, Rangers got their fourth. Amoruso powerfully headed home Albertz's cross, Rangers' third goal to come direct from a corner. The Italian celebrated in typically exuberant fashion, running the length of the pitch, arms outstretched, shrugging off the acclaim of his colleagues.

The goal capped a fine performance from Amoruso. He had strolled through the game, relishing the physical joust with the increasingly frustrated Sutton, who was eventually substituted before he was shown a red card. For all his faults as a player – the main one being an alarming tendency to imagine himself to be a rampaging left-winger – Amoruso never hid and was always prepared to put himself in the firing line. Powerfully built, dominant in the air and strong in the tackle, when he concentrated on his primary job of stopping opposition attackers he could be outstanding. On his day he was as good as any of the legendary centre-backs to have worn the light blue over the years. However, his many lapses of concentration prevented him from attaining such a status in his own right. Amoruso was also involved in the fifth goal, by far the best of them all. The goal was reminiscent of the sort of flowing, incisive move that Rangers had produced under Advocaat in his first two seasons.

It all stemmed from a weak long-range Celtic shot that was easily blocked by Amoruso, who calmly played it out of defence to Flo, deep inside the Rangers half. He laid it back to Reyna, who brought Albertz into the game on the halfway line. The German held it up before sending a diagonal pass to de Boer, who had made a run down the left wing. He allowed the ball to run into the penalty area before sending an inch-perfect cross into the path of Mols, who slid in to side-foot it past Douglas.

It was a sweet moment for the Dutchman, who was making his first appearance against Celtic despite signing from Utrecht for £4 million the previous close season. In his first four months at Ibrox, Mols had looked a phenomenal player, capable of turning defenders inside out with his ability to twist and turn with his back to goal. He also proved to be a clinical finisher and could easily have gone on to be a Rangers all-time great.

Then, in November 1999, he suffered a devastating knee injury in a Champions League game in Germany against Bayern Munich, a match in which he had been playing out of his skin. The injury ruled him out for the rest of the season, and, although he did return for the following campaign and remained at Ibrox until 2004, he never quite managed to recapture the form of his first few months. However, his goals in the 2002–03 season were crucial in propelling Rangers to the title and he was always a hugely popular figure among the fans.

Mols's goal marked the end of the scoring. Advocaat's side had regained their pride with a thrilling display of commitment and skill – both qualities that had been sadly missing for much of the season. The win sparked a revival, and Rangers went 13 games unbeaten in the SPL, a run that came to an end with a 1–0 defeat to Celtic at Parkhead, a result that left them trailing by 12 points.

By the end of the season, the gap had stretched to 15 points as Celtic won their first treble since 1969. Rangers were also beaten by their Old Firm rivals in the semi-final of the League Cup and were dumped out of the Scottish Cup in the quarter-finals by Dundee United. After two seasons of glory, Advocaat had suffered the ignominy of winning nothing in his third campaign. For Rangers, this was unacceptable, particularly when so much had been spent on the team.

Advocaat could point to injuries to key players like van Bronckhorst, de Boer and Mols, but the season raised serious questions over his man-management skills and judgement in the transfer market. In the longer term, the profligacy of the Advocaat era – sanctioned by David Murray – led to financial hardships that Rangers would still be struggling to overcome more than a decade later. At one point, the club's debts were said to have reached £80 million, with the record signing of Tore André Flo held up as the epitome of wastefulness.

Flo went on to score 13 goals in his first season, and in his second he hit the net 25 times. But, despite this decent scoring record, his time at Ibrox is considered by most observers to have been a failure, largely due to the high price tag. He was eventually sold to Sunderland at the start of the 2002–03 season for around £6.75 million and remains to this day Scotland's most expensive player, a title that he is unlikely to relinquish any time soon, given the current financial woes in the game.

FOLLOW, FOLLOW

It could be argued that the highlight of Flo's time at Rangers came in his very first match. As the Rangers fans celebrated the 5–1 triumph, they were convinced this was a return to normal service. But, as enjoyable as the win was for the supporters, it turned out to be something of a hollow victory.

22

THE LØVEN CUP

RANGERS 3 CELTIC 2
SCOTTISH CUP FINAL
PLAYED AT HAMPDEN PARK, GLASGOW
4 MAY 2002

Rangers team: Klos, Ross, Numan, Amoruso, Moore, Ricksen, Ferguson, Caniggia, McCann, de Boer, Løvenkrands

Rangers scorers: Løvenkrands (2), Ferguson

It was the sort of fairy-tale ending that Danish storyteller Hans Christian Andersen himself would have been proud of. The clock was ticking down towards extra time in what had been a gripping Scottish Cup final when Neil McCann collected a pass from Lorenzo Amoruso. There didn't seem to be too much danger as he carried the ball towards the Celtic penalty area. Two defenders closed him down, and another three were waiting in the middle to keep tabs on the only other Rangers attacker, Peter Løvenkrands.

McCann swung his left boot and flighted a perfect cross into the box. The Celtic defenders seemed to be taken by surprise and stood stock-still as the ball dropped from the sky and was met by the Dane. His diving header was perfectly placed beyond the despairing Rab Douglas into the corner of the net.

Rangers had won the cup with almost the last touch of the ball. All Old Firm victories are celebrated with gusto, especially cup finals, but it was clear from the way the players and fans reacted that this was even more special than usual.

It had been a difficult couple of years for Rangers. After two magnificent seasons under Dick Advocaat, things had gone horribly wrong in his third term. The arrival of Martin O'Neill as Celtic manager in the summer of 2000 had an immediate rejuvenating effect on the Parkhead club, and he led them to a treble in his first season.

It was clear that there were problems behind the scenes at Ibrox, with persistent rumours of dressing-room cliques and fallings-out. Fans' favourite Jörg Albertz was among those rumoured not to see eye to eye with Advocaat, and he left the club at the end of the 2000–01 season. Two other top-quality midfielders, Giovanni van Bronckhorst and the Turkish international Tugay also moved on in the summer, and their replacements, Christian Nerlinger and Russell Latapy, were not in the same class.

Claudio Caniggia, Shota Arveladze and Michael Ball were also recruited the following season but did not have the immediate impact that Advocaat would have hoped. The departure of Claudio Reyna and Kenny Miller later in the season was a sign that the financial situation at Ibrox was starting to be a cause for some concern.

By December 2001, Rangers were already 11 points behind Celtic and had failed to qualify for the Champions League. Amid a flurry of speculation, Advocaat moved into a director-of-football role at Ibrox and was succeeded as manager by former Aberdeen defender Alex McLeish, who had previously enjoyed some success in charge of Motherwell and Hibernian. His appointment was further evidence, if any was needed, that Rangers had entered a new era of austerity and that the big-spending days of Souness, Smith and especially Advocaat were now well and truly over.

The league race was effectively lost, but McLeish set about trying to restore some spirit in the squad while focusing on the two remaining domestic competitions, the League Cup and the Scottish Cup. In the former, his first task would be to overcome Celtic in the semi-final at Hampden. Since the 5–1 victory in November 2000, Rangers had lost five consecutive games against Celtic, and, despite a sixteen-match unbeaten run under the new manager, there was no great confidence among the support that this miserable derby record was about to end soon. However, a sensational 30-yard strike by Bert Konterman gave Rangers a deserved extra-time victory and they went on to beat Ayr United 4–0 in the final.

The Scottish Cup run got under way in less than impressive fashion. A no-score draw at Berwick Rangers in the third round brought back painful memories of the 1967 defeat, which had sent shockwaves around the world. This time, Rangers avoided an upset and won the replay comfortably. After the early shock, McLeish's men had a relatively comfortable run to the final, scoring thirteen goals and conceding just one in three matches.

Celtic, who had an equally stress-free progression to the final, were on their way to a record points total in the SPL and were overwhelming favourites to land the cup as well. However, McLeish was undefeated in the three Old Firm clashes in which he had been involved so far, including the League Cup semi-final.

His approach of playing a three-man forward line against O'Neill's favoured formation of 3–5–2 had paid dividends, with the three Celtic defenders struggling to cope with the pace of Løvenkrands in particular. Although a frustrating player, the Danish international had already scored three goals against Celtic during the season and was becoming a talisman in Old Firm games. Not since the days of Laudrup and McCoist had one Rangers player had such an impact against their Glasgow rivals.

The domestic cup competitions may have lost some of their glamour in recent years, but cup-final day retains a special allure for fans and players alike. The week before can be a busy time for players: as well as meeting the needs of the media, players also have to arrange tickets for friends and family, trying to ensure that no one important is left out while diplomatically fending off requests from long-lost acquaintances.

The management also has to balance the necessity of keeping the players ticking along after their final league match with the need to ensure they are as relaxed as possible for the big game. Alex McLeish chose to have the squad in at Murray Park for two light training sessions at the beginning of the week, before giving them a break on the Wednesday. Instead, the players, management and backroom staff headed to an Italian restaurant in the West End of Glasgow for a long lunch and a chat. The aim was to get the players in a relaxed mood and then drum home what was required of them on the coming Saturday.

Training was stepped up on the Thursday and Friday, as the match approached, but there was a growing sense of optimism among the players for the task ahead. Early on Friday afternoon, the squad headed to their regular base at the Moat House Hotel on the banks of the Clyde in the centre of Glasgow.

If the aim was for a relaxing night, it didn't quite work out that way. A fire alarm roused the hotel guests from their slumber at 4 a.m. and forced them into the car park for almost an hour. Not unreasonably, the Rangers players assumed this was an attempt at dirty tricks by a mischievous Celtic supporter hoping to disrupt their preparation. If so, it had entirely the opposite effect. Rumours spread among the Rangers group that the evacuation had been sparked by a hoax bomb threat, and, as Lorenzo Amoruso put it afterwards, 'It made us even more determined to win.'

A bleary-eyed but resolute Rangers party awoke the next morning to that rarest of things: a beautifully sunny Glasgow day. Long before the players surfaced, supporters club buses had been setting off for Hampden from all corners of the UK. Duncan Stewart arrived in Glasgow from Perthshire at 10 a.m., just in time for the unofficial opening of one particular city-centre hostelry. He says, 'These days, I'd normally treat a cup final just like any other game: get in the car a couple of hours before kick-off, drive to somewhere as close to the ground as possible and park up, then go straight to the ground and take my seat. If I get there a bit early, then I'll maybe push the boat out and meet up with pals in the pub for a soft drink.

'But, for some reason, this time we decided to make it into more of an event. So we arranged to meet at the pub first thing. I got there about ten o'clock, just after I was told they would be opening for business. It was all cloak and dagger, but I said the appropriate words to get through the door and went upstairs, expecting there to be a couple of people inside. But it was absolutely packed out already and it wasn't long before the singing started.

'There was a flute band over from Northern Ireland and a few dodgy looking characters from down south, but mostly it was just normal guys like me and my pals enjoying the chance to let their hair down in private. To be honest, the songs being belted out were not the sort I'd normally join in with nowadays, although not for PC reasons.

'If you read the lyrics, most of the songs are not actually offensive or bigoted or whatever you want to call it, anyway. It's just that, as a father in his 30s and someone with a responsible job, I think I've probably outgrown all that sort of thing. Living in rural Perthshire, I can't pretend I've got much knowledge of what's been going on in Northern Ireland either. But in that environment it was easy to slip back into it, and, no matter what the right-on types might think, I have to say I had a great time.

'As kick-off time approached, we piled onto buses and headed for Hampden. There was a real sense of anticipation among the crowds outside. Someone, somewhere, had decided it was going to be Union Jack day, and everyone seemed to be carrying, or wearing, a flag. With the sun shining down on Hampden, it all made for a colourful occasion.'

Inside the National Stadium, the Rangers end was awash with red, white and blue as the teams emerged from the tunnel. Craig Moore and Ronald de Boer were lacking match fitness after recovering from injury, but they had done enough in training during the week to deserve starting slots. McLeish also left out the much-ridiculed Tore André Flo in favour of his preferred three-man strike force of Caniggia, McCann and Løvenkrands. Flo was Rangers' top scorer, but his £12-million price tag made him an easy target for critics and he had never looked comfortable in games against O'Neill's Celtic.

The game plan looked to be paying dividends as the three Rangers forwards were linking well early in the game and causing the Celtic defence of Chris Sutton, Bobo Baldé and Johan Mjällby major problems with their movement. An early foul on Caniggia brought a Rangers free kick, and Barry Ferguson's cross was headed just over by Amoruso. McCann also came close with a long-range free kick.

But, just as Rangers looked to be getting a grip on the game, they suffered a double blow. First, Caniggia was cynically barged to the ground by Sutton as he burst through on goal and eventually had to leave the pitch injured. Then, a minute later, Celtic took the lead through a John Hartson header.

The goal had come against the run of play, and in normal circumstances it could easily have sunk Rangers. But Old Firm games are anything but predictable and, with Barry Ferguson in inspirational form, the Light Blues responded superbly. Within two minutes, the scores were level again, and, predictably, the scorer was Peter Løvenkrands.

Ferguson's long ball should have been easy enough for the Celtic defence to deal with, but Sutton and Mjällby managed to get themselves into a mess and the ball broke loose to the Dane. With one touch, he brought it under control and then drilled home a fine left-foot shot from 15 yards. A few minutes later, Løvenkrands came close again when his volley from a Fernando Ricksen cross was saved by Rab Douglas.

Hartson was then lucky to escape a booking or worse when he smashed his elbow into Craig Moore's face, and Rangers survived a penalty claim when Henrik Larsson went down theatrically in the penalty area. Television replays showed referee Hugh Dallas had made the right decision, the Swede having fallen with no contact from Amoruso. Those incidents apart, it was a relatively easy day's work for the referee, with both teams concentrating on the football rather than getting involved in needless altercations.

Rangers continued to make the best chances, with Arthur Numan hitting a long-range shot over the bar and then a cross from McCann narrowly evading Ronald de Boer with the goal at his mercy. But, when Hugh Dallas blew for half-time, the scores remained level and the stage was set for a dramatic second half.

Within three minutes of the restart, Dallas had shown two yellow cards, one to Hartson for a late and reckless challenge on Shota Arveladze and another to Amoruso for pulling back Larsson. It was from that foul on the Swede that Celtic regained the lead. Neil Lennon's cross was met by Baldé, who had outjumped Amoruso, and he headed home from six yards.

The goal was another bitter blow to Rangers, but they had 40 minutes remaining in which to find an equaliser and immediately set about cancelling out Celtic's lead. Captain Ferguson was the driving force behind everything his team did. It was a midfield masterclass that harked back to his performances as a teenager under Dick Advocaat, performances that had first brought him to the football world's attention. Ferguson was first to every loose ball and was always available for a pass from a teammate. One minute he was pushing Rangers forward, the next he was breaking up Celtic attacks. His opposite number, Neil Lennon, simply could not cope with his drive, vision and guile.

Ferguson almost had Rangers level after 15 minutes of the second half when he unleashed a swerving shot from nearly 30 yards that flew past Douglas but crashed back off the post. It was agonisingly close to an equaliser, but the Rangers skipper would not be denied and five minutes later he finally got his name on the scoresheet.

His performance was later described as 'Beckhamesque', so it was fitting that Ferguson should produce a goal from a set piece that the England star himself would have been proud of. Hugh Dallas awarded Rangers a free kick on the edge of the penalty area after Baldé recklessly barged into Amoruso. The foul merited a yellow card, and, having already been booked, Baldé was fortunate not to have been sent off. Furthermore, although Amoruso eventually landed outside the box, TV pictures showed the challenge actually took place inside the area. Nevertheless, the free kick was well within shooting range for one of Rangers' dead-ball experts like Amoruso, Ricksen, de Boer or Arveladze. But, to the surprise of the supporters, it was Ferguson who stepped up to take the kick. He had never previously shown any aptitude for the set piece, but it was clearly the sort of day when he felt capable of anything. His brilliantly executed free kick curled into the top left corner of the net, giving Douglas no chance.

The blue half of Hampden erupted as Ferguson whipped off his shirt and ran to the fans in the west stand to take their adulation. At last, Rangers had the lead and, in Ferguson, the game's best player by far. From that point on, there was never any doubt about who would come out on top.

Celtic appeared to give up the fight as Ferguson's free kick shook the rigging of Douglas's goal. For the last 20 minutes, Rangers dominated and had several opportunities to grab a winner. A shot from Ricksen was cleared off the line after Douglas spilled a McCann cross, then Løvenkrands was denied by the goalkeeper when he hit a volley from a tight angle inside the area after being picked out by Ferguson. With a minute to go, Rangers had appeals for a penalty turned down when Mjällby barged into the back of Løvenkrands as he met another Ferguson cross.

The game looked certain to be heading for extra time. Then came the dramatic ending and the goal that wrote Løvenkrands his place in history and sent the Rangers fans into ecstasy. As the Danish forward hurdled the advertising boards and ran to the Light Blue supporters, Duncan Stewart was among those in seventh heaven.

'It all seemed to happen in slow motion,' he recalls. 'I was sitting quite close to the front of the Rangers end so had a perfect view of the goal. When it hit the back of the net, my first reaction was that it was going to be disallowed for offside or something. Then, a split second later, my second reaction was to start jumping up and down like a loony and hugging the stranger I was sat beside.

'I remember seeing Løvenkrands run over in my direction, but after that it was all a bit of a blur. Next thing I knew, the game was over and we had won, but I don't think anyone had stopped cheering or dancing about since the goal had been scored.

'When I eventually got my bearings back, I noticed that, where a couple of minutes earlier there had been thousands of guys in green and white, now there were just plastic seats. It was unbelievable how quickly the Celtic end had emptied, but obviously they had no wish to see or hear us celebrate, even if it meant not hanging around to give their own players a round of applause. To be honest, I'd probably have done the same if the roles were reversed.

'After the last couple of years, we had begun to think that Celtic were unbeatable, but Big Eck had proved he was more than capable of matching O'Neill and it looked like the good times could be back again. When you look back at the players we had then – Ferguson, de Boer, Klos, Arveladze, Caniggia, to name a few – you can see that we really had been underperforming under Dick Advocaat. I'd be happy with just one player of that calibre in our team now.'

By the time Ferguson walked up the stairway to collect the cup, Hampden was half empty, but when he lifted the trophy above his head the 25,000 Rangers fans who remained made enough noise to fill the ground.

It was fitting that Ferguson should be the man to raise the trophy. Although Løvenkrands had scored two goals, his skipper had been man of the match. It was an inspirational performance from a player who had so often been the subject of criticism. Alex McLeish was in no doubt about the importance of Ferguson to his team. 'His goal was inspirational just when we needed it most,' he said. 'You need players like him in these games. His form has been sensational. He is a real class player, and we were thankful we had him in the final.'

Almost as soon as the game ended, speculation began about Ferguson's future at Ibrox. Despite talk of a move to the English Premier League, he remained at Rangers and the following season captained the side to a domestic treble, scoring 18 goals and winning both the Football Writers' Association and the Scottish Professional Footballers' Association player of the year awards in the process. After helping Rangers to qualify for the group stages of the 2003–04 Champions League, he moved to Blackburn Rovers for £7.5 million. His departure left a gaping hole in the Rangers midfield that wasn't filled until his own return in January 2005.

23

AWAY-DAY JOY

CELTIC 0 RANGERS 2
SCOTTISH PREMIER LEAGUE
PLAYED AT CELTIC PARK, GLASGOW
20 FEBRUARY 2005

Rangers team: Waterreus, Hutton, Ball, Andrews, Kyrgiakos, Buffel, Ferguson, Ricksen, Vignal, Pršo, Novo

Rangers scorers: Vignal, Novo

It had been five long years since Rangers had gone to Celtic Park and returned with a victory. Not since Rod Wallace gave Dick Advocaat's team a single-goal victory in March 2000 had the visiting Bears been able to leave Parkhead with smiles on their faces.

So when goals from Grégory Vignal and Nacho Novo secured a 2–0 victory in February 2005, the scenes of celebration were understandable.

The intervening five years had seen eleven visits to the East End of Glasgow, nine of which ended in defeat. The two draws that were achieved did not amount to anything that any Rangers fan would consider even close to acceptable. To be fair, it wasn't just the away form against Celtic that was awful. Alex McLeish's men had suffered seven consecutive derby defeats before finally securing a League Cup quarter-final win in November 2004.

FOLLOW, FOLLOW

The cost-cutting that had followed the Dick Advocaat era had been put into full effect at the start of the previous season. To the horror of fans, the treble-winning side of 2002–03 was effectively dismantled, with Barry Ferguson, Arthur Numan, Lorenzo Amoruso, Claudio Caniggia, Neil McCann, Tore André Flo and Bert Konterman all leaving. Most of the replacements – Nuno Capucho, Paolo Vanoli, Emerson, Zurab Khizanishvili and worst of all Egil Østenstad – failed miserably. Only the veteran defenders Henning Berg and Frank de Boer could be said to have been anything approaching a success, but their contribution failed to save a dismal season.

The squad was bolstered the following season with the arrival of two Bosman signings, Jean-Alain Boumsong and Dado Pršo. Both would have significant parts to play in the season, although in different ways.

French international defender Boumsong was an instant hit, with some supporters considering him to be one of the best central defenders ever to wear the light-blue jersey. His combination of strength, skill and positional sense ensured that he strolled through the first five months of the season. But hardly had he passed through the famous oak doors at Ibrox than the rumours linking him with a move to England began.

After weeks of speculation and denial from all parties, Boumsong was signed by Graeme Souness at Newcastle United for a fee of £8 million in January 2005. His loss was seen as a bitter blow to Rangers by most observers, but in retrospect it may have actually won them the title. The cash from his sale helped bring Barry Ferguson back from Blackburn, as well as securing the services of talented Belgian playmaker Thomas Buffel, Greek defender Sotirios Kyrgiakos and goalkeeper Ronald Waterreus. All four played crucial roles in bringing the championship trophy back to Ibrox.

While Boumsong was derided by many as a mercenary for his swift departure from Ibrox, Dado Pršo was immediately loved by the fans – and the affection was clearly mutual. The Croatian, who made his name by scoring four goals for Monaco in a Champions League semi-final, was a tireless worker who wore his heart on his sleeve.

He was also a very talented footballer, capable of producing great moments of individual skill, as his spectacular overhead-kick goal on his debut against Fulham showed.

The defining image of Pršo was perhaps the goal he scored against Celtic in the second Old Firm league derby of the 2004–05 season. His head swathed in bandages from an earlier injury, he battled to rise above three defenders and power a header into the net. The goal gave Rangers a two-goal lead in a match that was one of many twists in an astonishing season that saw the Old Firm's fortunes fluctuate on almost a weekly basis.

The match at Ibrox on 20 November was the second Old Firm clash in ten days. In the earlier contest, also at Ibrox, a Shota Arveladze goal in extra time had given the home team a 2–1 win in the League Cup quarter-final, breaking a run of defeats that stretched back to December 2002.

In between the two derbies, Rangers had gone to Edinburgh, where they won a hard-fought match against Hibs 1–0. Nacho Novo was controversially sent off in the first half following an off-the-ball incident spotted by the linesman and should have missed the following match against Celtic. The Spaniard, signed from Dundee in the summer, was already a huge fans' favourite, partly because of his excellent scoring record and partly because he had very publicly turned down a move to Parkhead before joining Rangers.

Thankfully for Alex McLeish, Novo successfully appealed against the red-card decision and was free to take his place in the starting line-up against Celtic. His inclusion paid early dividends when he won a penalty after being scythed down in the area. Novo took the penalty himself and fired Rangers into a deserved lead. Pršo's goal doubled their advantage and Rangers were never in any danger of being pegged back.

As is so often the case in Old Firm games, the scoreline told only part of the story. Celtic's Alan Thompson was sent off for a head-butt on Peter Løvenkrands, and Chris Sutton also saw red for two yellow cards – the second the result of an inexplicable deliberate handball that he must surely have known would see him ordered off.

It was later reported that Løvenkrands had been set upon in the tunnel by two Celtic players as the teams left the pitch at half-time. Henri Camara was given a retrospective red card for an off-the-ball kick at Vignal, while Novo was also punished for a similar offence against Stephen Pearson, despite the Celtic midfielder insisting he thought the incident was accidental.

But the real moment of madness came at the end of the match when Martin O'Neill, having seen his team well beaten, marched onto the Ibrox pitch, grabbed Neil Lennon round the neck and paraded him in front of the Celtic support, fists clenched as if they had just secured a great victory. It was a provocative act after such a heated match, but the Rangers fans were too busy celebrating to be angered and instead laughed it off.

O'Neill later said he was showing solidarity with a player he felt had suffered a disproportionate amount of abuse, but it was a bizarre act and one which certainly diverted much of the attention away from his team's poor performance and ill discipline. Likewise, his comments a few days later accusing Rangers fans of 'racially' abusing Lennon were guaranteed to move the story even further away from Celtic's failings. As so often after Celtic defeats, the newspaper headlines focused on issues other than football, a phenomenon that had been highlighted seven years earlier by Walter Smith.

Having been seven points behind at one stage, Rangers had now narrowed the gap to just one, and by the time the next Old Firm league match came around in February, they were level on points and ahead on goal difference.

Remarkably, with Stefan Klos out injured, Barry Ferguson was the only player in the Rangers starting 11 that day who had played in a winning team at Parkhead before. The chance to play in Old Firm games again had been part of Ferguson's motivation in returning to Scotland, and he played a vital role in Rangers' victory on enemy soil. Alex McLeish considered Ferguson's experience crucial in getting the best out of his teammates.

As a result of Martin O'Neill's comments following the previous league clash, the fans were under the spotlight of the authorities and the media more than ever. Apparently prompted by the coverage, the then first minister, Jack McConnell, held a so-called 'summit on sectarianism', branding the issue Scotland's 'secret shame', although quite what was supposed to be secret about it was unclear given the amount of column inches and airtime devoted to the topic over the decades. With a sense of timing guaranteed to maximise publicity, the summit took place in Glasgow days before the game. It brought together representatives from 40 of Scotland's most prominent organisations, including the churches, sport, business, the media and government.

Ahead of the match, Rangers' head of security, Laurence Macintyre, issued a warning to the travelling support:

> The police match commander has made it absolutely clear that his strict enforcement policy, particularly in relation to breaches of the peace aggravated by religious prejudice, will not be relaxed. It is clear, following the First Minister's summit on sectarianism, that the media will be particularly interested in how both sets of fans behave.
>
> By all means shout and sing in support of the team, but please consider very carefully what it is you're actually saying. Alternatively, you face the risk of appearing on television in a manner that might embarrass you and your family.

Rangers chairman David Murray weighed in with his own contribution to the debate, dismissing Mr McConnell's criticism of the Old Firm clubs and their supporters over sectarianism as a 'knee-jerk reaction'.

In the end, it wasn't sectarian behaviour by fans that grabbed the headlines but missile throwing from Celtic supporters.

Amid all the talk of sectarianism and bigotry, it was easy to forget that a football match was to be played, and quite an important one at that. The build-up was dominated by two players: Barry Ferguson, playing in his first Old Firm game since his return to Ibrox, and Craig

Bellamy, the controversial Welsh international signed by Celtic on loan from Newcastle.

For Ferguson, this was a return to the environment he had missed so much during his time in England, and it was clear from the moment he strode out onto the Parkhead pitch that he was in his element. Any Rangers fans who doubted the wisdom of his signing would surely have accepted that, on footballing grounds at least, he was a valuable addition to the squad.

Bellamy, on the other hand, was a newcomer to the manic world of the Old Firm and it showed at times. Rangers fans directed chants of 'Souness, Souness' at him, a reminder of his falling-out with their former manager at Newcastle, which had resulted in his loan move. His pace undoubtedly posed some problems for the Rangers back line, but once the defence got to grips with his movement they were able to nullify his threat.

On the occasions when he did break free, Bellamy found himself thwarted by Rangers' new last line of defence, Ronald Waterreus. The Dutchman had been signed from Manchester City to replace Stefan Klos, who was out injured for the rest of the season with knee-ligament damage. Any doubts as to whether he had the mental strength to cope with the unique pressure of an Old Firm clash were soon dispelled.

If the game had been billed as a battle between Bellamy and Ferguson, it turned out to be a tale of two goalkeepers. Waterreus, on his Old Firm debut, played like a seasoned veteran of these clashes, while at the other end Rab Douglas made a horrendous gaffe that set Rangers on their way to victory.

A ticker-tape reception greeted the Rangers players as they emerged from the tunnel before kick-off, but it was Celtic who started the game the stronger of the two. After just five minutes, Bellamy's blistering pace took him away from the Rangers centre-back Marvin Andrews, but his low drive was stopped by Waterreus. The Welshman was frustrated again ten minutes later when he was sent clear by John Hartson only to see the goalkeeper narrow the angle and block his effort.

Celtic continued to press forward, with Rangers struggling to get any rhythm into their game, resorting to sending long, hopeful balls to Nacho Novo, who was never going to have any joy in the air against the giant opposition defenders.

With Rangers pinned back into their own half, it required a heroic performance from Kyrgiakos to keep the Celtic forwards at bay. The Greek international kept his more eccentric tendencies in check during an epic battle with Hartson and as a result maintained the upper hand for most of the match.

On the rare occasions when Hartson was able to break free of his shackles, Waterreus came to the rescue again. The goalkeeper made a superb point-blank save in the 24th minute when Celtic's centre-forward latched onto a flick by Bellamy. And in the 67th minute, he got away from Vignal only to see his shot saved again.

By that time, Rangers had worked their way back into the game and were looking the more likely. Ferguson and Fernando Ricksen were pulling the strings in midfield, and when they got the ball on the deck their crisp passing moves were proving difficult for Celtic to deal with.

The breakthrough came in the 71st minute, after a scrappy passage of play in which Celtic failed to clear their lines properly and repeatedly gave possession back to the attackers. The ball was eventually worked to Grégory Vignal, who hit a powerful shot from 25 yards. Although the shot was on target, it was close enough to Douglas for it to be a relatively easy save, but he got his footing wrong and failed to get his body behind the ball, and it squirmed agonisingly out of his grasp and into the net.

As Vignal raced to the Rangers dugout to celebrate, Douglas hung his head in the knowledge that he had handed Rangers a major advantage in the race for the title. With almost 20 minutes to go, the Light Blues were now firmly in control and looked far more likely to increase their lead than concede an equaliser.

Ten minutes later, Nacho Novo got the second, decisive goal when he chipped the ball over Douglas after Celtic failed to deal with a high ball down the centre from Ricksen. The build-up to the goal summed up Rangers' performance, with first Ferguson then Ricksen harrying their opponents in midfield and forcing them to surrender possession before turning defence into attack.

Before the match was over, Ricksen needed stitches to a head wound inflicted by an object hurled at him from the crowd. A hail of missiles had rained down on the Rangers captain as he waited to take a late corner, one of them striking him just above the eye. His 'crime' was to applaud the Rangers fans as they chanted his name. The scenes of Ricksen being treated, with blood pouring from the wound, rekindled memories of the 1999 Old Firm game in which referee Hugh Dallas had been hit by a coin. Strathclyde Police launched an investigation but no one was ever caught, despite footage from CCTV cameras being scoured and an appeal for fellow fans to shop the culprit.

Teammate Thomas Buffel, who was making his first Old Firm league appearance since signing from Feyenoord in January, was shocked at the attack on the Rangers captain. 'What happened to Fernando was not good,' he said. 'If the missile had been one centimetre to the side, he would have got it in the eye and could have been blinded. We were all worried, but he is a hard one, and he didn't go down, so we knew he would be OK. He is a tough guy and handled it well, but no one should be throwing missiles in football grounds.'

Rangers fan Colin Brown was at Parkhead that day, sitting in the main stand, surrounded by well-heeled Celtic supporters. He recalls, 'I couldn't get a ticket for the game, then at the last minute a pal who worked with a business connected to a sponsor phoned to ask if I wanted to go to hospitality with him. I jumped at the chance. It was supposed to be neutral, but I knew it would be mainly Celtic supporters around me.

'I reasoned that if it was going badly, I could always just leave, and if it was going well, I'd enjoy the discomfort of the home supporters. Either way, I couldn't lose, as I wasn't paying anyway! As it turned out, it was a very enjoyable afternoon.

'Once the game got into full swing, and especially after we scored, the guys around me in suits showed their true colours. It was all "dirty orange bastards", "f★★★ing Mason in the black" and the rest.

'I was quite surprised as I expected it to be much more restrained, although I can't say I was shocked. You hear a lot worse walking down Sauchiehall Street on a Saturday afternoon. What did shock me, though, was the missile throwing. Before the game, so much had been said and written about sectarian singing, mostly aimed at the Rangers supporters. You'd be forgiven for thinking the Celtic fans were angels. But this was out-and-out hooliganism.

'I witnessed more than one incident before Ricksen was hit, and while I know it's difficult to pick out one culprit from a big crowd, it amazed me that it seemed to be something that was expected to happen and nothing could be done to stop it. Especially when so much effort was being made by the police to arrest fans singing sectarian songs. Let's face it, Ricksen could have suffered a career-ending injury that day. Is that less important than a few dubious lyrics?

'Anyway, in the end we won the game and for me that was good enough. I had a great time, even though I had to sit on my hands and force myself to look miserable for 90 minutes.'

The victory gave Rangers a three-point advantage in the title race, although they had still played a game more than their rivals. Defeat would have made it difficult for Rangers to recover, but the win put them in pole position, although there were still plenty of twists and turns to come.

Two weeks after the Old Firm game, Rangers went to Edinburgh to face Hearts. With the scores level at 1–1, the visitors were awarded a last-minute penalty after the linesman Andy Davis advised the referee of a foul by Hearts' Lee Miller on Kyrgiakos. The kick was converted by Fernando Ricksen, giving Rangers a vital win. But the decision sparked chaotic scenes, with the Hearts midfielder Saulius Mikoliunas receiving a red card for barging into the linesman as the teams left the pitch and missiles raining down on the officials. Dado Pršo was also red-carded during the incident.

The following days saw a remarkable amount of coverage given to the decision, fuelled largely by comments coming out of the Hearts camp. There was no TV footage of the incident, but newspaper photographs were cited as incontrovertible evidence that there was no contact. Radio and newspaper phone-ins were dominated by the issue for days, with a succession of callers making wild claims of bias and cheating by officials. A surprising number of calls appeared to be coming from Hearts fans based in the west of Scotland, leading some to wonder whether some of the more paranoid rants were actually coming from supporters of another club. The furore soon passed, but not before the linesman concerned was subjected to an unpleasant character assassination and trial by media.

Both halves of the Old Firm continued to drop points and by the time the teams went into the league split with five games left, Celtic were back in the lead by two points. A 2–1 victory for Celtic at Ibrox appeared to have handed the championship to the Parkhead men, and their fans were convinced that it was all over. But there was much more drama to come.

The following week, Celtic lost to Hibs, while Rangers beat Aberdeen, meaning the gap was back to two points. However, with both clubs winning their next two games, it seemed that Rangers' chance had gone. Celtic needed only a victory in their last match away to Motherwell to win the league, no matter what Rangers did at Hibs.

Rangers duly did what they needed to by winning 1–0 at Easter Road through a goal by Nacho Novo. But with two minutes to go, Celtic were leading by the same scoreline at Fir Park and the SPL title was heading for Parkhead. Then, suddenly, everything changed. Motherwell equalised through Scott MacDonald, sparking bedlam in Edinburgh, and when he struck again with the last kick of the ball, it was all over. Rangers were champions, in what was the most dramatic ending to a season Scotland had ever seen.

24

· ·

MILLER TIME

CELTIC 2 RANGERS 4
SCOTTISH PREMIER LEAGUE
PLAYED AT CELTIC PARK, GLASGOW
30 AUGUST 2008

*Rangers team: McGregor, Broadfoot, Bougherra, Weir, Papac, Davis,
Thomson, Mendes, Adam, Miller, Cousin*

Rangers scorers: Cousin, Miller (2), Mendes

The banner waved by the Celtic fans was supposed to be mocking,
but in the end the joke was on them. The spoof of the US cartoon
series *South Park* featured a picture of the hooded character Kenny
dressed in a blue strip, with the words 'Oh My God, They've Signed
Kenny'.

The target of the sarcasm was Kenny Miller, a former Rangers
striker who had signed for Celtic and then left after what many
considered a less than successful season at Parkhead. Now, to the anger
of many Rangers fans and the obvious delight of some of their rivals,
he was back at Rangers and about to take part in his first match
against his old employers.

Miller's signing was probably the most controversial by Rangers
since Maurice Johnston was brought to Ibrox in 1989. He was the
first player in modern times to cross the great Old Firm divide not
once but twice. For fans who considered him a traitor for moving to

Parkhead having previously earned his crust at Ibrox, any move to bring him back again was seen as a massive slap in the face. The fact that many believed his time at Celtic was a failure simply added to the discontent.

Miller had been signed by Dick Advocaat in 2000 after an explosive start to his career at Hibs under Alex McLeish. Despite scoring five times in one SPL game against St Mirren and netting a Champions League goal against Monaco, he failed to make the anticipated impact at Ibrox and was eventually farmed out on loan. Ironically, one of McLeish's first jobs as manager was to sanction a permanent transfer to Wolverhampton Wanderers.

Miller flourished in the English Championship, helping his new team reach the Premier League in 2003, and also became a mainstay of the Scotland international team under first Berti Vogts and then Walter Smith. In the summer of 2006, much to the annoyance of some Celtic fans, Gordon Strachan took him to Parkhead on a Bosman, making him one of a handful of players to have appeared for both halves of the Old Firm since the Second World War.

For a striker, Miller's time at Celtic was not hugely prolific. He suffered a difficult start to his career there, failing to score in his first nine games. When he finally broke his duck, the goal predictably came against Rangers in September 2006. Despite receiving praise for his hard-working performances, Miller scored just four league goals in a season in which Celtic won the league comfortably and at the end of which there was speculation that he wanted to leave. He remained at Parkhead over the summer, but amid rumours of a falling-out with chairman Peter Lawwell he signed for Derby County early in the new season. Strachan later said he had not wanted the player to go, but it was clear his relationship with the club was beyond repair.

Miller's Derby career got off to a good start, but with his team looking increasingly like relegation candidates, he quickly expressed a desire to leave. Speculation immediately began that Walter Smith wanted to bring him to Rangers. It was no surprise that the Ibrox boss was interested in Miller. He had been a mainstay of his Scotland team, where he regularly played the lone-striker role that Smith often deployed at Rangers.

However, as the rumours of a return to Ibrox persisted, there was a growing sense of unease among certain elements of the Rangers support. Some fans expressed their view vocally during games, with the chant of 'You can shove your Kenny Miller up your arse' leaving the Rangers management team in little doubt about their feelings.

'I have to say I was personally dead against Miller being signed,' says supporter Colin Brown. 'Of course, the usual critics tried to turn the opposition into a sectarianism issue, which was just ridiculous. Football is all about rivalry, whether it's Rangers and Celtic, Real Madrid and Barcelona or Arbroath and Montrose. If you take that out of the game, what does it leave? I'm sure the same people who criticised us for being opposed to Miller's signing would have been full of praise for the passion of the Barcelona fans who chucked a pig's head at Luís Figo when he signed for Real Madrid.

'I would have had no problem with us signing any other ex-Celtic player. In fact, there was a lot of talk of Shaun Maloney coming from Aston Villa, which I was in favour of. But with Miller the point was that he had already slapped the supporters in the face by going to Celtic, so I had no wish to see him back in a light-blue jersey. To me, it was just an insult to even consider it.

'In football rivalry, there is nothing worse than a "Judas", or a turncoat, and anyone who doesn't understand that doesn't understand the mentality of the football fan. It might be illogical and irrational, but that is all part of the deal. If fans weren't illogical and irrational, why would they keep parting with their hard-earned cash every week when their team isn't winning?

'To add insult to injury, Miller had hardly set the heather alight at Celtic and he was seen by fans on both sides as a "reject". His scoring record throughout his career was hardly anything to write home about, so you're not exactly talking about Ally McCoist or Henrik Larsson here.'

Thoughts of Miller's impending return were put on the back burner as Rangers moved into the closing stages of the season. Defeat in the UEFA Cup final against Zenit St Petersburg in Manchester was followed days later by the loss of the league on the final day of the season to Celtic, amid controversy over a crippling fixture backlog.

Miller eventually did sign for Rangers for around £2 million in the summer of 2008, and his second Ibrox career got off to a similar start to his time at Celtic. By the time the first Old Firm game of the season came around, he had still not managed to find the net and had done little to win over the doubters.

All the pre-match hype focused on Miller, with attention drawn to the fact that he'd scored his first goal for Celtic against Rangers. Surely he couldn't repeat the feat at Parkhead? 'It would be really ironic if I got my first goal for Rangers against Celtic,' he told reporters at the pre-match press conference. 'I always want to score, but if I have to wait for it, then that's just the way it has to be.'

Nevertheless, football being football, plenty of pundits predicted that this would be the game in which Miller would finally hit the net. The player himself was smart enough to know that he would receive a hostile reception from the home support whatever happened . . . and that he could hardly count on the 100 per cent backing of his own team's fans. 'I probably won't know who it is who's booing me!' he said, before adding, 'I hope the Rangers fans get behind me, as I know this is the game they look for the team to do well in most. I've come back here in special circumstances and I always knew a few people would oppose the move. That was to be expected – but I really don't think they've been that bad so far. I think the majority have been fantastic and the negative reaction there has been from some hasn't hindered my performances.'

Miller's inclusion in the Rangers starting 11 was no surprise, but the identity of his strike partner was. Kris Boyd may have been the club's top scorer and the fans' favourite, but as evidenced by his signing of Miller, Walter Smith has never been one to make decisions based on supporter demands. The manager's view appeared to be that Boyd did not have the attributes required for the big games, whether in Europe or domestically, especially when he adopted the tactic of playing one up front on his own. On this occasion, although Smith opted for a 4-4-2 formation, there was no place for Boyd even on the bench.

Instead of Boyd or one of Rangers' other forwards, such as £3-million signing Kyle Lafferty, Nacho Novo or Jean-Claude Darcheville, Smith unexpectedly turned to Gabon international Daniel Cousin, a controversial figure who had made no secret of his desire to exploit a clause in his contract that meant he had to be allowed to leave if a bid of a certain amount came in.

Cousin's attitude was often questioned by fans, but when he was in the mood his undoubted talents gave Rangers a dimension to their game that no other player in the squad could offer. His power and ability in the air had caused a major headache for Celtic the previous season, literally in Stephen McManus's case. An accidental clash of heads between the two players during an Old Firm game a year earlier had left the Celtic defender unconscious.

But there was much more to Darcheville's game than simply winning headers, as he demonstrated when he broke the deadlock eight minutes before half-time. Up until that point, the match had been fairly even, with neither team being able to create much in the way of clear-cut chances.

Cousin had been involved in a physical battle with Gary Caldwell through the middle for most of the first half, but on this occasion he found himself wide on the right against the left-back Mark Wilson. A magnificent volleyed pass from Pedro Mendes released Cousin just inside the Celtic half and he utilised his pace, power and skill to drive past Wilson towards goal. As McManus tried to block his path, the striker unleashed a shot from six yards that beat Artur Boruc at his near post.

Celtic got themselves level within three minutes. The Rangers defence failed to cope with an Aiden McGeady cross that eventually found its way to Georgios Samaras, who shot past Allan McGregor from seven yards. But seven minutes into the second half, the moment so many predicted duly arrived: Kenny Miller's first goal for Rangers.

With Rangers attackers swarming all over their penalty area, Celtic failed to clear the danger and the ball was eventually worked out to Saša Papac on the left. He played it into the penalty area towards Cousin, who appeared to be bundled to the ground by a defender as he tried to make himself some space.

Before the referee had to make a decision, the ball broke to Kevin Thomson, who sent a looping cross to the back post, where Miller was waiting, unmarked. The ball dropped out of the sky perfectly for him and he sent a downward volley into the corner of the net from the angle of the six-yard box. If Boruc had been culpable at the first goal for allowing Cousin to beat him at his near post, then this time he had no chance.

Miller and his teammates celebrated in front of the Rangers fans, and whatever misgivings there had been about his signing were forgotten about, temporarily at least. The Celtic supporters who had mocked Miller before the game and booed his every touch were now silenced.

'For all that I had said about Miller not being wanted, there was a part of me that knew he was going to get a goal that day,' says Colin Brown, who was in the Rangers end that Sunday afternoon. 'And believe me, I celebrated that goal just as much as I would any other against Celtic. Mind you, when the ball came over to Miller I wasn't confident it was going to go anywhere near the goal! In fairness, he showed brilliant technique to hit the volley just right and put it into the right place.'

Ten minutes later and it got even better for the Rangers followers. Pedro Mendes, a Portuguese international signed from Portsmouth early in the season, had been outstanding in midfield, bringing a creativity that had been lacking the previous term. He came with a reputation for scoring spectacular goals, and he certainly lived up to that with his first strike for Rangers.

Rangers won a corner on the left, and as the Celtic defence prepared for an in-swinger from Steven Davis, they failed to spot Mendes lingering outside the penalty area. Instead of launching the corner into the box, the ever-alert Davis instead pushed it out to the Portuguese, who had plenty of time to steady himself for a shot before blasting it low into the net from 30 yards.

MILLER TIME

The two-goal cushion allowed Rangers to express themselves, much to the delight of the 7,500 fans crammed into their usual corner of Celtic Park. There was no doubt that Rangers had played the better football and that Smith's decision to play two strikers had paid dividends.

However, it wouldn't be an Old Firm derby without a twist, and it came in the 75th minute when Cousin was sent off after another aerial joust with McManus. Referee Dougie McDonald appeared to believe Cousin had led with his elbow and showed him a second yellow card, although TV pictures proved it was a harsh decision.

The sending-off could have had a significant impact on the outcome of the game had it not been for a moment of madness from Jan Vennegoor of Hesselink just moments later. The substitute had been on the pitch for only minutes when he lashed out at Rangers defender Kirk Broadfoot and was shown a straight red card. With Celtic's numerical advantage immediately negated, there was now no doubt about the outcome, and any lingering uncertainty was dismissed with ten minutes to go when Rangers went 4–1 up. Miller again scored the goal, but this time it was a personal disaster for Boruc. He spilled a Broadfoot cross into the path of his former teammate, who prodded the ball over the line.

Much to the amusement of the Rangers fans, the Polish goalkeeper responded to their inevitable taunts with a single-fingered salute. The gesture was caught on camera and plastered all over the following day's papers, resulting in the SFA launching disciplinary action.

It was hardly the first time Boruc had found himself at the centre of controversy over his antics, and more often than not it was against Rangers that he decided to play up. The £500 fine he received for the gesture seemed somewhat derisory to some, given his track record.

His first brush with the authorities had come when he was cautioned by Strathclyde Police for indecent gestures made towards Rangers fans during a match at Ibrox in February 2006. Inaccurate claims that he had been rapped for blessing himself received widespread and damaging coverage throughout the UK and beyond, fanned by ill-informed politicians and attempts to turn the goalkeeper into a cause célèbre.

The following May, after a 2–0 defeat at Ibrox, Boruc found himself facing criticism again when he took a 'Champions' flag from the Celtic supporters and ran across the pitch with it. The next season, he refused to shake hands with Rangers players following another Ibrox defeat, explaining in a newspaper interview that he didn't like the club or its players. Then, after an Old Firm game at Parkhead in May 2008, he stripped off his jersey to reveal a 'God Bless the Pope' T-shirt.

His off-field antics were also landing him in trouble with his club and national team, and it appeared that his increasingly bizarre behaviour was reflected in erratic performances on the pitch. Needless to say, Boruc's behaviour at Old Firm games had endeared him to his own team's fans, but having once been a hate figure for Rangers supporters, his repeated gaffes meant he was fast becoming a figure of fun for them.

Boruc-baiting was only part of the fun for the light-blue legions as they celebrated a famous victory. It was the first time any visiting team had scored four goals at Parkhead since Rangers did it on New Year's Day 1994. Shunsuke Nakamura's last-minute free kick was little consolation to the home supporters, most of whom had already left the stadium by the time the ball hit the net. The ironic cheers from the away end drowned out the shouts from the Celtic fans.

After the match, Miller came in for much praise for his goalscoring performance and his mental strength in not allowing the mild hysteria that surrounded his appearance to affect his game. Rangers assistant manager Ally McCoist went so far as to compare Miller with his former teammate Johnston. 'It was brilliant for Kenny to score twice against Celtic and it brings back memories of Mo Johnston nearly 20 years ago,' said McCoist. 'The thing about Mo and Kenny is that they are both terrific players and good team players. And when you work as hard as they do, then you are always going to win the fans over.'

The aftermath of the game brought the usual post-Old Firm fallout. Among the incidents was an assault on a 29 year old who was set upon by a gang of Celtic supporters at Singer station in Glasgow.

The four assailants pursued their victim as he tried to make his escape on a train and continued the attack until they reached the next station. British Transport Police said the victim was left with a broken jaw.

Another incident, which took place several hours later, received far more media coverage. Former Celtic captain Neil Lennon, now a coach at the club, was set upon in the street in the early hours, having been out in Glasgow's West End. His two attackers were later jailed for two years each after being found guilty by a majority verdict at the city's Sheriff Court. Part of the charge – that the attack was aggravated by religious prejudice – was deleted. The attackers, who told the court they were Rangers fans, did not deny getting into a fight with Lennon.

The victory gave Rangers a three-point advantage over Celtic early in the season, but, having won the opening derby of the previous season, Walter Smith and his players were not fooled into thinking the title was already in the bag. Indeed, after a 1–0 home defeat in the second Old Firm match of the season two days after Christmas, Rangers fell seven points behind. By February, when the rivals fought out a goalless draw at Parkhead, the points gap had shrunk to two.

Going into the final meeting of the season on 9 May, Rangers were a single point behind and knew that victory would give them a two-point cushion with three games left. In front of 50,321 at Ibrox, a well-worked goal from Steven Davis in the 36th minute secured the vital win.

Kris Boyd played in Kenny Miller at the edge of the penalty area and he drove into the box, before picking out Davis, who had made a supporting run into the box. Davis slid in and put the ball into the net with his right foot from just a few feet. His momentum carried the Northern Ireland international into the back of the net, where he began his celebrations in front of the visiting fans.

Rangers soaked up Celtic pressure in the second half but could have increased their lead when Kris Boyd broke through on goal with only Boruc to beat. The striker's shot was saved, but in the end it had no bearing on the result as Rangers held on to their single-goal lead and took a massive step towards the title. The championship, the first in four years, was finally secured on the last day of the season, when Rangers beat Dundee United 3–0 at Tannadice while Celtic were held 0–0 by Hearts at home.

But while the league wasn't officially won until the final day, the two wins over Celtic – one at the start and one at the end of the season – made a massive contribution to the outcome. And after the heartbreak of the previous campaign, the Rangers fans could now enjoy a triumph they felt should have been theirs 12 months earlier.

25

IT AIN'T WHAT EDU ...

RANGERS 1 CELTIC 0
SCOTTISH PREMIER LEAGUE
PLAYED AT IBROX STADIUM, GLASGOW
28 FEBRUARY 2010

Rangers team: McGregor, Whittaker, Papac, Bougherra, Weir, Davis,
Thomson, McCulloch, Lafferty, Miller, Boyd

Rangers scorer: Edu (sub)

It would be fair to say the global significance of the Old Firm probably bypassed Maurice Edu as he grew up in California. It's unlikely that the monumental tussles that gripped Glasgow in the '90s and early 2000s made much impact on life in his particular corner of the Golden State, where basketball, American football and baseball continue to dominate.

When he signed for Rangers in the summer of 2008, Edu quickly came to understand that he was part of something big, but it wasn't until his last-minute winner against Celtic almost two years later that he fully grasped the enormity of the Old Firm phenomenon.

Texts, emails and phone calls flooded in from all corners of the globe to congratulate him on his strike, which all but guaranteed a second successive title for Rangers. But the moment it really hit home came during an international trip to Amsterdam for a friendly between the US national side and Holland.

FOLLOW, FOLLOW

In an interview with *Rangers News*, Edu said:

> What I did has reached out to more people than I
> expected it would. When we were over in Holland, for
> example, a few people talked to me about the game. Ryan
> Babel [of Liverpool and Holland] was one of them and he
> congratulated me on my goal. Back home in the States, a
> lot of fans saw the game on ESPN. It's been tremendous
> as there has been so much support for Rangers to the
> extent it has been global.
>
> I knew before the derby how big a club this is and I
> was aware the support we had was worldwide. But until
> something like that goal happens and so many people
> show their support for you, I don't think you fully grasp
> the whole situation. It has been unreal and it has made
> me feel proud to be a part of something so big and so
> special.

Born just three days after Walter Smith was appointed Graeme Souness's
deputy at Rangers in 1986, Edu is the epitome of the modern-day
footballer. A tall, powerful midfielder, he is a dedicated athlete, speaks
intelligently about the game and understands fully what is expected of
him as a professional sportsman, on and off the pitch.

Like most other people of his generation, Edu shares the
minutiae of his life on Twitter and Facebook, and in an era when
the vast salaries earned by footballers make them untouchable to
the average supporter, this makes him come across as more 'normal'
than other players. As a result, he is a hugely popular figure among
the Rangers fans. The downside of this celebrity status is that he
has become a target for the tabloids, and occasionally the candour
of some of his tweets has generated unwanted headlines.

Of course, for all the column inches, paparazzi snaps and Twitter
posts, it is what a player does on the pitch that really matters. Edu
suffered a faltering start to his Rangers career. He managed to
break his way into the team towards the end of the 2008–09 season

and played an important part in winning the title. But on the final day, he suffered a knee injury that kept him out for several months, meaning he missed a large chunk of the following season.

For the second season running, it wasn't until the closing weeks that he was able to play a part, mostly from the bench. Having started Rangers' previous match in the Scottish Cup against St Mirren, Edu found himself relegated to substitute for the crucial Old Firm game on the last day of February.

But a first-half injury to midfielder Lee McCulloch meant the American was given an early opportunity to make his mark, and, but for a controversial refereeing decision, he might well have made one of the most sensational Old Firm arrivals ever. With his first touch, just seconds after taking to the field, he struck a long-range volley beyond Artur Boruc into the net. But as the Rangers players and fans celebrated, referee Dougie McDonald disallowed the goal. During the build-up, the ball had broken off Kenny Miller's arm, although whether it was deliberate and merited a free kick was debatable.

Edu and Rangers would eventually get their goal, and it would take them ten points clear in the league table. But it was inevitable that refereeing decisions would come under the spotlight during the game.

Four days earlier, BBC Scotland ran a story based around quotes from an anonymous Celtic source highlighting the club's apparent concerns with refereeing standards in Scotland, specifically relating to major decisions they felt had gone against them and suggesting the club intended to make a formal complaint to the SFA.

Celtic were unhappy with decisions made in both their meetings with Rangers earlier in the season. When they lost 2–1 at Ibrox in October, they had a strong penalty appeal turned down by referee Craig Thomson, who later admitted he had got it wrong. And during the 1–1 draw in January, Tony Mowbray's team felt hard done by when Steve Conroy ruled Marc-Antoine Fortuné had fouled Rangers keeper Allan McGregor when heading into the net. Television replays showed there had been contact before Fortuné got his head to the ball.

In the BBC Scotland report, the Celtic source was quoted as saying: 'We are considering contacting the SFA to highlight our concerns at some of the major decisions we feel have gone against us this season. The refereeing performances are a concern and a frustration to us.'

While there had been widespread coverage of poor decisions during the season and an admission from the SFA that standards hadn't been as high as they would have hoped, there was nothing to suggest that Celtic had suffered any more than any other team. There were plenty who took the view that the complaints about referees were designed simply to draw attention away from Celtic's poor performances under their new manager, Tony Mowbray. He had taken over from Gordon Strachan in the summer, having previously been manager at Hibernian and then West Bromwich Albion, where he had forged a reputation for creating teams that played attacking football, and he arrived at Parkhead promising a similar approach.

But results are everything at the Old Firm and, however attractive their play might have been, Celtic were dropping too many points. By the time the February clash at Ibrox came around, they had lost five games and drawn six and were seven points behind, having played a game more. Defeat to Rangers would only increase the pressure Mowbray was under from fans and the media.

The timing of the story also led many to see it as a cynical attempt to put additional pressure on Dougie McDonald. The SFA's chairman, George Peat, described the comments by the unnamed source as 'ill-timed and fundamentally inaccurate', adding that he found it 'disappointing and somewhat bizarre' that someone at the club would 'seek to exert additional pressure on match officials'.

Former Celtic captain and manager Billy McNeill added fuel to the fire by claiming the club had been the victim of refereeing injustices for more than 50 years, the implication being that there was an institutional bias against Celtic that had seen officials conspire against them for decades. Such talk tapped into the paranoia that is rife among some Celtic supporters, but worse than that, it heaped even more pressure on the man taking charge of the weekend's game.

The attacks on Hugh Dallas and his family home in 1999 and the victimisation of other officials deemed to have made 'anti-Celtic' decisions, such as Mike McCurry and Andy Davis, demonstrated only too vividly what could happen when supporters took their obsession with referees too far.

Dougie McDonald insisted he was perfectly able to cope with the pressure of handling an Old Firm game, despite the added scrutiny that was sure to come his way as a result of the controversy stirred up by the story. In a feature on the SFA website a couple of days before the game, he acknowledged that the Old Firm 'feeding frenzy' meant his performance would be analysed even more than usual:

> You are aware it is the biggest game in the country and the TV coverage is much greater but you have the added aspect of phone-ins, websites and other media outlets. It is a constant feeding frenzy but, as Ally McCoist said recently, the refereeing and decision-making hasn't changed much – it's the exposure that is far greater.

For all his pre-match confidence, it would be surprising if the previous week's controversy did not cross McDonald's mind even briefly as he blew the whistle to get the game under way. Certainly, he seemed determined to stamp his authority on the match, issuing early yellow cards to Madjid Bougherra and Marc-Antoine Fortuné.

Someone else determined to make his mark early in the game was the Rangers midfielder Kevin Thomson. In his five previous Old Firm games, he had been on the winning side every time and his combative style was perfectly suited to the hurly-burly of the derby. Minutes into the game, he had launched into two thunderous, but perfectly fair, tackles on Celtic's expensive loan signing Robbie Keane that set the tone for his performance.

Republic of Ireland captain Keane had been signed on deadline day amid great fanfare, with hundreds of Celtic fans turning out at Parkhead to celebrate his arrival. Despite the fact that their team was trailing Rangers badly in the league, many fans reckoned he would be the catalyst for a Celtic revival and would drive them to the title.

In fact, by the time his first Old Firm game came around, the gap between Rangers and Celtic had actually widened by three points, and it was beginning to look like his reputed £65,000 weekly wage had been a hugely expensive mistake.

Keane actually had an early chance to score on his derby debut, when a rare mistake by Saša Papac after just 30 seconds was pounced on by Fortuné. His low cutback gave Keane a clear shooting opportunity, but he failed to make a decent connection and his shot was comfortably saved by Allan McGregor. Shortly afterwards came Thomson's tackles, which left Keane begging forlornly for greater protection. A half-chance later in the first period, which was again saved by McGregor, was the former Tottenham striker's only other significant contribution to the match. He was well policed by Thomson, Bougherra and Papac, and he looked a shadow of the player who had been one of the English Premier League's leading lights.

Thomson's first challenge on Keane sparked Rangers into action and they came close to opening the scoring moments later. A fine pass from Steven Davis picked out Kris Boyd, who charged into the Celtic penalty area. He took the ball round Boruc, but from a very tight angle he could only drive the ball into the side net.

Later, Boyd turned provider when his pass through the middle cut the Celtic defence apart and released Kenny Miller. He shrugged off the attentions of two Celtic defenders, but his shot was blocked by Boruc.

Four minutes into the second half and the referee was again called on to make a big decision. Steven Whittaker played an excellent pass in to Kris Boyd, who was well tackled just as he was about to release his shot. The ball broke to Edu, who was bundled over by Andreas Hinkel seven yards out, but Dougie McDonald ruled there was no foul and the danger was cleared.

Rangers stepped up their game in the second half, and on 55 minutes Boruc was forced to make a double save to deny Davis. Ten minutes later came another moment of controversy when Celtic's captain, Scott Brown, was sent off for head-butting Kyle Lafferty in the chest. The two players had been grappling with each other and some referees would have been tempted to simply give them both a ticking-off and continue the game. But McDonald clearly saw Brown's actions as overly aggressive and decided he deserved a straight red card. Given all that had gone before the game, it was – as Sir Humphrey used to say to Jim Hacker in *Yes, Minister* – a brave decision, although justifiable by the rules of the game.

By then, Rangers had already imposed themselves on the game and looked by far the likelier team to score. A draw would have suited the home team, but Walter Smith's men knew a victory would all but guarantee two in a row and they went for the jugular.

Edu, who was increasingly finding himself in attacking positions, came close at 82 minutes when he half-volleyed a shot over the bar following a cross from Papac on the left. But the American made no mistake in an incredible finale.

Three minutes into injury time, Rangers won a corner on the left after Boruc dived to keep out a Papac cross. Thomson's out-swinging corner was half-cleared, but only as far as the edge of the penalty area, where Bougherra took it down on his chest before driving a fierce shot at goal. It was straight at Boruc, but the goalkeeper spilled it and the ball fell to Boyd, whose attempt to bundle it over the line was thwarted by a combination of Boruc and Landry N'Guémo.

Eventually, the ball broke to Edu and, from three yards out and with the goal gaping, he had the easiest of tasks in tapping it over the line. The goal sparked wild celebrations on the pitch, in the Ibrox stands and in the dugout or, more accurately, outside the dugout. Even the normally restrained Walter Smith was out of his seat and haring down the track to join in the celebrations with the rest of his backroom team.

There was no time for any Celtic comeback and as the final whistle blew seconds later, everyone inside Ibrox, blue or green, knew that Edu's was the goal that had just won Rangers their 53rd league flag.

Lee McCulloch's first-half injury meant he had been forced to watch most of the game on TV in the dressing-room. But like the rest of his teammates, he had been fired up for the match. He remembers, 'We had the whole Robbie Keane hysteria because he was making his debut, but the Rangers players were right up for the game. Right from the first kick, our boys were flying into tackles. Then we started getting the ball down on the ground and passing it. I took the ball down on my chest and I think Kevin Thomson kicked me slightly, and the next thing I just felt my ankle roll. I thought the ligaments had gone and even though I wanted to play on, I obviously had to come off.

'I couldn't even go back out to the dugout to watch the rest of the match because I had to have the ankle in ice, so I was kicking every ball as I watched it on telly. For Mo to score the winner in the last minute was just brilliant. A few of the security guards and the masseur who was looking after me came running in and were jumping all over me after the goal. Words just can't describe the feeling properly.'

Inevitably, there was plenty of focus after the game on Scott Brown's red card, with Celtic immediately launching an appeal against the decision, which was subsequently rejected. A statement on the official Celtic website hours after the defeat appeared to question McDonald's impartiality over the decision, stating 'any fair-minded person looking at the incident at the time or subsequent TV replays could see it wasn't a red card'. Given that McDonald obviously did consider it a sending-off, the clear inference was that Celtic believed the referee was not 'fair-minded'.

Unsurprisingly, the refereeing row infuriated Walter Smith, as he once again saw his team's achievements overshadowed by other issues. He had refused to get involved in discussions about officials before the match, but afterwards he launched a scathing attack on the source behind the BBC story. 'It would have been nice if whoever complained, or wanted to complain, had come out of the closet to do it, rather than in an anonymous manner,' he said in his post-match press conference.

The victory was Smith's twenty-sixth against Celtic in his two periods as manager, and so often had those victories been followed by controversy over one thing or another that it was understandable that he felt the need to voice his frustration.

Rangers fan Colin Brown sees the Celtic reaction as nothing more than bad sportsmanship: 'I applauded Walter Smith for speaking out. For too long, it's simply been accepted that when Celtic lose to Rangers it is evidence of some massive conspiracy against them. Obviously the media have an interest in stoking it up because it provides great copy and sells more papers, but for me it just undermines the credibility of the game.

'Of course, we only hear about the terrible decisions that go against Celtic, not the ones that go in their favour. Lee McCulloch had what looked like a perfectly good goal ruled out in a derby at Ibrox in 2007. It would have made the final score 4–0, and with the title race so tight that could have made all the difference. Imagine if Celtic had won the league by one goal . . . then imagine if the roles were reversed and it was Celtic who had the goal chopped off and Rangers won the league. There would be questions in Parliament and cases being brought to the European Court of Human Rights. We just get on with it because we know that there is no conspiracy – just bad luck, bad decisions and bad performances.'

Rangers had proved over the course of the season that they were by far the best team in the country, despite the fact that the management team were operating under stringent financial restraints. Smith had not been able to sign a player since bringing Maurice Edu in at the start of the 2008–09 season but had still managed to land two consecutive titles.

In fact, his record since taking over from Paul Le Guen in January 2007 was quite remarkable. Under Smith, and his assistants Ally McCoist and Kenny McDowall, Rangers had won six domestic trophies, including two SPL titles, and reached a European final. In his first full season in charge, they were beaten to the league only on the last day, having been forced to play nine games, including a UEFA Cup final, in twenty-four days.

Given his success over the preceding two years, it was easy to see why he reacted angrily again, when, ahead of the final Old Firm clash of the season, the German full-back Andreas Hinkel claimed that Celtic were better than Rangers. Smith pointed out that during the same spell in which his team had been so successful, Celtic had won just two trophies. 'I have to ask Hinkel if he's been proud of the way his team's played over that period,' said Smith. 'I know I'm proud of my players and how they've done. If Hinkel's going to make comments like that about us, then he should have a look at himself first before he opens his mouth. It's patently obvious that Celtic are not a better team than Rangers and that's because our approach and attitude have been better than theirs.'

Attitude. It's the word that sums up both of Walter Smith's periods as Rangers manager, especially in matches against Celtic. Over the years, he often saw his teams outplayed by their city rivals, but they were rarely found lacking in application. That is why, even in matches during which Rangers were on the back foot for long periods, more often than not they found the resolve to salvage something from the game.

The match that followed Andreas Hinkel's comments ended in a 2–1 defeat for Rangers, but with the league already won and Celtic secure in second place, there was nothing at stake for either team.

That's not to say the match was meaningless. It is a cliché, but there is no such thing as a meaningless Old Firm clash. Celtic were desperate for victory to salvage some pride from a shambolic campaign and provide evidence that they would be capable of overcoming Rangers in the season ahead. Meanwhile, Smith would have been determined not to give his rivals any crumb of comfort or encouragement for the future. Defeat means weeks of misery for the fans, while a victory gives the opportunity for some serious gloating.

26

TWENTY GREAT OLD FIRM GOALS

1. Davie Cooper, Drybrough Cup final, August 1979. Rangers 3 Celtic 1

It says much about the quality of this goal that despite the fact that it was scored in a relatively obscure pre-season competition, the fans voted it the greatest-ever Rangers goal in 1999. If all the Rangers supporters who have since claimed to have been at the Drybrough Cup final that August afternoon to see it in person are to believed, Hampden would have been filled three times over. As it was, there was a crowd of 40,000 to see Rangers lift the trophy after a 3–1 win.

Frustratingly, the only pictures in existence hardly do it justice. The grainy images were apparently shot on a Super 8 camera by someone sitting at ground level behind the goal line. As a permanent record of one of the most memorable moments in Old Firm history, it leaves something to be desired. Compared to today's high-definition TV coverage, it's more home movie than home cinema, but somehow that just adds to the aura surrounding the goal.

The goal itself was Cooper at his mesmerising best. The move started with a chipped cross from the right from Alex MacDonald. From then on, it was all Cooper. Eight yards out and with his back to goal, he controlled the ball with his chest, pushing it back towards the edge of the penalty area, away from the defender tight on his back.

Without letting the ball touch the ground, he flicked it high into the air with his left foot, allowed it to bounce once, then hooked his foot round the ball, in the same movement spinning away from his marker. By now, other Celtic players were alert to the danger and two lunged in on the winger. But with another deft flick of his left foot, he dinked it over both of them, and before the ball landed, chipped it over the head of a fourth onrushing defender. He then brought it down with his chest and from seven yards slotted it past the goalkeeper.

Teammate John MacDonald recalled later, 'That was my first Old Firm game and it was the best goal I ever saw. It was brilliant. But I still wish I had pushed him out of the road, because I had been waiting for ages for a pass.'

In 2008, listeners to Real Radio's football phone-in voted it the best Scottish goal ever.

2. Ray Wilkins, Premier Division, August 1988.
Rangers 5 Celtic 1

For power, accuracy and technique, it would be difficult to better this spectacular strike by Ray Wilkins. The England international arrived at Ibrox with the disparaging nickname 'The Crab' because of his supposed tendency to move only sideways across the pitch. But in his time at Rangers he proved that he was a midfielder of class and creativity, and he played a vital role in the championship-winning season of 1988–89, the first of nine in a row.

Probably his finest moment in the light blue was this goal in a 5–1 demolition. Rangers having gone behind to an early goal, Ally McCoist equalised and took command of the game, with 32-year-old Wilkins pulling the strings.

Nine minutes before half-time, a long throw into the penalty area from right-back Gary Stevens was headed on by Terry Butcher. It was headed out of the penalty area by a defender, but the ball went only as far as Wilkins. He met it perfectly from 20 yards and volleyed a tremendous shot past goalkeeper Ian Andrews into the net.

The goal helped cement Wilkins' place in the hearts of the Rangers fans, and when he left during the following season he received an emotional send-off. 'It was a pleasure to play for that support,' Wilkins told the *Daily Mirror* in 1997. 'And the games against Celtic will be etched in my memory banks for ever.' He continued:

> I was an outsider, born in London, but it is impossible not to get caught up in these occasions. The fervour is something else. I remember when I scored one of my rare goals in our 5–1 win over them in 1988 at Ibrox. I slammed in a first-time drive past Ian Andrews and was astonished when one half of the ground erupted and the other went absolutely silent. A fascinating sensation, believe me.

Seven years later, Wilkins returned to Ibrox as a forty-year-old Hibs player and was given a standing ovation by the home fans. And in 2007, fellow Englishman Ugo Ehiogu, who was at Rangers at the time, commented on the continued impact of that goal. He told the *Evening Times*:

> Ray Wilkins was up at Ibrox recently to do the half-time draw. He was announced to the crowd as having scored a goal in a 5–1 win in 1988. That was nearly 20 years ago. I suppose it just shows you how important scoring a goal in a win against Celtic is to Rangers fans.

3. Bert Konterman, League Cup semi-final, February 2002. Rangers 2 Celtic 1

Bert Konterman was an unlikely Old Firm hero. He arrived at Rangers in the summer of 2000, fresh from the European Championships, where he'd been part of the Netherlands squad. His international credentials and the price tag of more than £4 million led Rangers fans to believe he was going to be a top-class centre-half. Sadly, it didn't work out that way. He struggled from the beginning and was widely derided – his cause not helped by some of the bizarre comments he made in interviews and on his personal website.

Konterman started to show signs of improvement when he was moved into midfield, and he played there in the League Cup semi-final against Celtic at Hampden in 2002. Rangers had lost five consecutive games against Celtic but had embarked on a sixteen-match unbeaten run under new manager Alex McLeish. Rangers had been the better team, but the 90 minutes finished with the teams level at 1–1 and the match went into extra time.

Shortly before the end of the first period, Konterman picked the ball up and played it to Shota Arveladze. He lost control, but the ball broke loose to Konterman. From almost 30 yards, he struck it magnificently and the ball rocketed into the top corner, leaving Rab Douglas grasping at thin air. Rangers held on to the lead and went on to beat Ayr United 4–0 in the final.

Konterman later told *The Herald*:

> That goal is a fantastic legacy to leave behind. It's crazy how you can be remembered for one thing, but it made a huge impact among the supporters. Things had been really difficult for us until that point but it really set us up, when you look back on it now. I still get photographs of the goal from fans wanting me to sign it. In terms of importance, it was the best goal I have ever scored.

4. Willie Henderson, Scottish Cup quarter-final, March 1964. Rangers 2 Celtic 0

Rangers' classic team of the early '60s were sweeping all before them on their way to a treble when they met Celtic at Ibrox in the quarter-final of the Scottish Cup. They had already beaten their city rivals four times in the season, scoring nine goals and conceding just one, so they were hot favourites to progress in the cup.

In front of 85,000, Rangers took the lead a minute before half-time through a close-range diving header from Jim Forrest, but it was the second goal, from winger Willie Henderson a minute after the restart, that would live long in the memory.

John Greig started the move after breaking up a Celtic attack deep inside the Rangers half. He hooked a 60-yard pass to Forrest, who laid it back to Henderson just inside the Celtic half. The winger then set off on a dazzling 50-yard run through the heart of opposition territory, easing effortlessly past defenders before pushing the ball into the penalty area. As two more Celtic men closed in on him, he blasted it past Fallon into the net from fifteen yards.

Almost as memorable as the goal were the celebrations. After being mobbed by his own players, the little Number 7 stood in the middle of the pitch, arms outstretched, taking the adulation of the crowd. The only trouble was, he was saluting the away support!

Henderson said later, 'A television company asked me to do a rerun of the moves in that goal. They took me onto the park at Ibrox and when I actually stood and looked at where I had run from I said "I must have been some player!" And then when I scored it I went straight to the Celtic end. But my eyesight was never the best ...'

5. Barry Ferguson, Scottish Cup final, May 2002.
Rangers 3 Celtic 2

Despite having the better of the game, Rangers had fallen 2–1 behind to their Old Firm rivals in the cup final. Twenty minutes into the second half, Lorenzo Amoruso was barged to the ground by Bobo Baldé and a free kick was awarded.

Despite having no prior reputation as a dead-ball expert, Rangers captain Barry Ferguson stepped up to take the kick. He curled it into the top left corner of the net, giving Douglas no chance. The strike was likened to David Beckham's dramatic last-minute goal against Greece a few months earlier, which took England to the World Cup finals, and the comparisons didn't end there.

Both Ferguson and Beckham had put in magnificent individual midfield performances to drive their respective teams towards triumph. Rangers went on to win the cup with a last-minute goal from Peter Løvenkrands.

6. Jonas Thern, SPL, April 1998. Rangers 2 Celtic 0

Rangers desperately needed a victory to keep alive their bid to win a tenth successive league title, and Jonas Thern's thunderous volley helped them achieve their target. The win, in the last Old Firm derby of Walter Smith's first term as Rangers manager, took the Ibrox side back to the top of the Premier Division table by one goal. It was also their second victory over Celtic in a week, after beating them in the Scottish Cup semi-final the previous weekend.

Celtic were gaining the upper hand in the Ibrox clash without seriously troubling the Rangers goal when Thern unleashed his shot after 25 minutes. Defender Marc Rieper's headed clearance from a Lorenzo Amoruso free kick went straight towards the Swede, who was standing unmarked 25 yards out.

He watched the ball intently as it came towards him, allowing it to bounce once before hammering it back towards goal. Keeper Jonathan Gould threw himself across the goal in a desperate attempt to keep the ball out, but he had no chance of stopping the shot and the ball flashed past him into the top corner. Jörg Albertz added a second in the sixty-sixth minute to seal the win.

It was Thern's fourth goal in five games and he joked at the time, 'Something must be wrong. I was very pleased with the goal, because it came at exactly the right time, when Celtic were playing a bit better than us. I think some of my recent goals have been very good, but this was one of the most important goals I've ever scored.'

In the end, the victory wasn't enough for Rangers to secure the much-sought-after record of ten consecutive title victories, with Celtic winning the league on the last day of the season.

7. Pedro Mendes, SPL, September 2009. Celtic 2 Rangers 4

Pedro Mendes will always be the player who scored the infamous Goal That Never Was. But his magnificent strike at Parkhead for Rangers against Celtic, in only his second appearance for the club, ensured that he will be remembered by the Ibrox legions for a goal that definitely did count.

Playing for Spurs, Mendes was the victim of one of English football's most controversial incidents of the last twenty years, when his speculative shot from fifty yards was fumbled over the line by Manchester United goalkeeper Roy Carroll. The goal was not given because officials deemed the ball did not cross the line, although TV replays clearly showed it should have stood.

Mendes came to Rangers with a reputation for scoring spectacular goals, and he lived up to that with his first strike in the sixty-second minute of his Old Firm debut. In what appeared to be a training-ground move, Steven Davis played a corner to the edge of the penalty area, where Mendes was lurking unmarked. He steadied himself before driving a shot low into the net from 30 yards that gave Artur Boruc no chance.

The goal put Rangers 3–1 ahead and they eventually went on to win 4–2. The victory was an early boost to the Light Blues' title hopes, and Walter Smith's men eventually went on to land their first championship in four years.

'That was one of my best; it was a good goal,' Mendes said later. 'It was a special one and a beautiful one because it was my first Old Firm game. To score in that game was important for me and because it was our third goal, it helped the team to settle a little bit.'

8. Kai Johansen, Scottish Cup final replay, April 1966. Rangers 1 Celtic 0

Danish defender Kai Johansen's goal won Rangers the Scottish Cup in 1966 and won him the title 'King Kai'. With his powerful strike 20 minutes from the end of the replay, he wrote himself into the history books as the first foreigner to score the winner in a cup final and gave Rangers, who had gone into the final as underdogs, their 19th triumph in the competition.

The strike that flashed past Ronnie Simpson was of the highest quality in itself, but the move that led to the goal was equally impressive. The build-up began on the right with Willie Henderson before John Greig took over and drove forward into the Celtic half.

He released a pass to Willie Johnston on the left-hand side and the winger weaved past three defenders before cutting it back across the penalty area. The ball ran through to Henderson, who had continued his run to the back post, and he hit in a shot that was cleared off the line by a defender.

The ball rebounded into the path of Johansen, who was lurking just outside the penalty area. He brought the ball under control, carried it forward to the edge of the 18-yard box and then thrashed an unstoppable shot into the net.

William Allison's official history *Rangers: The New Era* described in colourful terms the reaction to the goal:

> In one blinding flash, more than half of Hampden became
> a deliriously happy, singing chorus to a background of blue.
> Staid old men were on their feet cheering, ignoring their
> blood pressure in the majesty and drama of the moment,
> while the youngsters went hoarse as they added their
> hosannas.

It was the last trophy Rangers would win for almost five years.

9. Ugo Ehiogu, SPL, April 2007. Celtic 0 Rangers 1

Veteran defender Ugo Ehiogu was Rangers' unlikely match-winner at Parkhead in a game that meant little in the championship race but laid down a marker for the following season. The former England international's spectacular overhead kick brought about Celtic's first home league defeat for 16 months and won him the club's goal of the season award.

Ehiogu had been signed to stiffen up the Rangers defence in January, along with fellow veteran Davie Weir. Walter Smith had returned as Rangers manager the same month, after the short and unsuccessful reign of Paul le Guen.

Rangers had been on the back foot in the first half, but four minutes after the break Ehiogu put Rangers into the lead with a goal that was as extravagant as it was unexpected. Celtic failed to clear a Charlie

Adam corner and after a sequence of headers the ball fell to Ehiogu, who hit an acrobatic overhead kick. Goalkeeper Artur Boruc could only push the ball against the crossbar on its way into the net.

Rangers took control of the game and rarely looked like relinquishing their lead. At the end, the clearly frustrated Celtic captain Neil Lennon reacted to a comment from a home fan by hurling a plastic bottle into an empty dugout.

After the game, Ehiogu told reporters, 'It was incredible. To score in such dramatic fashion to decide my first Old Firm game – I couldn't have written a better script. It was probably my best goal ever. It was one of those surreal moments. I thought the keeper had actually saved it because I saw him get a hand to it. It wasn't until I heard the roar that I realised that it had crept in.'

10. Ralph Brand, Scottish Cup final replay, May 1963. Rangers 3 Celtic 0

The 1963 Scottish Cup final replay is often remembered as Jim Baxter's final, the night the Rangers legend toyed with Celtic at Hampden. But the contribution of Ralph Brand to this famous win should not be forgotten.

The forward scored the goal that set Rangers off on the road to victory and he also got the third, which sealed the win and sparked a mass exodus from the Celtic end. The first was a relatively easy tap-in but his second was a fine effort worthy of winning any cup final.

Twenty-five yards out and with his back to goal, Brand pulled a high pass from Jimmy Millar out of the air with his left foot and in the same movement span and shot on the turn. Celtic goalkeeper Frank Haffey appeared to be taken by surprise and couldn't get down quickly enough to prevent the goal.

Haffey, who had enjoyed probably his best-ever match in the drawn first game, came in for heavy criticism from fans and the media for failing to stop the shot, but that is harsh both on him and Brand, who showed great technique to bring the ball under control and hit the powerful volley.

Scottish Cup final goals were a Brand speciality. He remains the only player ever to have scored in three consecutive finals, having netted against St Mirren in 1962 and Dundee in 1964 as well as his 1963 double against Celtic. In fact, he also scored Rangers' goal in the 1–1 draw that led to the '63 replay.

11. Brian Laudrup, Scottish Cup semi-final, April 1997.
Celtic 1 Rangers 2

A classic sucker-punch. Celtic had been pressing for an equaliser when Brian Laudrup picked up a pass from Paul Gascoigne just inside the Rangers half. He flicked it first time to Gordon Durie on the right, then carried on running through the middle. By the time Durie's expertly weighted return pass reached him, Laudrup's pace had taken him beyond the Celtic defence. Without breaking his stride, the Dane controlled the ball on his chest and, as goalkeeper Gordon Marshall charged out of the penalty area, coolly chipped it over him into the net from 20 yards.

Rangers won the game 2–1 and went on to thrash Hearts 5–1 in the final, with Laudrup again the star of the show.

12. Jörg Albertz, Premier Division, January 1997.
Rangers 3 Celtic 1

It was stunning free kicks like this one that earned Jörg Albertz the nickname 'The Hammer' and made him such a favourite with the Rangers fans. Nine minutes into the traditional New Year derby at Ibrox, David Robertson was fouled thirty yards out and Albertz stepped up to take the free kick.

Fearing the worst, Celtic set up a five-man wall, but there was nothing the defenders could do to stop the German's left-footed thunderbolt. The ball barely rose more than a foot off the ground as it flashed past the wall and beyond goalkeeper Stewart Kerr's outstretched fingers into the bottom corner. It was hit with such pace, ferocity and accuracy that the ball was almost past the keeper before he had even begun to move.

On a bitterly cold January night, a flu-hit Rangers side went on to win the game 3–1, the first of four victories they inflicted on their old rivals that season.

13. Paul Gascoigne, Premier Division, August 1996.
Rangers 2 Celtic 0

This counter-attacking goal was started and finished by Paul Gascoigne. With Rangers a goal ahead, the midfielder collected the ball in his own penalty area after John Hughes had hit the crossbar with a header. He charged forward out of defence, playing a short ball to Stuart McCall, who in turn passed it to Laudrup wide on the left. He rolled it short to Jörg Albertz, who whipped in a perfect cross from 18 yards out.

Gazza had continued his lung-busting run from one end of the pitch to the other and arrived at the edge of the Celtic six-yard box at precisely the same moment as Albertz's cross. His diving header bulleted past Gordon Marshall into the net to seal a 2–0 victory, as the Light Blues stormed their way to a ninth title in a row.

14. Alex Miller, Premier Division, August 1980.
Celtic 1 Rangers 2

Alex Miller's last-minute winner at Celtic Park was a rare bright spot during a dark period for Rangers. With the scores level at 1–1 and the game heading for a draw, Rangers won a throw-in on the left, a yard from the corner flag. Everyone expected Willie Johnston to hurl the ball deep into the penalty area – including Celtic's Davie Provan, who stood on the touchline directly in front of the veteran Rangers man in a bid to prevent the long throw.

Instead, Johnston threw it back to the edge of the area, where Miller met it with his left foot on the half-volley and sent a curling shot beyond Pat Bonner into the top corner.

15. Ian Durrant, Premier Division, August 1986.
Rangers 1 Celtic 0

Critics accused Graeme Souness of buying success when he came to Rangers, but he enjoyed victory in his first Old Firm game thanks to two players who had already been at the club for several years. Davie Cooper, whose skill created the winning goal, and Ian Durrant, who provided the clinical finish, were both key players in Rangers' first championship win for nine seasons.

Cooper picked the ball up twenty-five yards out and danced past two defenders before sliding a delicate reverse pass into Durrant's path with the outside of his left foot. The young midfielder burst into the penalty area and calmly slotted the ball past Pat Bonner to score the only goal of the game.

16. Arthur Numan, SPL, March 2002. Rangers 1 Celtic 1

Dutch international left-back Arthur Numan didn't score often in his five seasons at Rangers, but this goal will live long in the memory. Rangers were already well out of the title race when Celtic visited Ibrox but were playing for pride under new manager Alex McLeish.

With half an hour to go, Rangers were a goal down when Numan collected the ball 30 yards out on the left-hand side of the pitch. He took one touch then unleashed a fearsome shot into the top right corner that gave Rab Douglas no chance. The goal inspired Rangers, but despite piling on the pressure in the closing stages of the match they were unable to find the winning goal.

17. Ronald de Boer, SPL, September 2002.
Celtic 3 Rangers 3

In a thrilling game at Parkhead, Celtic had come back from a goal down to lead 2–1 early in the second half and looked to have dealt Rangers a massive psychological blow. But straight from the restart after Celtic's second goal, Alex McLeish's men went onto the attack.

Neil McCann was released down the left and sent over a perfect cross for Ronald de Boer to head home. The instant response to going a goal behind summed up the spirit McLeish had instilled in the team since taking over from Dick Advocaat the previous season. The game finished 3–3 and the point was vital in a league race that went down to the last day of the season, when Rangers eventually won the title by just one goal.

18. Dado Pršo, SPL, August 2005. Rangers 3 Celtic 1

Croatian striker Dado Pršo gave Rangers the lead in a fiery derby at Ibrox with an expertly taken volley. Centre-back Marvin Andrews set up the goal with a pinpoint long-range pass that belied his reputation as a player lacking in technical ability.

Pršo drifted in from the left and met the cross virtually on the penalty spot, hooking his shot past Artur Boruc into the corner of the net.

19. Derek Parlane, Premier Division, November 1975. Celtic 1 Rangers 1

Derek Parlane's goal merits inclusion for its sheer impudence. Late in the game, and with the match apparently heading for a goalless draw, Celtic had a free kick just inside their own half. Andy Lynch rolled it short to Tommy Callaghan, but the ball didn't reach its intended recipient. Instead, Tommy McLean, who had been running back into position, nipped in from behind the two Celtic players and stole the ball away, before releasing Parlane through the middle.

The stunned defenders could only watch in horror as the Rangers forward burst through, rounded goalkeeper Peter Latchford at the edge of the penalty area and nonchalantly rolled the ball into an empty net.

Celtic claimed Parlane was offside, but TV pictures showed that he was clearly onside when McLean played the pass. Whether or not McLean should have been allowed to intercept the free kick in the first place is another matter, as he was obviously less than ten yards away when the kick was taken. However, the goal stood, although Celtic would have considered that justice was done, as they equalised three minutes later.

20. Jim Bett, League Cup final, December 1982.
Rangers 1 Celtic 2

Jim Bett's perfectly executed free kick just after half-time turned out to be little more than a consolation, as two first-half strikes from Celtic won the League Cup final. But it was a goal worthy of winning any final.

Gordon Smith was fouled 25 yards out and dead-ball specialist Davie Cooper lined up to take the free kick. But instead, he ran over the ball and Jim Bett stepped forward to strike it. His delicate right-footed shot curled and dipped over the wall into the bottom left corner, leaving Bonner with no chance.

BIBLIOGRAPHY

Allan, John, *The Story of the Rangers: Fifty Years of Football*, Rangers
Football Club, 1923

Allison, William, *Rangers: The New Era*, Rangers Football Club,
1966

Burns, Tommy, with Hugh Keevins, *Twists and Turns: The Tommy
Burns Story*, Sportsprint, 1989

Duff, Iain, *Follow On: 50 Years of Rangers in Europe*, Fort
Publishing, 2006

Duff, Iain, *Temple of Dreams: The Changing Face of Ibrox*, Breedon
Books, 2008

Gallacher, Ken, *Playing for Rangers No. 3*, Stanley Paul, 1971

Johnston, Maurice, and Chick Young, *Mo: The Maurice Johnston
Story*, Mainstream Publishing, 1988

McCarra, Kevin, *Scottish Football*, Polygon Books, 1984

McPhail, Bob, with Allan Herron, *Legend: Sixty Years at Ibrox*,
Mainstream Publishing, 1988

Mason, David, *Rangers: The Managers*, Mainstream Publishing,
2000

Young, Chick, *Rebirth of the Blues*, Mainstream Publishing, 1986